A DIFFERENT KIND OF STRENGTH

BEVERLY LaHAYE & JANICE SHAW CROUSE

HARVEST HOUSE PUBLISHERS
Eugene, Oregon 97402

Cover by Koechel Peterson & Associates, Minneapolis, Minnesota

Published in association with the literary agency of Alive Communications, Inc., 7680 Goddard Street, Suite 200, Colorado Springs, CO 80920

A DIFFERENT KIND OF STRENGTH
Copyright © 2001 Beverly LaHaye Institute
Published by Harvest House Publishers
Eugene, Oregon 97402

Library of Congress Cataloging-in-Publication data

LaHaye, Beverly.
    A different kind of strength / Beverly LaHaye and Janice Crouse.
      p. cm.
    Includes bibliographical references.
    ISBN 0-7369-0651-7
    1. Women in the Bible—Bibliography. 2. Christian women—Religious life.
  I. Crouse, Janice. II. Title.

BS575 .L34 2001
248.8'43—dc21   2001024257

Printed in the United States of America.

01 02 03 04 05 06 07 08 09 10 / DH-MS / 10 9 8 7 6 5 4 3 2 1

To the women in our families
who have been a strength and inspiration to us—

From Beverly

To my sister, Barrie Lyons,
Daughters, Linda Murphy
And Lori Scheck,
Daughter-in-law, Sharron LaHaye,
And granddaughters,
Jenny Murphy Larson
Emily Scheck

From Janice

To my mother, Sarah Ruth Baird Shaw,
Daughter, Charmaine Crouse Yoest,
Daughter-in-law, Naomi Liles Crouse,
And granddaughters,
Hannah Ruth Yoest
Helena Gilbert "Gibby" Yoest
Sarah Shaw Carr Yoest

Acknowledgments

We want to express heartfelt appreciation to our husbands,
Tim LaHaye and Gil Crouse,
whose love and support give us encouragement
for the tasks God puts before us.
We are also grateful for the support and encouragement
of the CWA leaders—
the board of directors, state leaders, and the wonderful staff
in the Washington, D.C., office.
And to the prayer warriors
who made this book a special prayer concern—
especially Nancy Huston Hansen and Barbara Miller.

Contents

Finding Strength
When Life Falls Apart

My heart rejoices in the Lord; There is none holy like the Lord,
Nor is there any rock like our God.
The Lord makes poor and makes rich; He brings low and lifts up.
He raises the poor from the dust
To set them among princes
And make them inherit the throne of glory.
For by strength no man shall prevail.
HANNAH'S PRAYER

*S*uddenly, out of the blue, life can fall apart. With stunning swiftness we can be left staring numbly into the void...the death of a loved one...the illness of a child...the loss of a job...the treachery of a friend...depression...divorce...cancer. When disaster strikes, we ask, "Where is God? Why does He let things like this happen? Doesn't He care about us?"

We rarely wrestle with these questions when times are good. We earnestly teach our children to pray before meals: "God is great. God is good." Countless tiny tots in homes all around the country murmur this simple grace long before they understand what the words might mean or comprehend their profound implications. Eventually, though, when life falls apart, we must all come to grips with the seeming incongruity between our circumstances and this simple prayer. If God is great...and if He is good...then why...why?

God is not indifferent to our struggles, our defeats, or our pain. He is not silent, and He is not idle. He is always working in every circumstance of our lives to bring the good plan He has for us to completion. Even when we cannot see Him working, or even imagine that anything good remains in life for us, He is working.

But this, of course, is not the message we are hearing in our postmodern culture. The prevalent messages today are all about seizing control of your life, learning to control others, and, most of all, achieving that always-elusive goal of personal fulfillment through your own determined efforts.

This is a different kind of book about a different kind of strength and achievement—the kind God had in mind when He created us in His image. "For I know the plans I have for you," God promises through Jeremiah, "plans to prosper you."

Yes, there is a different kind of strength—God's strength. "Have you not known? Have you not heard?" asks Isaiah. "The everlasting God, the LORD, the Creator of the ends of the earth, neither faints nor is weary" (Isaiah 40:28 NKJV). What an assurance! And a blessed promise follows: "He gives power to the weak, and to those who have no might He increases *strength*" (verse 29).

God has given us many examples in His Word of His concern for the weak and needy, particularly for those battered by hardship and pain. You may be enjoying unprecedented opportunities and enviable comforts at the dawn of the twenty-first century, or you may be fighting just to keep your head above water in the midst of the darkest circumstances of your life. Whether you are at either end of this spectrum or somewhere in between, we believe you will find something in the lives of the five unusual women we describe in this book that God can use to give you a different kind of strength.

The True Path to Strength

We want to take you on a journey to see just how much God cares about the smallest details of our lives. On our way we'll discover how to find strength and meaning in our circumstances even when things fall apart. And we'll see God's faithfulness and the importance of spiritual discipline in the daily exercise of our faith.

We begin in the first book of the New Testament, chapter 1, verse 1. Generally, we tend to skip right over Matthew's rather dry recitation of Christ's genealogy and move on to what we perceive to be the real Christmas story that begins in verse 18. But perhaps we shouldn't be so hasty. It could be we miss something significant if we skip over the words God inspired Matthew to use as the beginning of the account of His Son's birth.

"Abraham begot Isaac...and Judah begot Perez and Zerah by Tamar...Salmon begot Boaz by Rahab...Boaz begot Obed by Ruth.... David the king begot Solomon by her who had been the wife of Uriah...and Jacob begot Joseph the husband of Mary, of whom was born Jesus who is called Christ" (Matthew 1:1-16 RSV). Then Matthew summarizes for us saying, "Now all this was done, that it might be fulfilled which was spoken of the Lord by the prophet, saying, Behold a virgin shall be with child, and shall bring forth a son, and they shall call his name Emmanuel, which being interpreted is, God with us" (Matthew 1:22 KJV).

God with us! All this was done that God might be *with us!* What an amazing story...what an amazing promise. *God has a plan and it cannot be thwarted.*

But wait! Mary is understandable. Of course Matthew would give special prominence to the virgin prophesied by Isaiah. But what about these other four women? Tamar, Rahab, Ruth, and the unnamed but immediately recognizable "wife of Uriah," Bathsheba. Between Abraham and the birth of Christ, there were 52 generations. Hundreds of years of men and women, but *these* five women are highlighted. Why? "All this was done..." Clearly their names are included because of their special place in God's plan. *Who were these five women?*

In a day and time when women were often relegated to the background, Matthew placed them center stage—in the spotlight. Mary and Ruth we can understand, but what was his purpose for including the other three when he omitted such prominent names as Sarah and Rebecca?

Several of these women were not like the women we generally consider worthy of emulation: Tamar was an abandoned widow who seduced her father-in-law and bore him twin sons. Rahab was a prostitute. Bathsheba, an adulterer. Strange choices. An intriguing puzzle! And yet, there they are...through God's grace...and their stories are immortalized in His Word to teach us truths about His power, His pardon, and His plans.

Note that Scripture does not blush to show us a completely unvarnished picture of humanity in all of its sinfulness. Throughout the Bible the principle characters are described in brutally honest terms—again and again we see them fall short. They vividly illustrate our need for redemption. At the same time, they amazingly reveal the fact that our limitations cannot thwart God's sovereign plan.

Despite their flaws, there is much we can learn from the experiences of the three women with less-than-admirable reputations who are listed in Christ's genealogy. First and foremost, God does not require perfection in us to accomplish His will. He uses fallible human beings for His purposes. Moreover, in the lives of these ordinary people, we can find sterling qualities alongside their human failings.

A Great Mystery

In addition to the mystery of why bad things happen, there is another great mystery: How is it possible for God to allow us to have free will—the very means by which most of the bad things in our lives come about—and at the same time accomplish His divine purposes...purposes that spring from His unfathomable love for us? In the biblical stories revisited in this book, we see the documented record of how this puzzling paradox of God's sovereignty and human freedom coexisted and how these two elements played out in the lives of the women whom Matthew highlighted in his genealogy of Christ.

The scriptural account of the unfolding of God's Divine plan to rescue His fallen creatures is something too incredible to be the product of human imagination. Understanding and appreciating the mysterious way God works might not be so difficult to comprehend if it were not for the fact that Scripture records how it unfolded in the lives of ordinary people who, more often than not, were as willful and disobedient as you and me. The outworking and fulfillment of God's plan in their lives was as much a surprise to them as it is to us!

Of course, it is even more likely that these pivotal biblical characters lived and died never knowing the eternal significance of their lives. It is important that we not look at these women's stories entirely in terms of hindsight—where in the end, things do finally come together. If we are to find hope, inspiration, and instruction, if we are to gather our own courage to face our own trials, we must walk through these stories the way the characters lived them—full of uncertainty, not knowing the ending.

The biblical characters were authentic human beings—people like us. We can never really know them until we grasp their humanity and see it as equal to our own; until we see in them our own needs, fears, passions, hopes, and hurts; until we see them as real flesh-and-blood persons who bled and wept just as we bleed and weep. Then, and only then, can we find inspiration from their pain, troubles, and uncertainties, from seeing in hindsight that God was working out His purposes. Then, and only then, can we find the reassurance that the narrative of our own lives has a coherence beyond our comprehension. God is indeed great. And He is good. But as He reminded Job and his friends, it is He who scatters the east wind over the earth. We stand in relationship to the Almighty as mere dust. "For My thoughts are not your thoughts, nor are your ways My ways," says the Lord. "For as the heavens are higher than the earth, so are My ways higher than your ways and My thoughts than your thoughts" (Isaiah 55:8,9 NASB).

And yet the stories of the women in Christ's genealogy show God, in His great mercy, working to redeem sinful people…people who lie, steal, deceive, and commit adultery and murder. These stories demonstrate that God is at work even when lives are falling apart. Even when His people could not see His hand of mercy, He was working. Isaiah assures us that God offers us a place of peace, a haven from the world's struggles: "In returning and rest you shall be saved," says the Lord God, the Holy One of Israel. "In quietness and confidence shall be your strength." (See Isaiah 30:15 NKJV.)

But Isaiah also records the response of a "rebellious people," those who "trust in oppression and perversity." The reply is, even for us as modern people, an all-too-recognizable defiance: "No, for we will flee on horses—We will ride on swift horses!"[1] Nowhere is it more evident that our ways are not God's ways than when we look at the ways women pursue strength in their own power.

The Counterfeit Path to Strength

The cover story of the first *Newsweek* magazine of 2001 was "The Age of Oprah." The headline proclaimed, "She's changing more lives than ever."[2] Oprah Winfrey, of course, is the blockbuster television talk show host and founder of the most successful start-up publication in history, *O* magazine.

Oprah has always centered her career on finding meaning for life's journey, and today through her varied forums she offers up her make-it-happen-for-yourself philosophy to a culture searching for meaning and direction. The purpose of *O* is to "encourage readers to revamp their souls the way Martha Stewart helps them revamp their kitchens."[3]

Oprah's back-and-forth kind of conversation with celebrities and women across America and her transparent attitude toward her personal struggles with issues like childhood abuse and weight control have established an unprecedented intimacy with her predominantly female audience of 14 million viewers and 2 million readers.

In contrast to other talk shows and women's magazines that seek out the lowest common denominator in personal behavior, Oprah has targeted women who want to take charge of their lives, who want to have successful relationships, who long for a sense of self-esteem, and who desire meaning outside of themselves. In her quest to reach others where they are, Oprah offers a brand of spirituality that sets feeling at its center. She once said that she was "guided by a higher calling." Oprah, however, defines the calling as a feeling, not a voice. "If it doesn't feel right to me, I don't do it."[4]

Oprah's philosophically bland, motivationally hyped combination of New Age, feminist, humanistic, shamanistic spirituality focuses on her audience feeling good and teaches them to believe they can do better without placing any limits or demands on themselves. It also appeals to the human desire to be in control of your own destiny. Acknowledgment of the "goodness of life" by writing entries in a "Gratitude Journal" is an indicator of the fact that even if they haven't yet arrived, at least they are headed in the right direction.[5]

Oprah has certainly hit her target audience! Not since 1963 and the release of Betty Friedan's *Feminine Mystique* has anyone so captured the heart and soul of American's women. But what becomes increasingly clear with a look back over the decades is that no matter who brings the message, women then and women now are searching for the same things: meaning, purpose, strength to endure life's challenges, encouragement of their dreams, and power to become who they were meant to be.

It All Began with Betty

In the early '60s, the *Feminine Mystique* took the women of American by storm. By becoming an advocate for women's power, Betty Friedan brought her cause into the living rooms and bedrooms of America and launched the so-called "women's movement." Claiming that frustrated and thwarted women were downing tranquilizers "like cough drops," she said, "Some people thought I said, 'Women...you have nothing to lose but your men.' It's not true. You have nothing to lose but your vacuum cleaners."

Friedan obviously struck a responsive nerve over 40 years ago. Women of the '60s were happy to have a secular analysis that sounded sophisticated for their spiritual hunger, and thousands sought to fill their emptiness with feminist manna. In contrast to Oprah, who teaches women to seek power from within, Friedan sought to find power in the external marketplace. Strong women pursued power, she proclaimed—power provided the path toward self-actualization and happiness.

Far too many women, including Betty Friedan herself, crashed their lives on the shoals of faulty reasoning about the path to power. Their grasping attempts to seize power led not to self-actualization but disillusionment and cynicism. In the wake of this frustration, a bright and beautiful woman appeared in the '70s to refine the message, cloak it in sophistication, and propel it forward on the wings of celebrity.

The Allure of Liberation

Gloria Steinem has been called a feminist "icon," "diva," and "matriarch." Her style, sophistication, and media savvy paved the way for her to earn a place among the "beautiful people" and made her a celebrity. In the 1970s, her star-power moved feminism's focus away from the well-educated but less fashionable middle-class suburban mothers who wanted simple respect and dignity, to the glamorous elite and urban intelligentsia who were more interested in crushing "patriarchy" and championing "victims." Through her high-profile speaking and writing, Gloria helped make extremism radically chic and politically correct.

During the 1980s and 1990s, Gloria published bestselling books and launched *Ms.*, a magazine that has been described as the "journalistic linchpin of the American feminist movement."[6] Her uncanny ability to fascinate the public assured the success of her work and took her ideology into the mainstream. Unmarried, childless, and wealthy, she had almost nothing in common with the majority of women whose cause she advanced, yet one young fan said of Gloria, "She's like the president of all women."[7]

Ironically, after 30 years of marriage-bashing, Gloria married in the summer of 2000. Early in her career, she had said, "You become a semi-nonperson when you get married." She also talked about married women being "part-time prostitutes" and called marital bedrooms "settings for nightly rape."

Steinem's own divergence from the values she lauded for over 30 years should be a red flag to any person who looks for life's meaning in the principles she so adamantly and forcefully paraded before women for three decades.

What's the Truth?

With the advantage of hindsight, two questions must be asked: Why has radical feminism's message of self-absorption and focus on personal power been proclaimed so loudly? Why have the radical feminist messengers been so celebrated when their messages have not stood the tests of time?

According to conventional wisdom, women have been an oppressed class throughout much of history. There is no denying the truth in this characterization. But then how do we explain the seemingly contradictory sayings: "Never underestimate the power of a woman," and "The hand that rocks the cradle rules the world"?

History is replete with examples of women who have had a powerful impact on the world around them. And amazingly few of these powerful women have held positions of status and worldly power.

Motherhood today is often disdained. Mothers report feeling disrespected or patronized. But witness the books that have been written and the monuments erected in homage to the influence of mothers whose children grew up to change the world.

Radical feminists have argued for decades that a woman's search for power and her struggle for equality can only be satisfied externally—in the marketplace, in relationships, in monetary terms. Phrases like "my goals," "my body," and "my self-fulfillment" run like threads through most radical feminist writings.

In our modern culture, many women consider self-fulfillment a basic entitlement. The concept of "doing your own thing" has been lifted to the level of a constitutional right or a theological truth. As a result, many are engaged in a relentless pursuit of pleasure and self-fulfillment, or domination and oppression, or of simply trying to live life on their own terms regardless of the consequences or personal costs. It's a seductive, fruitless philosophy that confounds and often ensnares women—sometimes even the most ardent women of faith. Jesus demonstrated that all "power and authority" belong to Him.[8] Therefore, nothing could be clearer: Any philosophy or form of deceptive thinking which places self at the center instead of adopting the servant's posture modeled by Christ—the One who humbled Himself and washed the feet of His disciples, disciples who called Him "Master"—is diametrically opposed to the wisdom of God and doomed to fail.

Betty Friedan's biographer asserts that prior to Friedan and the women's movement, "women celebrated in American history books were footnotes."[9] While there is again some truth in that observation, the problem, of course, is in the writing of history books, not in the accomplishments of women.

As surprising as it may seem to some, radical feminists did not invent the idea of the powerful woman. God did. Long before Betty Friedan, Gloria Steinem, Oprah Winfrey, and others brought their definitions to bear on who we are as women, God raised up women who exemplified His definition of a woman's true strength and power. And long before there was any kind of feminism, Jesus established real women's liberation. Paul wrote to the Galatians emphasizing that through faith we all now share in God's glorious new covenant that provides freedom for those who believe: "There is neither Jew nor Greek, there is neither slave nor free, there is neither male nor female; for you are all one in Christ Jesus."[10]

Toward a Right Understanding

We believe it's time to take a closer look at the power of a woman. We are convinced that at the start of a new millennium women are still hungering for truth and searching for answers about who they can become and how their lives can have meaning. Regardless of the packaging, the issues remain the same. And God's promises and answers are the same as well: They are timeless, unchanging, and absolutely certain to be fulfilled.

No matter who we are individually or what gifts we possess as a woman, the Bible promises that our true value and meaning come from belonging to Jesus Christ, our Creator and Redeemer. God promises a different kind of strength—a strength that doesn't depend on our own frail efforts, a strength that will empower every woman who desires to serve Christ and His Kingdom. We can become vessels of honor because He will live and serve through us. That is real strength. Strength that is eternal and righteous.

Ephesians 2:10 expresses our highest calling: "For we are God's workmanship, created in Christ Jesus to do good works, which God prepared in advance for us to do." God has a plan and a purpose for our lives, and He will empower us to accomplish that purpose by His grace. God will "make all grace abound to you, so that in all things at all times, having all that you need, you will abound in every good work."[11] Thankfully, God has provided His role models for us to follow (Tamar, Rahab, Ruth, Bathsheba, and Mary), ensuring that His Word preserved their stories. You may be surprised and inspired by the challenges God gave them the strength to overcome. When God wrote His history book, women were far more than footnotes! The lives they led, mistakes and all, are central to "The Story."

A Fresh Look

We believe that this fresh look at the lives of the five women listed in Christ's genealogy will help to clarify for today's women the powerful ways in which we can be used for God's purposes in spite of our human frailties and failures. We believe that these stories and the emphasis on the character traits of these five women will teach us much about God's power and His desire to redeem the lives of women. An understanding of these women who lived in a time vastly different from ours will reveal a different kind of strength!

Each section begins with a creative account of the life of one of these women. While we rigidly adhere to the documented facts of each woman's life, the aspects of her life that are not described in Scripture have been filled in as we've imagined them. Our purpose in creating a story is to make the individual and her unique personality, character, and relationships come alive so you can identify with her uncertain circumstances and tremendous challenges.

After we see the story of each woman's life and how God used her to fulfill His purposes, we will look more closely at those character traits that define each woman's unique strength and how each of us can develop these qualities in our own lives.

While God's work within us is His doing, our role is to strengthen our relationship with Him and grow in our personal discipline and devotion. Our challenge is to see how we can cooperate with what He is doing in us as He builds these qualities of true, godly strength into each of us.

From the Two of Us to You

As we think together and try to apply the clear lessons as well as grapple with the ambiguities and unanswered questions in the lives of these women, we pray that you will discover more about the powerful ways God can use your unique gifts and abilities during our own time in history. And we pray that you will be challenged and inspired to seek God's power for influencing the world around you. It is essential for us to see, in the end, that the centerpiece of these stories is neither the character flaws nor the achievements of the human personalities occupying the foreground, but it is the boundless grace, mercy, and forgiveness of God who works unceasingly in the background.

Just as the apostle Paul prayed for his friends at Ephesus, it is our prayer that through this book the truths of Ephesians 3:16-21 (NIV) will become real to you:

I pray that out of his glorious riches he may strengthen you with power through his Spirit in your inner being, so that Christ may dwell in your hearts through faith. And I pray that you, being rooted and established in love, may have power, together with all the saints, to grasp how wide and long and high and deep is the love of Christ, and to know this love that surpasses knowledge—that you may be filled to the measure of all the fullness of God. Now to him who is able to do immeasurably more than all we ask or imagine, according to his power that is at work within us, to him be glory in the church and in Christ Jesus throughout all generations, for ever and ever! Amen.

For we are all called to strength...but a strength that has as its source the empowering of the Holy Spirit in every aspect of our lives.

We are all called to greatness...but a greatness that is defined as faithful obedience, walking humbly in the paths God opens up before us.

We are all called to success...but a success that is measured by an enduring faith in God. As Scripture says, "Without faith it is impossible to please God" (Hebrews 11:6 NIV). But with faith, it is possible for our lives to be pleasing to the infinite Creator of the universe. That is true success! That is life's highest goal.

Sometimes that walk of faith will require great courage. The lives of Tamar...Rahab...Ruth...Bathsheba...and Mary will show us the way—not the way of perfection, but the way of faith, hope, and obedience.

God gave them power, even in their imperfections.

God valued them. And He values you.

He has put down the mighty...and exalted the lowly...

The Lord makes poor and makes rich; He brings low and lifts up...

God had plans for these unlikely women, and He has a plan for you! God chooses unlikely people to accomplish His will. Today, God is choosing you.

For He who is mighty has done great things for me...
And His mercy is on those who fear Him...
He has put down the mighty...
And exalted the lowly....
He has helped his servant...
In remembrance of His mercy...
MARY'S MAGNIFICAT

When Life Falls Apart

The Power of Courage
The Power of Fortitude

Tamar

When Life Falls Apart

*E*noch watched the wind toss Tamar's hair as she hurried up the trail toward him in the late afternoon sun. Even at a distance, he could see the happy glow on her face. When she was excited, her smile was so incandescent it nearly took his breath away. She was at the stage where one moment she was still his little girl, and the next she was an incredible vision of young femininity—a re-creation of his wife when he married her.

Tamar was bringing a message to her father. A visitor would be joining them for supper. Enoch already knew that the family would entertain tonight. From where he stood high on the side of the hill, he had seen a man leave the main road and take the winding path that led to their home. Even from a great distance, Enoch had been reasonably certain that the visitor was Judah—no one else he knew cut such an imposing figure.

Enoch could never see Tamar come up the trail beside the winding creek without his mind flashing back to a day long ago. She had been only four or five years old then. Ordinarily, when she climbed the trail to the upper pasture to bring him a loaf of freshly baked bread for his lunch, he watched from the outcropping that gave him a view of the trail below.

However, on that eventful day, flashes of lightning danced across the mountaintops foretelling possible rain and interrupting Enoch's usual routine. He spent the morning guiding the ewes and their lambs up to the western slope where they would be safe from the water that could soon come rushing through the lower parts of the meadow. Once his task was accomplished and he settled in against a rock to rest, he thought longingly of the warm bread Tamar usually brought to him. His gaze turned toward the sun-drenched valley below and then to his left at the pouring rain in the eastern hills. Suddenly, his heart froze in horror. He realized that possibly in the beauty of the sunlight below, they had not heard the thunder or seen the storm clouds in the distance. What if Tamar was coming up the trail?

Already the creek was beginning to rise and run brown with mud stirred by the rushing current now racing off the mountains. In an instant Enoch was on his feet and running toward the top of the trail leading down the hillside. At his lookout point, he saw Tamar nearing the part of the trail that followed along beside the creek. He could hear the distant roar of the water thundering down out of the mountain. In a matter of moments, the flash flood would fill the lower side of the meadow and would sweep away everything in its path as the torrent rushed down the hill.

Enoch saw Tamar's little legs pumping as she fought to keep her feet under her. The rising water of the creek was rapidly turning the trail into a slippery, muddy mess. Instantly, Enoch hurtled down the mountainside, praying with every step that he would not lose his footing as he raced to reach his little girl before the rising water swept her away.

As the flood swallowed the trail, a surge of water spun her around. The current now began to push her down the hill. Unable to resist the force of water, she threw her arms around a small shrub to keep from being swept off her feet.

As he closed the distance between them, Enoch was horrified to see the shrub begin to flatten under the combination of her weight and the growing force of the water. Frantically, he lunged and grabbed

Tamar around the waist and lifted her up. Clinging to his precious cargo, he worked to regain his balance as the knee-deep rapids pushed him further and further down the hill. Enoch pulled Tamar up against his chest. He desperately fought the surging force of the current as it beat against his legs and threatened to take them out from under him. He could hear in his ears even today the chant that he had repeated to her over and over as he had gasped for breath, "Hold on, Tamar. Hold on."

Enoch could feel Tamar's little arms locked around his neck as he stumbled along trying to escape the battering flood. Then he spotted a fallen tree wedged against a huge boulder just below him. Holding Tamar with one arm, and grabbing a large limb of the tree with the other, he caught his breath. Very slowly he managed to move along the tree from one limb to the next until he was finally able to reach the boulder the tree was trapped against. Using its limbs as handholds, Enoch climbed up on top of the boulder out of the grip of the current.

When he could finally breathe easier, he took stock of their situation. They were about three feet above the water. Enoch was thankful for the boulder that he had seen survive many floods. Relieved that their perch would keep them safe, he turned his attention to Tamar. Though her little face was scratched in several places, she appeared to have no serious injuries.

As Enoch tilted her head back and looked carefully into her eyes, he was surprised to see grim determination, not terror, in Tamar's beautiful face. He had seen that expression many times before when she set her mind on doing something—but now! He gently pulled her arms from where they were still locked around his neck, and, as he did, he saw clutched in one tiny little fist the knotted cloth containing their lunch.

"Mommy told me not to drop it," she said. "I promised I would hold on tight."

Enoch pulled her close as the tears welled in his eyes.

Enoch looked up from his memories as Tamar, now a lithe young woman, climbed the last few yards of the trail, quickly closing the distance between them. Eagerly, she told him the news that Judah had come to see him and would be staying for dinner.

Enoch drew in a deep breath to still the feeling rising in him. He had known this day would come. But so soon? His daughter was a beauty, a prize that a father could not hold onto forever.

Judah was a rich man—a proud, fine man. But everyone had heard stories about his sons, especially Er, the eldest. Judah was also an affable man, perhaps too affable. Some suggested that he should have taken a stronger hand in raising his sons.

Enoch frowned pensively as he pondered the coming conversation with Judah. Perhaps the marriage could be a good thing. If the young buck only needed straightening out, Tamar could do the job. Maybe she could have a happy life in Judah's family. Still, Enoch could not return Tamar's glowing smile.

As they walked back down the trail in the evening's soft light, Tamar tucked her arm in her father's, and her happiness engulfed him. It was a bittersweet moment. One that Enoch would relive many times in the years to come.

Judah was a man's man—a natural leader, a man whose size and brute physical strength were matched by the force of his personality. Most men automatically deferred to him. His self-assurance inspired confidence in those around him.

In his final deathbed blessing, Judah's father, Jacob, would skip over his three eldest sons and bestow the leadership of the family clan upon Judah saying, "Your father's sons shall bow down to you."[12] It was, thus, through this son of Jacob that there would one day come a shepherd boy who would fight a lion and a bear to save his sheep, a shepherd boy who would fell a giant to defend Yahweh's honor,[13] a shepherd boy who would become a king that mighty warriors of Israel would gladly follow into battle. Eventually, from this line, in the fullness of time, a Savior would be born in the city of David, a Lion of the Tribe of Judah.[14]

But that blessing lay far in the future. The man Enoch encountered on this warm, summer evening was still not reconciled to his father.

As a prideful young man, Judah left his father and brothers[15] in the hope of putting the past behind him. Given his easy good cheer, few would have ever guessed the dark memories tightly locked in the deepest recesses of his soul.

Judah had put many miles and many years between him and his father, Jacob, a man whose great wealth had not been able to heal the grief he felt over the loss of his beloved Rachel[16] and their firstborn, Joseph. On rare occasions, when word came about his brothers or his father, deeply buried memories were unlocked—especially memories of his father's grief-stricken face on the day Judah brought Joseph's blood-soaked coat to him.[17] The memories of his father reminded Judah of Yahweh, his father's God—a just God, a God who rained fire and brimstone on Sodom and Gomorrah for their wickedness.[18] Judah understood that this just God demanded retribution for wickedness. The memories always resurrected his old guilt and stirred up his fear of God's possible judgment for his sin.[19]

No hint of these darker facets was evident in the warmth of Judah's presence tonight. After their meal Tamar had stood with her mother in the shadows of the other room listening to the two men talk. Judah was expansive, heaping praise on Tamar's youthful beauty and grace. Enoch countered hesitantly that she was barely a woman, maybe not yet mature enough for the responsibilities of marriage.

Judah's smile indicated that he understood Enoch's reluctance to give up the radiant warmth of his daughter's presence. Clearly Tamar was the pride of his life. Judah cleverly shifted the topic to the wonderful grandchildren his handsome Er and Enoch's beautiful Tamar would give them. Here he found Enoch more receptive.

Sensing that he was gaining ground, Judah proudly offered Enoch a bride price that he knew was double anything previously paid in the region. To Judah's amazement, Enoch's eyes had grown cold. Enoch's voice cracked like a whip as he told Judah that the extravagant price he offered meant nothing. His words were hard and clipped as he spat out that he cared only for his daughter's happiness. Then with a sad resolve, he announced that he would rather Tamar never marry than be mistreated or neglected.

Judah tensed at Enoch's open suggestion that Er might not be a fit husband. Enoch expected anger at his thinly veiled insult, and he braced himself. But the explosion didn't come. While Judah fully understood Enoch's reply, he respected this man's fierce love for his daughter and his determination to protect her. And, truthfully, he himself was sadly aware of Er's reputation. One other reality, too, held Judah in check: While he had no daughters of his own, he could never forget what had happened to his sister.[20]

Judah sat quietly, for what seemed like an eternity to Tamar, before he responded in a low but passionate tone, "Enoch, you have my word: Tamar will always be treated kindly." Then, glancing upward toward the heavens, he added deliberately and solemnly, "May God require it at my hand if any harm should ever come to her."

Enoch said nothing. He didn't need to. His expression told Judah that the deal had been struck. The men shook hands in silence. Judah's wealth had been meaningless in these negotiations. In the final analysis, only his oath before God to protect Tamar had won a wife for his son.

Tamar's trip to Judah's home began quietly. Judah spoke first, "Tamar, tell me, what do you like to do?"

She gave him a smile bright with the excitement of the adventure and said, "Well, I especially like to help my father with the sheep during lambing season." Then quickly, wanting him to think her grown-up, she added, "I always enjoyed helping mother with my little brothers, particularly when they were tiny babies. I guess babies and lambs are my favorite things. And I also love listening to my father sing and tell stories."

Judah asked what kind of stories she liked.

She blushed as she told him that she liked stories about princes and princesses. That response brought an amused smile to his face.

"So," he said after another comfortable silence, "tell me one of your favorite stories." He added with a grin, "I'll need to know what kind of stories to tell my granddaughters."

Embarrassed, she genially protested, "No, you will laugh at me. Besides stories are only for children."

He looked at her warmly and said, "Oh, but you are wrong. Stories are very important to adults as well." Then he added lightheartedly, "I used to tell my sons many stories when they were small, and I would enjoy hearing one for little girls. I haven't had that opportunity since I overheard my mother, Leah, telling bedtime stories to my baby sister, Dinah."

For some reason, the image of Judah as a boy eavesdropping on a little girl's bedtime story made her smile. She began to tell him the story he had asked to hear.

Tamar had barely begun her story before Judah recognized it. The story was not an imaginary tale at all. It was, in fact, a story about his great-grandmother, Sarah, who had been such a beauty that more than once in her travels with her husband, Abraham, they encountered a ruler—even the great Pharaoh of Egypt—who had tried to take her for his wife.[21]

Tamar didn't have all of the details straight, but her version was close enough to the actual facts that there could be no mistaking the origins of the story.

When Tamar completed her tale, Judah surprised her by asking, "Would you like to know more about the princess in your story?"

Tamar, curious and eager to hear more, replied, "I would love to! Have you heard this story before?"

Judah nodded and began to tell her more of the history of Abraham and Sarah. Tamar was mesmerized. He could not have delighted her more. Judah talked until it was time for them to rest and enjoy a bit of bread and honey.

As they relaxed in the shade, Tamar eyed him carefully. Some of the details he had included in his stories were identical to events she had purposely left out because she hadn't wanted to bore him with too many particulars.

Baffled, Tamar questioned, "How is it that you know so much about the princess in my father's story? Did your mother tell that same story to Dinah?"

"Well, yes," he replied, "but my father also told that story repeatedly to me and my brothers as we worked beside him in the fields with the herds. You see, the princess, Sarah, was actually my great-grandmother."

Tamar was slightly annoyed that he seemed to be toying with her. She smiled politely and stiffly replied that she would love to know more about his family.

Judah was an enthusiastic, sociable man. He enjoyed seeing Tamar's eyes flash as she listened to him talk. Her enjoyment of his tales was all the encouragement he needed to spend much of the rest of the trip telling her the old stories of the wanderings of his father, Jacob, his grandfather, Isaac, and his great-grandfather, Abraham.

Tamar noted the pride in Judah's voice when he told the story of his great-grandfather's triumphs in battle. It was particularly obvious when he recounted the time Abraham rescued his nephew, Lot, from Chedorlaomer, the king of Elam, and how after the battle he had received the blessing of Melchizedek.[22] Tamar was a keen listener and peppered her future father-in-law with question after question.

Judah casually avoided certain questions. But Tamar was not the least bit fooled by his seeming nonchalance as he sidestepped her questions about why he left his brothers and father to come down to the land of Adullam.[23] Judah's responses about his father and brothers were vague and imprecise—quite unlike other parts of his stories that he told in rich, dramatic detail. Tamar easily saw that there were some aspects of his family relationships that he simply was unwilling to discuss.

Later in the afternoon, he asked Tamar about her childhood. A warm bond began to grow between them as they learned more of each other's families—and of each other. Judah's stories of Abraham, Isaac, and Jacob stirred Tamar's imagination and left her in awe, especially the part about the covenant with Yahweh. Judah said that He alone was the one true God—the God above all other gods.

While Judah's stories had captured Tamar's imagination, she could barely comprehend the meaning of all that he had told her. As a silence finally fell between them, she turned her attention to wedding plans and to thoughts of fitting into a new family.

When Tamar arrived at Judah's encampment after her pleasant hours with Judah, she discovered that blending into her new family would be more of a challenge than she expected. Tamar was amazed at the number of people in Judah's camp. Judah had his father's talents as a herdsman and had so many sheep and other animals that he had hired a great many bondsmen. Once the wives and children of these men were counted, the camp numbered 56 besides Judah's own family. As she suspected, everything seemed to revolve around Judah when he was there. But when he was not—which was often— Bathshua, Judah's wife, ruled everyone and everything.

Bathshua showed one face to Judah. When he was present, she was full of wit and charm. But the face she showed to most of the encampment in Judah's absence was quite another. She was cold, aloof, and imperious—an unapproachable woman with a will of iron. No one ever interrupted her when she spoke, and none of the servants spoke to her until given permission. Her sons were a partial exception. One moment she would shower them with affection, then she would coldly manipulate them the next.

The encampment took special care not to give any offense to Bathshua. The servants were particularly careful not to cross this tyrannical mistress. It was clear that they had learned the hard way not to so much as exchange a glance with Judah, at least not in Bathshua's presence. Tamar noted though that Judah eyed several of the prettier ones very appreciatively.

Tamar did not know exactly what Judah had told the encampment about her, but it was clear that he had let it be known that Tamar was under his personal protection. He obviously had made it clear that no one—not even Er or Bathshua—dared be anything less than extremely polite to her.

While she was warm and kind with everyone, including the servants, her efforts to make friends were met with wary politeness. Slowly, she became aware of an underlying tension. Fear flowed like an unseen current beneath the surface of the otherwise peaceful camp.

Tamar remembered her mother's last words of advice to her as she was preparing to leave home. She had warned Tamar that she would need to be patient, that she should not expect too much of her young husband. She had advised that after the first child was born a young husband would start to settle down. She had assured her daughter that many things would change for him when he saw his wife caring for their new baby. Oh, how she wished her mother were here now so she could ask her what to do! She felt her life falling apart…and she could not figure out how to pull it back together.

Er was a big man and handsome like his father, but he had none of Judah's warmth and enthusiasm. Like any new bride, she had tried at first to be attractive to her husband. In time, Tamar settled for doing her best not to trigger his anger—a feat that proved impossible. Being near him was like being near a serpent that could strike unpredictably at any time. He had his mother's eyes, and the cruelty that Tamar saw in them made her blood run cold. The more she learned of Er's wickedness, the more it was a relief to see him drink himself into a stupor. Tamar began to look forward to the frequent times when he would leave the camp in the evening and not return until the next morning.

Tamar shuddered at the thought of how his touch made her skin crawl. Sadly, she recalled how as a child she had run to her father and leapt into the warmth of his arms. She remembered how she would squeal with delight as he tossed her high into the air. She thought back to how she had loved playing tag with her brothers and wrestling with them when they were small. She thought, too, of Judah's warmth and of how safe and content she felt in his presence. She had never been uncomfortable around men. She had dreamed of being close to her husband. Er's wickedness, however, filled her with fear and loathing.

Er had more than his mother's cold, calculating eyes. The changes in Bathshua's chameleon-like personality were so radical that Tamar was puzzled that Judah never seemed to have learned about his wife's dark side.

The bondsmen's families had good reason to fear Bathshua. When she was displeased or simply in a certain mood, someone was going to suffer. She was, however, an extremely clever woman at hiding her intentions. She did not shout or even raise her voice when she planned to mete out discipline. She would simply summon Er or Onan.

Bathshua would lean close to the son she had drafted for her purpose, and in a voice barely above a whisper she would give instructions. A malicious smile would flit across her face. Her eyes would glitter with intentions more cruel than any Tamar had ever seen. What followed was far more than just harsh discipline; it was cruel and vicious punishment. Tamar was horrified to see the pleasure that Er took in all of this. In some strange way she could not begin to understand, the opportunities to administer his mother's twisted form of "discipline" seemed to energize Er.

Did Judah not know about what happened when he wasn't around? She couldn't picture this man condoning what was being done. Or could she?

It seemed to Tamar that there were two sides to Judah, too. There was the man who had graciously sworn an oath to protect her, and then another man who ignored his wife's brutal, tyrannical rule that took over in his absence. Obviously, Bathshua's behavior wasn't a new phenomenon. It was clearly a long-standing practice. Maybe he knew and simply didn't care enough to do anything about it. It perplexed Tamar.

One day, looking for a way to keep Er's mind from drifting off into unpleasant things, as was so often the case, she told him that she was proud to have married into a family so favored by Yahweh.

Er had snarled back, "What's so wonderful about Yahweh? I worship the gods of Canaan."

Tamar was taken aback and thrown off balance by his response. She was also frustrated by her failure to divert him. Thus, she stammered out bits of the stories that Judah had told her. But her reply only made him angry, and he snarled, "But there's a lot more he hasn't told you."

Seeing that he was spoiling for a fight, she decided to give him one. Nothing else had worked so far. "Like what?" she spat back at him.

"Did he tell you about his sister, Dinah...and Shechem?" Er drawled sarcastically with a wicked glint in his eye.

Tamar's mind raced back to the trip with Judah. She had been hoping for an opportunity to learn more about the family history because she knew Judah had avoided telling her parts of it. Even in the face of Er's anger, Tamar's curiosity was too much for her to hide.

Sensing the opening, Er pounced. His eyes glittering with malicious pleasure, he remorselessly told the story of Dinah's abduction and rape by Shechem.[24] Tamar noted that there was not the slightest hint of sympathy or grief evident as he spoke. But as he began telling about how his uncles, Simeon and Levi, had slaughtered Shechem, Shechem's father, and all the other men of the town, his eyes danced with a manic intensity. He went on and on and on, reporting grizzly details of murder after murder after murder. It was clear to Tamar that her husband would have relished taking part in the killings.

As he became more and more excited, he pulled his knife from its scabbard and started to act out the drama. He violently slashed at imaginary figures and drove the blade first into a tent post and then into a nearby carob tree. Kneeling on the ground astride an imaginary body, he drove his knife into the ground again and again. He was now totally consumed with the reenactment. Tamar could see beads of sweat beginning to cover his forehead and cheeks. When he straightened, he whirled around toward her with his knife raised above his head and lunged forward. At the last possible instant, something stopped him from striking her. Her knees buckled. Tamar had to steady herself against a nearby table.

Tamar's eyes went wide with fright, and her face turned pale as she stood there trembling. Her response brought a jeering look of triumph to Er's face. Clearly pleased with the effect of his performance, he announced that he was leaving, that he was ready for a drink. Slamming his knife back into its sheath, he wheeled around and marched away.

It was the last time she saw him alive.

Marriage to Er had been almost more than she could bear. Privately, she had felt relief when Er died.[25] Her innermost thoughts were that if Judah's God, Yahweh, was just and loved righteousness as she had heard Judah say, then He must have taken Er's life. Er's wicked heart, so full of hatred, seemed out of control.

But witnessing Judah's grief was deeply painful. The floodgate of her tears, tears for Judah's grief, rushed open. But mixed with tears for his grief were tears for her own shattered dreams. She knew that she could only guess at the pain a mother or father would feel to bury their firstborn son. Watching Judah, however, she could not help feeling that he was possessed, not only by grief over Er's sudden, mysterious death, but by something more as well, some mixture of guilt and fear. But what would a man of Judah's strength be afraid of?

At the burial she felt many eyes on her. But the look of suspicion in one set of eyes frightened her—Bathshua's cold stare was unnerving. Suddenly, Tamar's heart was filled with fear for her future. Over and over, Tamar kept telling herself that there was absolutely nothing that she could have done to prevent Er's death. It was Bathshua who had seen nothing to blame in her son's wickedness. However, Bathshua's stare was so intimidating that Tamar struggled to hold onto the reality of her innocence.

She found herself wondering if perhaps her argument with Er had resulted in his death. She wondered, too, if Er eventually would have lost control and harmed her. If so, what would Judah have done to his son? What would her father have done?

Tamar forced herself to control her wild thoughts. She knew the truth: Bathshua's influence and dominance over Er had turned him against his father's God. And that, more than anything else, was what ruined him.

Tamar felt suspended in reality. Being a widow so suddenly, and at such a young age, seemed impossible. She was not merely a widow, however. She was doubly cursed. She was a childless widow.

She wondered if Judah had any inkling what her marriage to Er had been like. What had Er said to his father about her? Or to Bathshua?

When she learned that Judah had ordered Onan to take her as a wife to fulfill his obligation to produce an heir for Er,[26] Tamar experienced tremendous relief...at first.

After the disaster of her marriage to Er, her shattered little girl's dreams of happily-ever-after were beyond repair. But her hopes for a baby and a legitimate place in the family were rekindled with the new marriage.

She quickly discovered, however, that Onan only intended to placate Judah with a show of marrying her. He had learned well from his mother how easy it was to deceive his father. Onan slept with her often enough. But after using her, he would withdraw in time to prevent her from getting pregnant.[27] It was clear that Onan had no intention of producing offspring for Er. Giving Tamar a child would only serve to reduce Onan's share of Judah's wealth when his father died. He clearly planned to have the best of both worlds: He wanted to appear to be an honorable brother, and he wanted to indulge in pleasure with Tamar as well. But there would be no baby. That dream, too, was not to be.

Tamar knew she was under constant scrutiny. Everyone searched for any sign that she might be pregnant. She also knew they gossiped about the question of her fertility. Whenever possible, Tamar studied Bathshua closely to see if she could detect any knowledge on her part of Onan's efforts to prevent her from conceiving. But her face was always a mask that gave nothing away.

Tamar was certain that Judah didn't know of his son's ploy. She debated whether she would have the courage to tell him, given the chance. Onan continued to make a point of being obvious when he slept with Tamar. So even if she were able to tell Judah, it seemed likely that he'd think she was making an attempt to shift the blame for her infertility to Onan.

Why debate the issue? There never was an opportunity to talk with Judah in private anyway. Since their trip together when Judah had come to pay her bride price, Tamar had never been alone with him. Whenever Tamar saw Judah, Bathshua or one of his sons was always at his side. Bathshua carefully saw to that.

When Tamar first pleaded with Onan to give her a child, he flatly denied his attempts to keep her from conceiving. He accused her of imagining things. He was not as clever at concealing his intentions as his mother, but he had learned much from her. In the end he simply ignored all of her protests. Appeals to his honor, to his manhood, to his obligation to his father, to his dead brother were summarily dismissed. He turned a deaf ear to Tamar's pleadings with amused disdain. Failing in these appeals, she tried to convince him that Bathshua would be happy to have a grandchild. This attempt produced even greater derision. On those occasions when she burst into tears, he seemed to derive great pleasure from her distress. She guessed that her outbursts made him feel dominant and in control—a welcome status after years of being in his mother's iron grip.

Regardless of the variety of pleas she made, nothing changed. Once, in her distress, she even held him as tightly as she could in an attempt to prevent him from withdrawing. Her frantic efforts made him laugh out loud as he easily slipped out of her clasp.

As a final desperate measure to persuade him to give her a child, she reminded him of the promise of Yahweh to make a great nation of Abraham's seed. She thought she saw a flicker of fear cross his face at the mention of Judah's God. But she wasn't certain. However, there was no doubting the raging anger her comment produced—anger thick enough to choke a man.

It had been Judah who had told her about Yahweh and the promise to make a great nation out of Abraham's offspring. But when God took Onan,[28] Tamar could only wonder if Judah's seed would indeed be a part of this grand promise.

With the death of Onan, Bathshua's suspicions increased, and Judah's distraught eyes were full of perplexity when he looked at Tamar. Now, not only did they think that their daughter-in-law was infertile, it appeared they were wondering if the curse she was under was also the reason for their sons' deaths.

She was helpless. There was nothing she could say, nothing she could do to erase their suspicions. No matter how many times she reviewed the events, no matter how many times she asked, "What if," she could not understand how everything in her life had come undone. All of the dreams that were born with Judah's visit to arrange her marriage to Er had been swept away, drowned in raging currents from which there seemed to be no escape.

She had tenaciously held on to the hope that one day she would be able to send word to her father and mother that she was pregnant, that she would soon present them with a grandchild. But that day had never come.

Now Judah was telling her that she was to return to her parent's home as a widow. That she would now have to wait until Shelah, his only remaining son, was old enough to marry her. But something in his eyes troubled her.[29]

As Tamar prepared to go, she thought back over the years since she had joined Judah's family. Even as miserable as the marriages had been, she did not remember ever once wishing for either of her husbands' deaths. All she had hoped for with either Er or Onan was—despite their lack of love for her—that they would give her a baby and then leave her in peace to raise her child.

Even though there was no evidence that she had done anything to contribute to the death of either of her husbands, Tamar knew many in Judah's household assumed she was at fault. Feeling Judah's questioning eyes on her back as she walked away, Tamar made an extra effort to hold her head high.

As Judah watched Tamar begin her journey down the path accompanied by one of those bondsmen, he thought of the eager young bride he had brought with him to the camp so short a time ago. Her young eyes had been so bright and full of wonder. Now her young eyes were grave and troubled. He thought of the heavy burden she carried as she returned childless to her parents. She was so obviously trying to be brave. His heart softened momentarily.

Then his mind raced to his sons...Er...Onan. Images of them as young boys painfully floated through his memory. He'd been so proud. Suddenly, an unwelcomed face replaced them in his mind's eye. Joseph. *Joseph!*

Judah frowned and shook his head in an effort to clear his mind. Could God possibly be punishing him? He heard Joseph's youthful voice calling him from the pit. The same question that had plagued him for years pushed its way to the surface once again: "Why didn't I join Reuben and protect him?" The two of them together, he knew, could have held off Simeon and Levi, and then the other brothers would have backed down.

No! It wasn't his fault. Joseph deserved what he got for being so high and mighty. He took such pleasure in his dreams where everyone bowed down to him.

Oh, but how crushed, how heartbroken his father, Jacob, had been as he had looked helplessly at Joseph's bloody coat in his trembling hands. Now Judah understood—twice over—how it felt to lose a treasured son.

Yes, but what of his mother's feelings? Judah thought of the quiet longing he had seen day after day in his mother's, Leah's, lonely eyes as she had watched his father's obvious preference for her sister, Rachel. No, Jacob only got what he deserved for being indifferent to his mother and for the preference he'd shown to Rachel's son, Joseph!

Judah shook himself out of his reverie. He had left his father and brothers behind. He had no intention of digging all that up again.

He was sending Tamar away. He had to protect his only remaining son. He needed an heir. It was God's promise. It wasn't his fault that her future would be barren. Instead of dealing with his own guilt, Judah concentrated his attention on the reasons for believing that his sons' deaths were Tamar's fault. Shifting responsibility was an old, comfortable habit. Digging around in his failures as a man and a father to try to find things that had contributed to his sons' deaths would only add to his grief and pain.

The night before, as the plan had unfolded in her mind, Tamar had been energized. She had felt as if she were awakening from the long months and years of waiting to hear from Judah. But the only word she had heard from Judah's camp was the news of Bathshua's death.

Now in the predawn darkness, she worked quickly, gathering together the things that she would need for the coming day. Long before the rest of the household stirred, she set out in the cool morning air. As she briskly walked toward her destination, a myriad of thoughts played through her mind.

She contemplated how strange it seemed that one who had enjoyed such a happy childhood should end up where she was now. Her mind wandered back to the evening when she had listened breathlessly to Judah talking to her father about marriage. She thought bitterly of how, at the time, she had resented her father's reluctance. She recalled Judah's assured voice as he had spoken about his strong young son, Er. She remembered now that she had wondered on that night why Judah's assurances had not served to totally calm her father's doubts.

She relived how flattered she had been that night to realize how taken Judah was with her. She reminisced over her total amazement at the incredible bride price that he had offered for her. Then, her mind raced through every detail of the oath he had sworn to protect her.

She was startled that tears welled up as she thought of the early days in Judah's camp. She remembered the days when everyone carefully watched for signs of pregnancy, a pregnancy that had never happened. She recalled the argument Judah and Bathshua had after Er's death over whether to give Onan to her in levirate marriage. For once Bathshua had gotten so loud that everyone in the camp knew they were fighting. Judah's ominous rumblings echoed in her mind even now. She recalled how he had insisted that it was the right thing to do and that it would be done. That argument replayed itself point by point. Bathshua's one last attempt at resistance was especially vivid in the replayed event. All of her arguments, including her trump card—her argument that Tamar was probably not fertile anyway—were recounted. The memory of how Bathshua had scornfully reminded Judah that he had gotten her pregnant on their wedding bed stung bitterly as it paraded through her mind. Tamar's memory of the fact that not even a raging Bathshua could change Judah when he made up his mind brought a moment of pause.

Tamar physically shook herself and roughly rubbed her temples to regain control of her present thoughts. She urgently needed to go over all her options one last time. She wanted to see if there was anything she had overlooked, anything she had not considered. One final question had to be answered: Was there any other choice?

She stopped abruptly and gazed back down the path she'd just covered. She momentarily entertained the possibility of simply turning around and going home. She had come quite a distance. Still there was time to return before everyone prepared to go to the fields for the morning and wondered why she was sleeping so late. She had to work to resist the temptation to think that it would be better if she just turned around, went home, and continued to wait. Simpler, yes. But better? Options marched back and forth in her mind.

Better? Better than what? Better—or just less risky? And wait for *what?* Wait for Judah to fulfill his promise? She had been waiting, waiting silently, for a very long time.[30] Shelah had long since attained the age when he was old enough to marry her, and yet Judah had sent no word.

She had often wondered since the fateful day when Judah had sent her home to live with her father if it would have been better if she had protested and asked to stay. But after Onan had been struck dead and buried beside Er, all the warmth had drained from Judah's eyes. Tamar had felt so alone that she had been relieved—at first—when Judah had told her it would be best if she returned to her father's house to wait until Shelah was old enough to marry her. What a fool she had been not to realize he had never intended to fulfill his promise! If she had demanded to stay, her very presence would have made ignoring her more difficult. And it would have made Shelah's obligation to marry her more obvious. She had been so lonely and unhappy at that time, however, that she had not been able to see the possible ramifications of leaving. She had not wanted to stay in the tense atmosphere of Judah's camp. Home had seemed a welcome shelter. So she had meekly followed Judah's instructions without protest.

No, she thought as she started walking as fast as she could, she would *not* go home this morning to continue the futile business of waiting on Judah. Clearly, just waiting was not going to force Judah to live up to his word. What he was doing was not right. It was not fair. Something had to be done.

As she walked on, her mind sorted though her options one by one. She could continue on this journey, find Judah, and demand that he make good on his promise to have Shelah marry her. That, she knew, would be quite a scene. She would be embarrassed, and Judah would be embarrassed. She smiled wanly as she thought about how surprised Judah would be to have her stand up to him. She could handle an argument now—endless heartache had made her much stronger. She was no longer the blushing young woman he had brought home to marry his son.

But what if Shelah died, just like Er and Onan? If there was a curse, she thought, it was on Bathshua and her sons—even she was dead now! If Shelah died after marrying her, she would definitely be blamed—maybe even killed. Could she rely on Judah to protect her from Bathshua's relatives if yet another son died while married to her? Maybe it was Judah who was cursed.

Next, she had thought of demanding a divorce from her betrothal to Shelah. This approach would require going before the elders and further embarrassment. And what would be the point? What man would marry a divorced woman who had already had two husbands, both having died, and who was, to all appearances, infertile? *Not a chance,* she thought, *not a chance.*

Question after question seemed to pound against the walls of her mind. What if Judah demanded that her father return the bride price? Her one last shred of pride came from the memory that she had once been considered worth a small fortune.

Were there any other options? No. She now settled on the plan that she had rehearsed carefully and repeatedly in the night. It seemed her only option. No other plan made sense—only the one that had exploded in her mind when the word had come of Bathshua's death.[31] When she was told that Judah was going up to Timnah to visit his sheepshearers, the timing for the plan seemed to be right, and in the night the details had come to her.

Tamar knew just the spot along the road to Timnah where she could intercept Judah—just outside the gate to Enaim.[32] There was a spring nearby, and a short distance away, there was a cave where she and her brothers had played as children.

Dawn was breaking as she neared Enaim. The closer she came to the spring, the more feverishly her mind rehearsed again every detail of her plan. Only now the plan that had seemed so clear the night before seemed far less certain. Finding that the cave had not changed in all the years since she had last visited helped calm her a bit. Moving quickly, she undid the bedroll of blankets she had slung over her shoulder and began to make a pallet in the back of the cave. It needed to be far enough out of sight that anyone who happened by would have to actually enter the cave to find it.

She took the change of clothing she had wrapped inside from the blankets. She quickly changed from her widow's garments into a beautiful brightly colored robe. As she wrapped the heavy veil across her face, she realized that her hands were shaking.

As she made the final preparations, she began to fully confront the realities of what she was planning. Tamar's shaking hands made her wonder if her nerves might fail her. She knew if she would simply keep moving that her anxiety would lessen. So she tucked her widow's garments out of sight between the blankets and headed to find the spring she remembered from so long ago. As she strode in the direction of the spring, she was struck by the beautiful colors of her robe. She had worn her widow's garments for so long that it seemed strange to be wearing anything else. Strange, but also exhilarating.

When she found the spring, she saw that it flowed freely. She was relieved that it had not dried up. Water to offer Judah was an important part of her plan. The good clear water flowing from the spring bolstered her courage and firmed her resolve. However, when she closed her eyes and took a long drink, she could feel her heart pounding in her head. As she started to straighten up after drawing the water, she felt herself trembling inside.

Tamar took a deep breath and struggled along the faint path until she found a place where she could look down on the highway. It was the perfect spot. She could wait here in the cool shade, and she was positioned far enough from the highway that she could see long before being seen. She found a place to sit, settled in, and took another sip of the water.

Where had the sudden surge of fear that was threatening to undermine her plan come from? What was the fear? Was she afraid that Judah would recognize her? The veil covered all but her eyes, and she didn't think her eyes would be enough to give her away. But her voice? What if he recognized her voice?

Her plan, which had seemed so simple, so perfect the night before, now seemed treacherous. Then it came to her. She could mimic her mother's voice like she used to do when she was trying to fool her little brothers into keeping their eyes closed long enough to fall asleep.

It took her several tries before she thought she sounded fairly natural as she said in her mother's very mature voice, "Good day, sir. Would you care for some water?" Maybe it wasn't a perfect imitation, but it didn't sound like her voice either, and that was the point.

She sat in her sheltered position straining to see as far down the road as possible. She was searching for a traveler who looked like Judah. Seeing a group of travelers approaching, she searched to determine if any of them might be Judah. None had a figure of his imposing proportions. Her doubts began to plague her again. What if he came along in a large party? What if he were talking and didn't notice her? Questions tormented her reason. What if he were not coming by today at all? What if she had already missed him though she was so early? Or what if he had Shelah with him?

Was what she was planning to do really wicked? Didn't Judah's failure to have Shelah marry her in effect nullify the betrothal? Certainly, she told herself, it was no more wicked for her to deceive Judah than it was for him to break his word to her. Certainly, he owed her a debt that he was ignoring. Certainly, she had no other good option that she could think of. But did that make it right?

Try as she might, she could not resolve the dilemma or sort out all the questions. God would have to judge her. She did not know how to judge for herself.

What she knew for certain was that Judah had not kept his word. She was also absolutely sure that he would not honor his promise if she did not do something. He had made a promise, sworn an oath, and it wasn't right for him to leave her a childless widow. She had done exactly as he had instructed. But he had left her to live a life of shame, a disgrace to herself and to her family, and she was not going to leave things as they stood.

He owed her. He owed her, and it wasn't fair. *It wasn't fair.*

Her feelings of defiance spurred her to her feet. She moved closer to the road for a clearer view. Then, she saw the two men. Without doubt one of the two could only be Judah. The other she guessed was Hiram. Now that she had Judah in sight, the possibilities of her plan suddenly seemed real, so real, in fact, that a new idea confounded her, one that she hadn't had time to think through.

What if her long shot plan succeeded? What if she did conceive, then what? How would she ever explain what she had done? How would she tell her father? Her mother? She had barely managed to convince herself that this was the only option left. How would she ever convince her family? Would anyone understand? She told herself that these questions could wait until she saw what happened. But as the two figures climbed the hill, these questions kept creeping back into her mind.

The men paused at the turnoff to Enaim, and her heart sank. Her realization that they were going to stop in the village was almost more than she could bear. Her sudden awareness of her own hunger made her realize what a fool she had been. Of course, the men would be hungry after walking all morning. They would want to stop to eat. She had overlooked this possibility.

As the two men started up the long hill, Judah, who still had the eyes of a hawk, spotted movement beside the road ahead—a flash of bright color. The movement reminded him of a special place. It was just beyond the turnoff that led into Enaim—a little-used path that led to a small spring located not too far from the road. The water was a little hard to reach, but he remembered how clear and sweet that water was. Usually when he traveled this way, he went into the village where he could get a meal and something stronger than spring water to slake his thirst. But today the water and rest in the cool shade beside the spring sounded perfect.

He could tell Hiram had not seen any movement. All Judah had heard from him for the past 30 minutes was how hungry he was, how his feet were sore after their long walk, and how he looked forward to a long nap after they had something to eat.

Tamar's heart was pounding so hard that she had to take deep breaths and concentrate on not fainting. One small flaw, and her entire plan was unraveling! She was cursed! Then suddenly, to her amazement, she saw Hiram head into the village while Judah moved on up the road in her direction.

Judah had sent Hiram on ahead, saying that he first wanted to check and see if the little spring up ahead was still flowing and whether the water was as sweet as he remembered it being. He assured Hiram that he would join him in half an hour's time.

Spring water? Judah? Although Hiram thought this choice awfully strange, he kept his peace. Perhaps so soon after his wife's death, Judah's appetite wasn't what it once had been. Maybe he just wanted to be alone for a while.

But being alone was not what Judah had in mind. No one, he knew, but a woman would be wearing clothes as bright as what he had glimpsed. And only one kind of woman would be alone outside of town near the path to the little spring.

Tamar looked down at the staff she clutched tightly in her hand. Judah had given her his staff as a pledge. She thought of his signet and cord that she had wrapped tightly in the sash around her waist, and she was amazed, afraid, joyful, and sorrowful. As she hurried along, she silently cried out in prayer to Judah's God for a child to come out of her desperate gamble. What if her plan hadn't worked? What if she wasn't pregnant? She didn't even want to think of that possibility.

If she were with child by Judah, he would have proof that she was not infertile. Plus, her pregnancy would erase the lingering question in her own mind that some lack in her as a wife could have contributed to the deaths of Er and Onan. She *had* to be pregnant. This was her last hope. Now, she prayed, "Please God!" Tamar's legs were shaky as she made her way along the trail that would take her home. If she arrived home before dark, her parents would think little of her absence. Otherwise, she would be uncomfortable answering their questions tonight.

She slowed down and breathed easier as she marveled again—Judah had not recognized her! If he had discovered her identity, all would have been lost—most probably, even her life. With a small smile, she remembered her concerns about how to entice him. She needn't have worried. All she had to do was stand there. He had walked up and taken charge. She should have known he would. Her heart had pounded furiously as she realized that her planning had not gone beyond the logistics involved in luring him—what to wear, where to stand, where to take him if she managed to catch his eye. How naïve she had been! She had not even considered the issue of payment.

As Tamar continued to replay the events of the last hours struggling to grasp their reality, she felt again the sense of panic that had run through her body as she had been leading Judah to the cave and suddenly realized that a "real" harlot would ask for payment in advance.

Upon recognizing her oversight she had quickly asked, "What will you give me to lie with you?"

Judah had replied, "I will send you a young goat from my flock."

She had been amazed to hear herself say in a brazen tone, "And what will you give me as a pledge until you send it?"

As she thought it over now, she was astonished at herself. Why had she asked for the pledge? She had asked for payment only to try to make herself sound like a real harlot. She certainly didn't want a goat from him, so why, she wondered, had she asked for a pledge when all she really cared about was having a child? Worse still, remembering the look on Judah's face, she had known her request had struck a nerve that threatened disaster.

She couldn't remember the next part as clearly. She did remember that she had been improvising furiously when she reached for his hand and started away from the road as if to say, "Forget about the pledge." Her memory of the next few moments was too choked with fear to even guess how far Judah had let her lead him before he had stopped and pulled his hand away, but it seemed like only a few steps. She could vividly remember though how her heart had dropped to her feet as she had turned slowly to face him…it made her tremble even now as she relived the horrible moment when she had expected the worst.

She recalled the astonishment she had felt when she had heard him say in a gruff tone that had told her he was bent on reasserting himself, "What pledge should I give you?"

Tamar remembered that with these words, her spirits had soared. She had known that he was determined to have her—whatever it took. Her intuition had given her the answer. Instinctively, without thinking, she had casually said over her shoulder, as though it were a matter of no consequence to her, "Your signet and cord…and the staff in your hand."

She recalled the niggling fear she had felt when Judah had made no reply. Now that the encounter was behind her, she remembered every unexpected difficulty. She marveled how at each moment, as though guided by an unseen hand, there had been a solution even though it had seemed that disaster was just one step away.

The sound of her own footsteps now reminded her of the sounds of Judah's footsteps that had told her he was still following her along the path toward the cave. She recalled how the sound had been all there was to reassure her because he hadn't responded when she asked for the staff and signet. She could still feel where Judah had placed his big hand on her shoulder when he at last had said, "Just a minute."

It had been one of the most dramatic moments of her life. She thought of how his touch had startled her. She realized again now that she had had no idea what to expect next. She recalled how when she had turned to face him that every nerve in her body had stood on end and every muscle had been taut. She remembered that she had felt as though she couldn't breathe. She thought of how she had looked into his face and tried to read his intentions, and how it had seemed as though time had slowed to a crawl.

Now thinking back on it, she wasn't sure whether she had been expecting to see lust or anger. But in that moment she knew she had been amazed at how much Judah had aged in the few years that she had known him. She thought of his face and of how it had always been weather-beaten. But she recalled now, in her memory, the deep lines she had seen in it today, and how they were carved into his cheeks. She thought, too, of the streaks of gray she had noticed running through his hair, and she could see that his eyes were now forever shadowed by loss.

She tried to remember if she had looked into his face for only an instant or longer. So many thoughts had rushed through her mind at that moment that she couldn't say how long it had lasted. In that moment her memories of the past—Judah bargaining with her father, Judah at the graves of first Er and then Onan, Judah sending her away—had come so fast that it had hardly registered with her when he handed her his staff.

She could picture how he had removed the signet from around his neck. With both hands, he had placed the cord holding it around her neck. She mulled over how he had taken particular care not to disturb her veil, and how at that moment all of her preconceptions of this encounter had shattered. It had been such a small gesture of respect, but it had shaken her to the core. She remembered how she had suddenly recognized that the aging man standing before her was not the Judah of her thoughts—her anguished thoughts since that day when he sent her away. She realized afresh, now in her memory, that standing there in the shaded glade, she had seen a very different man, one who had lost two sons and a wife. She remembered how seeing him that way had forced her to confront anew a familiar question that she had thought of and repressed many times in the long days since she had returned to her father's house: If I had been Judah, would I have given my only remaining son to a woman whose first two husbands had died so suddenly?

She recalled now how realization had hit her like a thunderbolt in that moment, for she had known immediately that she was no longer angry with Judah. She relived the freeing feeling she had experienced at that instant when she had known that she likely would have done the same as Judah. She recalled how she had been liberated from the resentment and bitterness that had held her captive. Remembering that moment again made her heart sing. She felt alive, she felt free.

Tamar relaxed. She felt certain she was pregnant. Somehow she knew that Judah's God had heard and answered her heart's cry for a child.

*About three months later **Judah** was told,*
*"**Tamar** your daughter-in-law has played the harlot;*
and moreover she is with child by harlotry."
*And **Judah** said, "Bring her out, and let her be burned."*
As she was being brought out, she sent word to her father-in-law,
"By the man to whom these belong, I am with child."
And she said, "Mark, I pray you, whose these are,
the signet and the cord and the staff."
Then Judah acknowledged them and said,
"She is more righteous than I, inasmuch as
I did not give her to my son Shelah."
And he did not lie with her again.
When the time of her delivery came, there were twins in her womb.
And when she was in labor, one put out a hand;
and the midwife took and bound on his hand a scarlet thread, saying,
"This came out first."

But as he drew back his hand, behold, his brother came out;
and she said, "What a breach you have made for yourself!"
*Therefore his name was called **Perez**.*
Afterward his brother came out with
the scarlet thread upon his hand;
and his name was called Zerah.
GENESIS 38:24-30 RSV

*Now these are the descendants of **Perez**:*
***Perez** was the father of Hezron, Hezron of Ram,*
Ram of Ammin'adab, Ammin'adab of Nahshon,
Nahshon of Salmon, Salmon of Bo'az,
Bo'az of Obed, Obed of Jesse,
and Jesse of David.
RUTH 4:18-22 RSV

The Power of Courage

Be strong and of good courage;
be not frightened, neither be dismayed;
for the LORD your God is with thee,
wherever you go.
JOSHUA 1:9

Albert Camus, the Nobel Prize-winning existentialist writer, once said, "If, after all, men cannot always make history have meaning, they can always act so that their lives have one." But can we really? Sometimes when life falls apart, we gaze into the future and can see nothing but emptiness. Can acting create meaning? Can something come from nothing? In the face of a shattered loss, the search for meaning is far more than a perplexing philosophical question. *Why* can become a very piercing question. When that anguish echoes in your soul with no answer, the next question is *how?* How do we face tomorrow without hope?

When life falls apart, it takes courage to believe that there is an answer to that question. But even in the depths of a Babylonian dungeon, sunk in the mire, the prophet Jeremiah spoke of a gracious God who has "loved us with an everlasting love." Great is His faithfulness! We serve a God who provides "strength for today and bright hope for tomorrow,"

At its heart, Tamar's story is about having the courage to act when life falls apart. It is the story of how God taught a woman to trust Him in the small, myriad details of her life and how God used a woman to strip a man of his excuses and self-justification and to make a new man of him. In the face of total uncertainty and the possible threat of death, Tamar faced the "whys" of her life and acted with courage.

We tend to think that courageous people face the challenges of their lives without fear or uncertainty. Our culture defines courage as bravery based on fearlessness. Most of us *could* face our challenges and problems with courage and uncommon valor if we knew ahead of time that the outcome of our difficulties would be positive. Unfortunately, we rarely have that luxury. In fact, it's in the "not knowing" that true courage finds its opportunity. We know the miraculous outcome of Tamar's story, but Tamar had no idea what the conclusion would be when she entered into her bold plan.

Courage That Faces Fear

Try to imagine Tamar's emotional state. Surely she felt anger at Judah. He sent her back to her father with a promise that Shelah would be her husband when he was old enough. Shelah had become a grown man, and Tamar still had not heard from Judah again. She must have despaired of her situation. She was a widow—twice over. Her first husband was wicked, and her second husband was unwilling to provide a child to continue his brother's line. God slew both men because of their wickedness. And on top of her plight as a childless widow, Tamar was blamed for being childless and suspected of being the cause of her husbands' deaths.

She existed on the fringes of a community where life revolved around families and children. There seemed little hope for a positive resolution. Widowed twice, there was yet another brother alive to marry her, but that wasn't happening. Under those circumstances, no other man could marry her. She saw her future as one of lonely isolation.

Tamar was desperate to find a solution to her dilemma. She could come to only one possible way out as she debated and deliberated in her mind. She must have been frightened as she planned her strategy. There were too many uncertainties to have a fixed plan. She knew that she had to remain flexible and be able to "go with the flow." Her objective was clear, but the twists and turns along the path to realizing her goals made her heart skip a beat.

She had to face the possibility that Judah would not be fooled by her costume. Even in the prostitute's clothing she envisioned and hurriedly pieced together, Tamar knew that Judah might recognize her as his daughter-in-law. If so, there was no way to predict Judah's reaction. Yet her fate rested in his hands. If her disguise failed, would she face death? On the other hand, if she failed to seduce him and conceive a child, she had nothing to live for.

Judah's inadequacies were evident even before Tamar came on the scene. All through this man's life, there had been a pattern of shifting responsibility to others and providing alibis for his own failings. There are two significant examples that demonstrate Judah's lack of character.

The first time we encounter Judah's failures, he and his brothers are deciding what to do about Joseph, the much-desired and long-awaited first child of Rachel. Next to the youngest of Jacob's sons was his father's favorite, a fact that had bred a smoldering hatred in his brothers' hearts for years. He also annoyed them by his accounting of dreams suggesting that he, as the youngest, would one day rule over all of them. Joseph's very existence reminded them of the inferior status of their lives—that Rachel was their father's favorite wife and that her firstborn son was his favorite son.

Reuben, the eldest, had sternly cautioned his brothers to lay no hand on Joseph. But in Reuben's absence, Judah took over and schemed to get rid of Joseph without actually killing him. He suggested to his brothers that they sell Joseph to the Ishmaelites as a slave. The others jumped at this bloodless means of getting rid of the hated brother. Judah's solution seemed an easy way out.

But Judah's scheme was not without hard and bitter consequences for him. Unable to face either the distance he now felt between himself and his brothers because of their shared guilt or the grief his father suffered at the loss of Joseph, Judah abandoned his family, shirking his responsibilities for a second time as he left his brothers to care for their father and the family business. This was no small failing. It was a major abandonment.

When Tamar came into the story, Judah was looking for a wife for his oldest son. She knew nothing of Judah's propensity to shift responsibility and escape the consequences. With typical irony, God used unlikely circumstances to finally get through to Judah.

At the time Tamar became a part of Judah's family, he had three sons, and we see in the telling of the story that the two eldest sons were out of control. His firstborn son was wicked, and the next was disobedient. God pronounced judgment on both of them and struck them dead. Rather than face up to God's judgment on the two sons, Judah blamed their deaths on Tamar.

The old pattern of Judah's dealings with difficult circumstances surfaced again. On top of his failure as a father, Judah did not live up to his obligations to his daughter-in-law. Thus, Tamar was forced to live in her father's house as a burden on her family, with neither a husband nor a child.

Tamar went through great despair and grief, but she summoned her courage, took off her widow's weeds, and set about to seduce Judah. And when the seduction was complete, two things had been established: Judah had incontrovertible evidence that it was not a lack on Tamar's part that caused the death of his sons, and he knew firsthand that she was fully capable in every respect to be a wife and become a mother. Through Tamar's high-risk masquerade, God finally stripped Judah of all of his self-serving alibis and set him on the road to becoming a man who takes responsibility.

When the day of accounting came, Judah finally took responsibility for his actions. He could have tried to cover things up. He could have tried to create an alibi as his way out. But, here we see him, *for the first time*, taking things head on...and he becomes a new man.

How do we know this change occurred? Years later during a period of famine, Judah went down out of Canaan to Egypt to replenish the family food supply. When his long-lost brother, Joseph, threatened to keep Benjamin as a hostage, Judah stepped up and offered himself to be a slave in return for the release of his father's only remaining child—he thinks—by Rachael, who is dead.[33] Finally, he was a leader who put others ahead of himself.

Because Tamar had the courage to pursue what was rightly hers, Judah finally humbled himself, faced his failings, and turned to God. In death, Judah's father, Jacob, gave Judah his "blessing"—skipping over Reuben, the older son, and naming Judah the leader of the family clan.

God at Work...in the Details

The story of Tamar shows God, in His great mercy, working to redeem sinful people. The story clearly illustrates that God is at work when lives are falling apart. And even as He is working out His plan, He is working courage into our lives.

In hindsight, when we look at all of the elements of the story of Tamar and Judah, we can clearly see the hand of God at work. How amazing that God made all of the broken fragments fit together—such unlikely events pieced together in the most surprising fashion, a quilt so intricate as to defy human origin. God was working in ways that certainly were not evident to either Tamar or Judah at the outset. And, even more amazing, they are incredible to us centuries later.

One of the many striking examples of this is the fact that when Judah arrived on the scene of his encounter with Tamar—disguised in her veil as a prostitute and waiting for him on the road to Timnah— he was carrying no means of payment. Since Tamar's sole goal was to get pregnant from this encounter, it strains the imagination to think that she had planned in advance to seek a pledge for future payment from Judah in the form of his signet and staff. It is only because we know the ending that we understand that down the road she was going to need these items. Without them to prove that she was pregnant with his child, the final pieces of the puzzle would not have fit into place: Tamar would not have survived Judah's unjust death sentence; Judah would have killed his own unborn sons; and Perez would not have carried on Judah's line as God intended.

Tamar's wary response to Judah's promise to pay her later is certainly understandable given Judah's earlier failure to keep his promise to her, but it was surely a spontaneous reaction rather than a planned response. If her demand for a pledge was a premeditated means of guaranteeing payment in the future, it was an ill-conceived and risky move. Her implication that he was untrustworthy, while true, could have easily insulted Judah's dignity, and he could have responded in anger or simply walked away in indignation.

If Tamar had made Judah angry, all would have been lost. She would have failed in her principal objective—to conceive a child by Judah, a child who, as the legal heir of Judah's firstborn son, Er, would have full rights of inheritance. She would also have lost the opportunity, as the mother of the heir, to once again be restored to her rightful place in Judah's household.

As further evidence that God was providing for her in every detail, we note that while Judah's signet was an object she could easily hide under her clothing, his staff, on the other hand, was a far more difficult object to conceal. Here we see God at work in three ways. First, the staff and signet were the closest things to DNA evidence available to Tamar in that day and time. They were her best bet for convincing Judah that he was the father of her child. Second, in the face of her aggressive demand, Judah could have been either angered by her challenge to his honor or attracted by her feisty take-no-prisoners boldness. As we know, he was attracted to her despite her demand.

Third, God set Judah up by giving him a potent dose of time-delayed medicine. In the past, Judah had succeeded in rationalizing his cruelty, selfishness, pride, and unreliability by blaming others. Somehow, Judah had managed to shut out the memory of his father's grief as well as Tamar's pain. But now God brought into his daily life a visual reminder to force Judah to confront himself, to face up to who and what he had been. Every time he reached for his staff—first the replacement one he used for three months and later the original staff after it had been reclaimed—he would have to confront his weakness.

God was not going to let Judah escape his sinfulness until he faced the truth and became the man God intended him to be, one who would take on the responsibility of leading and putting the well-being of those for whom he was responsible above his own. Clearly, Tamar's obtaining the signet and staff from Judah has all the earmarks of a mini-miracle...surely God was at work to accomplish His purposes.

When Things Go from Bad to Worse

Tamar's experience seems to illustrate the importance of seeing God's love and provision in the small details of our lives. We can more clearly see this from the following aspects of her story.

When a month had passed and Tamar found that she had conceived, she must have finally realized that she had moved from one desperate situation to an even more desperate one. Instead of being a barren widow with no hope of marriage in sight, she was now pregnant and unmarried—a very precarious circumstance for a woman in that day and time. And yet she does not appear to have been consumed by fear because it appears she let it be known early on that she was pregnant.

The author of Genesis didn't think it important to tell us by what means it was told to Judah that Tamar was pregnant, but the account is quite specific about the fact that Judah found out about her condition when she was only about three months pregnant. That early in her pregnancy, Tamar should have had little difficulty in concealing her condition if she had wanted to. While it is possible that she was so elated that she rashly trumpeted the news without any thought for the trouble that might result, it is not likely. By now she had been educated in the school of hard knocks. She had lived through the death of two husbands and knew the pain and suffering of banishment from Judah's encampment to the lonely life of childless widowhood.

Tamar's decision to let the fact of her pregnancy become known would make the most sense if it were true that she had come to faith in Judah's God and that she had seen in all of the small everyday details of her recent encounter with Judah that God was taking care of her. Perhaps she had even glimpsed that she was a part of the mighty miracle-working Yahweh's plan to fulfill the covenant He had made with Abraham, Isaac, and Jacob. This latter insight may have been beyond Tamar's grasp. But with all of the story before us from beginning to end, we can see an incredible puzzle being brought together piece by piece.[34]

Moreover, even though letting it be known at three months that she had conceived was early in terms of her pregnancy, it does not represent a snap judgment on her part. She had had a good six to eight weeks to consider what her next move should be. As further evidence that she was not acting rashly or emotionally, we should consider that she could have announced her pregnancy even earlier, but that she apparently waited until she had safely passed the early stages where the risk of miscarriage is highest. Coupled with the timing of her decision to let the fact of her pregnancy be known, we have further evidence of the likelihood that Tamar had developed faith in God by the nature of Tamar's response to Judah's hypocritical demand that she be burned.

She was cool, measured, and devastatingly effective. She did not plead with her family to protect her. She did not try to flee. She did not lash out at Judah in anger or terror. Tamar simply produced the signet and staff and announced that she was with child by the man to whom they belonged. Then, she was inspired to add what was essentially the same question that Judah had asked his father Jacob when he presented him with Joseph's bloody coat: "Do you recognize whose are these?"[35] God gave Tamar the words that would cut through all of Judah's hypocrisy and selfishness.

What a picture of determination and courage! Tamar was a woman who was prepared to take things head on, a woman convinced of the justice of her cause and prepared to risk all to see her part of God's promise to Abraham fulfilled. She was a woman who came to see God working in the smallest details of her life. We believe it was this faith that gave her the courage to calmly face Judah's wrath and lay claim to her rightful place in his household as the mother of his heir. She truly was a woman with a different kind of strength.

Let God Be God

Despite difficult, unanswered questions in this story, who can dispute that Tamar's request for Judah's staff and signet is evidence of God at work in the small things to accomplish His divine purposes. Tamar's story speaks to us of a courage that consists of learning to see God in the way He chooses to reveal himself.

There are many instances in Scripture of God speaking or acting in the most dramatic fashion we could imagine. Among these, there are few occasions more spectacular than in the heroic story of Elijah's contest with the prophets of Baal on Mount Carmel. In the first stage of the contest, the 450 prophets of Baal prayed to their god, pleading all morning and all afternoon for Baal to send fire down to consume the sacrifice that they had placed on the altar. Then, after their lengthy efforts proved futile, Elijah prayed to Yahweh at the time of the evening sacrifice...and the fire of the Lord fell from heaven, consuming not only the sacrifice prepared by Elijah but also the wood and the stones of the altar and the 12 barrels of water Elijah had ordered be poured over the sacrifice.[36]

Let's stop just a second and take note of the impact this incredibly dramatic event had. Instead of seeing a man inspired to new levels of faith and courage, we find Elijah fleeing in terror from the wrath of Queen Jezebel, whose prophets of Baal he had just executed. We shake our heads in wonder at how a prophet who had just seen God answer his prayer by raining fire down from heaven could possibly be afraid of anything or anyone.

The answer undoubtedly lies partly in Elijah's sheer physical and emotional exhaustion after the rigors of the day. Reading further, we find an intriguing final episode in this drama. After a brief time of rest during which God twice put Elijah to sleep and afterward provided him with food and water, we see Elijah journey to Mount Horeb in the Sinai.

Here, full of self-pity, Elijah ascends the mountain and takes a front-row seat for a divinely orchestrated spectacular event. "And behold, the LORD passed by, and a great and strong wind rent the mountains, and broke in pieces the rocks before the LORD; but the LORD was not in the wind; and after the wind an earthquake; but the LORD was not in the earthquake; and after the earthquake a fire; but the LORD was not in the fire; and after the fire a still small voice."[37]

Out of this experience where God first provided for his small, ordinary daily needs for food and water and then spoke to him in a still small voice, Elijah regained his courage and sense of purpose. As you think about these events, ask yourself the following question: Which event strengthened Elijah's faith more—the 40 days of quiet solitude in the wilderness that prepared him to hear the message of the still small voice on Mount Horeb or those incredible, climactic moments on Mount Carmel when the fire of the Lord fell? And what of us today?

We want to see God rain fire from heaven. And, sometimes, at times of His choosing, He does. But more often, it is the intricate arrangement of the ordinary details of our lives that point to His loving care. Sometimes, He reaches us most deeply in a still small voice. We tend to think that we would believe more readily if we could have been on Mount Carmel to see the fire rain down. We think that if we had stood alongside the disciples and seen Christ heal the sick and raise the dead that our faith would never falter. But if we are to judge from the experiences of Elijah and the disciples, unwavering faith does not come easily—even when God works mighty miracles.

It requires the discipline of faith to learn to see the working of His hand, however He chooses to act. But it also requires courage to accept God's right to reveal Himself in the manner of His own choosing without us questioning His goodness or love for us. One reason that the apostle Paul so often instructs us to give thanks—and not just give thanks for the pleasant things, but in all things—is to help us to grow in our capacity to see God's power and love at work in all of the details of our lives, great and small.

The Path to Courage

Tamar's story and many other diverse examples in Scripture clearly show that God is always at work to bring us into a right relationship of obedience to Him, and that He speaks to us at different times in different ways in a manner of His wise choosing. Believing that God is both *great* and *good* means accepting that it is God's prerogative, not ours, to define what is good. Part of the discipline of faith is to accept His choice of what is good for us as the right choice—even when our lives fall apart as Tamar's did—even when we simply don't understand.

C. S. Lewis once wrote that "courage is not simply one of the virtues, but the form of every virtue at the testing point."[38] This was true in biblical times, and it remains true today. Thankfully, we are not required to somehow manufacture courage from within ourselves. Rather, God promises us, "My power works best in your weakness."[39]

In the story of Tamar, the two major figures barely escape a tragic ending. If Judah had not faced up to the truth regarding Tamar and taken responsibility, he never would have become the leader God intended for him to be. Even more tragic would have been the deaths of his own unborn twin sons by whom his line was to continue through to David. Without Tamar's courage, Judah may well have sacrificed his place in God's eternal story.

Our awareness of God's loving concern for us is the prime ingredient that will nourish our faith, our courage, and our determination. If we really believe that God is loving and good, and if we really believe that God is great and powerful, we can face hardship and uncertainty without letting our fears gain control and, like Tamar, courageously persist through the bad times until God brings us through our trials to triumph and joy either in this life or in the life to come.

As we try to develop the courage we need to face our challenges, we can learn from the powerful prayer of St. Francis of Assisi:

> God, grant me the Serenity to accept the things I cannot change, the Courage to change the things I can, and the Wisdom to know the difference.

The Power of Fortitude

I have been young, and now am old;
yet have I not seen the righteous forsaken,
nor his seed begging bread.
PSALM 37:25 KJV

All through the long period of waiting for Judah to fulfill his obligation to give her to his youngest son, Shelah, Tamar was growing. She
may not have realized it, but God was developing in her one of the
highest forms of courage—fortitude. He was strengthening a part of
her character that had been evident even when she was a child, and
that would now prepare her for action.

When Tamar set out to entice Judah into giving her the child he
had, since Shelah achieved maturity, deprived her of the opportunity
to have, her cause was just, and her tenacity drove her to tremendous
measures to accomplish her righteous goal. She was becoming a
woman of fortitude—a woman with a tenacious refusal to give up
hope in the face of great adversity.[40]

For sheer audacity and raw courage, there are few parallels in
Scripture to Tamar's pursuit of justice. One incident, however, rivals
her daring and tenacity—the story of the young stripling shepherd
who, though untrained in the arts of war, did not hesitate to fight
single-handedly a battle-hardened, heavily armed giant. This remarkable shepherd boy was none other than David, Tamar's own descendent. David went into his deadly duel with Goliath carrying nothing
but his staff, a sling in his hands, and a passion for the honor of God
in his heart.[41]

Hundreds of years before David courageously took on the ferocious Philistine giant in a duel to the death, his ancestors, Tamar and Judah, were locked in a near mortal conflict that sparks the imagination to wonder "what if." What if Tamar had not been determined and courageous? What if she had given up hope during those long months of waiting? What if she had not been wise in her actions and, most particularly, in her choice of words by which God was able to convict Judah of his sin and ward off the death sentence he had so hypocritically pronounced upon her and her unborn child? No Perez. No Boaz. No Obed. No Jesse. No David!

One of the greatest orators in American history, William Jennings Bryan, once said, "The humblest citizen of all the land, when clad in the armor of a righteous cause, is stronger than all the hosts of error."[42] His remarks certainly could be applied to the young David, but, of course, in our reading of the story, they apply to David's great-great-great-grandmother as well.

Becoming like Tempered Steel

"Fortitude" is not a word we hear very often in our culture of ease and comfort. And yet it is as vital for our lives as it was for Tamar's. It is a quality in a person's character that is like the temper in steel that gives it the capacity to retain its flexibility, shape, and cutting edge despite hard usage.

The potential for temper in a piece of steel may be there from the outset, but the realization of that potential depends upon the right circumstances to develop it. Nothing short of being put through the fire and being hammered on again and again will produce the finest tempered steel. And so it is with fortitude. This sterling quality of character can only be forged through long periods of struggle and patient waiting.

Waiting was definitely part of the program for Tamar, just like it is for each of us. Waiting unsuccessfully to have her firstborn child with Er. Waiting futilely to conceive with Onan. Waiting pointlessly for Shelah to mature. Then not only was there the period of waiting before her encounter with Judah, but another waiting period followed afterwards as well. There were several anxious weeks before she had confirmation of the hoped-for conception. And then there were another couple of months of waiting and thinking about how to handle what would come next. Here we see another parallel with the life of her famous great-great-great-grandson, whom the prophet Samuel anointed to be the next king.

Years before David would sit on the throne, he spent long periods in the wilderness on the run from King Saul. During these days, David had ample time to think about how he should act when he became king of Israel. He did not want to repeat Saul's mistakes. David surely recognized that in order for him to be treated with respect as God's anointed, it was imperative that he not set wrong precedents in his dealings with Saul.[43]

When Saul pursued David into the wilderness of En Gedi, Saul went into the very cave where David and his men were hiding. At this point, David had the opportunity to kill Saul. But despite the urgings of his men to do so, he merely crept up and cut off a part of Saul's robe without being seen. After Saul had left the cave, David called to him, showed him the piece he had cut off his robe, and told Saul, "Even though you are trying to kill me, I didn't kill you when I had the chance. I'm leaving it to the Lord to judge between us and avenge me." Then, Saul wept and said, "You are more righteous than I."[44]

David, like Tamar before him, confronted the man who sought his death, but he did it in a spirit that provided an opportunity for Saul to repent. Saul, like Judah before him, found the grace to admit the wrong of what he intended and acknowledged his own moral failings in the same words that Judah had used hundreds of years before.

What is amazing and instructive about this parallel is that both Tamar and David wisely chose the long-run good over short-run satisfaction. Without rancor, each confronted an adversary who was bent on their destruction. Either of them could have focused only on survival or revenge. But both were able to look to the long run, to wait for God's timing.

Tamar wanted a child as desperately as any woman might, but in the long months of waiting she had doubtless recognized that it was not enough for her just to conceive and bear a child. For that child to have any future, it had to have a father. Yet, her response to Judah's condemnation of her was miraculously free of any trace of hostility or vengefulness.

We can only wonder how she found the strength to frame her response in such a nonconfrontational manner to the judgment Judah had pronounced on her. It was carefully calibrated so as not to embarrass Judah or otherwise diminish him. Despite the way he had failed her in the past, she somehow managed to hope that he would be more in the future: the strong father her child would need.

Just as David would later be respectful of King Saul despite his failings,[45] Tamar did not rail at Judah for his duplicity. Instead, she respectfully asked whether he could identify the signet and staff of the man by whom she had conceived. Some might ask whether she did this tongue-in-cheek. But given the deference and respect of Judah's response, it seems only logical to assume that Judah did not take Tamar's response to be an attempt to emasculate him. She was both humble and strong in her approach.

Is it any great surprise, then, that the bold warrior-king David felt such a strong affinity for his great-great-great-grandmother that he named his own daughter after Tamar? It was David's tribute to the legacy left by her example of courage and fortitude.

In Spite of Human Weakness

But you may be thinking, even as we praise Tamar's tremendous fortitude, "What about the deception?" How can this element be reconciled in light of what we know about God and His call for righteousness in our lives? What are we to make of the fact that this woman who appears in the genealogy of Christ seduced her father-in-law in order to conceive an heir for her dead husband which by custom was her duty? Perhaps the answer can be found in Judah's response and, further, in something else we know about God and His plan.

In scriptural stories, God sometimes gives an immediate and direct blessing or He metes out swift judgment in response to particular deeds. In other instances, we have to ferret out the lesson that God is trying to teach us. Sometimes the reason for His judgment about a particular deed is not revealed. Then we have to figure out why in His wisdom He responds immediately in one situation and delays in another or reacts positively in one and negatively in another. To us, the situations may appear to be similar,[46] however, "man looks at the outward appearance, but the LORD looks at the heart" (1 Samuel 16:7 NKJV).

And, we can rejoice at the psalmist's words, "the LORD is merciful and gracious, slow to anger, and plenteous in mercy" (Psalm 103:8 KJV). Knowing that God is merciful should not lead us to believe that we will be immune from the natural consequences of our sins, mistakes, poor choices, and bad decisions.

Tamar's story is not the only biblical story that challenges our understanding of deception and duplicity. We encounter those sins in the lives of Abraham,[47] Sarah,[48] Isaac,[49] Rebekah,[50] Jacob,[51] Rachel,[52] and Judah.[53] We can understand how Abraham and Isaac were moved to deception out of fear of physical harm and Sarah out of fear of embarrassment. It is harder to have sympathy with Rebekah, who conspired with her favorite son, Jacob, to trick Isaac into giving him the blessing that belonged to Esau, the less-favored brother. Such greed is not a pretty sight! Nor would many of us sympathize with Judah, who sold his brother Joseph into slavery and then compounded his father's grief by leading Jacob to believe his favorite son had been eaten by some wild animal.

While our carnal selfishness, pride, and anger—like Judah's—have caused each of us to sin, the shame we feel at the sins that spring from such base motives makes us quick to rationalize and make excuses. We certainly are not inclined to identify with others who sin so blatantly and basely.

Tamar's story is distinctly different than any of those previously mentioned. Her motivation does not seem to have been fear, greed, pride, or selfishness. Instead, hers was a righteous cause, and we can identify with that. Who among us has not been denied something that we believed was our due? For Tamar, it was a broken promise—Judah made a promise and didn't keep his word. His verbal contract was not fulfilled. He lied to Tamar about her future. Judah violated his pledge of Shelah as Tamar's surrogate husband and apparently gave no thought to the fact he was cheating her out of her rights to a child.

And yet, in the end, when Judah discovered that Tamar was the woman who had enticed him along the route to the sheepshearing and that her pregnancy was the result of that encounter, he declares Tamar "more righteous" than he. Even Judah recognized that she was right to demand that he live up to his obligations to her.

But what did Judah mean when he said that she was "more righteous than he"? The custom of the time, which would later be incorporated by Moses in the law,[54] called for a childless widow to be given in marriage to the dead husband's brother to produce an heir who would carry on the deceased man's line. Judah had violated the custom, and

Tamar was determined to see the tradition satisfied and her destiny fulfilled. Tamar, even in a prostitute's disguise, acted in pursuit of truth and justice. Judah, even in his role of authority and power, was perpetuating a lie.

She had engaged in deception by tricking him into giving her a child. His declaration was certainly not a vindication of her method, but it did go to the heart of the matter because Tamar's tenacity and fortitude had resulted in the fulfillment of God's plan.

While we do not celebrate the deception of this imperfect biblical woman, we can recognize the godly motives of her heart, as Judah did. These qualities constitute strength of purpose against overwhelming odds. But most importantly, we can celebrate the fact that God can redeem even bad decisions, situations, and circumstances when our heart is to accomplish His good. We can celebrate the way God accomplishes His plan in history.

Tamar's decision—to obtain by deception the rights she lacked the power to gain straightforwardly—leaves the modern Christian, who lives in an entirely different culture, with many unanswered questions. But one thing is clear: God in His wisdom and mercy allowed Tamar to become pregnant from this single instance of intercourse with Judah.[55] God honored her heart and fulfilled His plan.

Taking the Measure of Our Lives

Life will fall apart. We will fail and fall short. Yet, the biblical record illustrates not only our need of redemption, but the fact that nothing will thwart God's ultimate plan: He is committed to developing His character in us.

To more fully understand His plan for imperfect men and women and why developing fortitude is a high priority in His plan for our lives, we must go back to the beginning. We must study the aspects and purposes of God's creation. When God created the animals, He endowed them with the drives necessary for their physical survival both individually and as a species: the drive for self-preservation and the drive for procreation.

When God created human beings, He decided to go a step further and make us in His image. This dimension endowed us with a capacity for choice arising out of an ability to think. With the capacity for thought came self-awareness. So, unlike the animals, we draw pictures and compose stories to communicate who we are and what we have done.

Early men and women drew pictures on the walls of their caves— pictures that said, "I was here" and "I fought the lion and the bear and I survived." These pictures are indicative of the fact that God—along with the capacity for thought—placed in human beings a drive for "meaning" in their lives (a drive that will never be fully satisfied aside from being in relationship with Him). Another important fact that these pictures illustrate is that to find meaning in our lives we look for ways to measure ourselves. The picture of the cave dweller killing wild animals says that he faced the challenge and terror of the lion and the bear and prevailed.

Clearly, Tamar exhibited a strong desire for procreation. But we see more than just this biological drive operating in the events of Tamar's life. Tamar was a farsighted and intelligent woman. She showed a keen understanding of her situation, and she took incredible risks to overcome the injustice heaped on her. Plus, she managed to pull off her courageous gambit without alienating the very person who was to blame for the injustice.

God uses our struggles as a conduit to bring meaning to our lives. When we struggle, we grow. When we overcome the challenge of dis- couragement from within as well as threats from without, we, like the cave dweller battling wild beasts, obtain a measure of ourselves. This measurement adds meaning to our lives by increasing our under- standing of the potential God has placed within us. It also brings with it an understanding of our dependence upon Him.

The enemy wants us to believe that it is out of cruelty that God allows us to encounter struggles. But this perspective is a lie. God knows that in order for us to grow into our full potential, especially in the areas of character development and spiritual awareness, we must be tested and tried. The enemy knows that if he can deceive us into believing that the God who created us is a cruel tyrant who does not love and is not worthy of love that he will succeed in robbing us of the ultimate basis for meaning in our lives. When we believe this lie, it cuts us off from the real ground for meaning in life: under- standing *who* we are by accepting *whose* we are.

The classic example of someone who faced the lies of the enemy and believed God instead is that of Job. Stripped of all their children and possessions, the enemy's lie even came from the lips of his very own wife when she wailed, "Curse God, and die."

Forgiveness—The Key to Fortitude

Without his struggles, Job would have lived and died and passed unnoticed from the scene. He left behind no great monuments. He did not conquer great kingdoms. As far as we know, Job did not do anything heroic. But he provides us with priceless inspiration because, in the face of disastrous loss, he conquered hopelessness. His monument is his life's story—the story of a man who fought a great battle with the demons of despair. It is a story that helps us even today to cope with one of life's most difficult and vexing questions: Why do bad things happen?

God wanted us to know that in this fallen world the troubles we encounter are not always a sign of divine judgment upon us for wrongs we have committed. To this end, God allowed Satan to strip Job of everything in his life that he valued. Job's trials can be likened to those of the infant's trauma as it is painfully forced from the warmth and comfort of the womb through the birth canal into a world that must at first seem cold, hostile, and terrifying.

It is far too easy for us to picture God as some cruel tyrant who takes pleasure in the pain of Job's struggle. But the image we need to form is that of God as a midwife who diligently attends a long and difficult labor and is silently cheering for the tiny bundle of life that is struggling to be born. When this tiny infant has at last been brutally expelled from its comfortable nest, the midwife then "lovingly" smacks the infant on the bottom to make it cry out in protest in order that it might fill its lungs. Startled, the wailing infant sucks in life-giving air.

In like manner, we need to picture the Almighty watching Job's pain-filled struggle as he is squeezed through a spiritual birth canal to emerge gasping for spiritual breath, the breath of life-giving faith. God was not indifferent to the pain Job felt when he contended with the advice of his wife that he should give up hope, that he should accept life as meaningless because the Almighty is neither great nor good. God was not indifferent when He allowed Job to be discomforted by his friend's false accusations that his troubles must be God's judgment for his sin. God saw and cheered as Job argued with them that they were wrong. And He cheered again to hear him crying out in agony, "Though he slay me, yet will I trust in him."[56] Through this experience we see Job suck in the spiritual air of faith and enter into a new level of spiritual life until he is able to proclaim: "I know that my redeemer liveth."[57]

Like Job, Tamar experienced great hardship, heartbreak, and an extended period of barrenness. Like Job, Tamar undoubtedly had to do battle with the voice of Satan whispering in her mind that her life was useless and would never be anything more. Just like Job, Tamar was stripped of everything good in her life. And then on top of this dilemma, she was left in a prison of hopeless barrenness. Her long wait for Shelah to achieve maturity likely lasted a minimum of two to three years. Yet, she did not give up. Even when it became apparent that Judah had lied to her, she did not give up. Tamar's struggles defined who she was. Through those struggles, God brought meaning to her life.

It would appear that Tamar had one thing more in common with Job. Regarding Job, we read: "And the LORD turned the captivity of Job, when he prayed for his friends: also the LORD gave Job twice as much as he had before."[58] Here, we see directly that forgiveness was critical to Job's triumph over his misfortunes because it was when Job prayed for his friends that God delivered and restored him. Remember that these friends for whom he prayed are the very ones who had tried to "comfort" Job by arguing that his troubles represented God's righteous judgment for his sins. God directly rebuked them for this false counsel and commanded them to go to Job and have him intercede for them.[59]

Judah had sinned against Tamar. But when she confronted him with the evidence that he was the father of her child, she was able to do this in a gentle spirit without bitterness so that God was able to bring Judah around to admitting his wrongdoing. It does not seem possible that this could have happened unless by God's grace she had forgiven him. In her long days of waiting, she had not only grown in fortitude, but she had learned how to turn away from the temptation to wallow in bitterness and resentment.

Just as God turned the captivity of Job, He restored Judah and gave Tamar the longing of her heart: a son. Rather, He gave her and the contrite Judah two sons. We note that just as God restored all that which Job had lost, God replaced both of the sons that Judah had lost. Tamar, though a Canaanite woman, became the mother of the celebrated Perez[60] and earned a place in the lineage of David.

The Path to Fortitude

What was it in her time of waiting for Shelah to reach manhood that prepared Tamar for her daring action to lay claim to the fulfillment of Judah's promise? What was it in her time of waiting to see if she was pregnant and the two months afterwards that prepared Tamar for her confrontation with Judah when he learned she was pregnant? How shall we account for her fortitude, her tenacious determination to fulfill her destiny?

We are privileged with knowledge she certainly did not have—the extent to which the enemy was working to destroy Jacob's seed. While in our fictionalized account we have imagined Er telling Tamar of Simeon and Levi's slaughter of Shechem,[61] it is very doubtful that she knew of how Reuben had sinned by sleeping with Bilhah, one of Jacob's concubines, and, in doing so, had lost his claim to leadership.[62] Nor is it likely that she knew Judah and his brothers had sold Joseph into slavery.[63] One by one Satan was working to prevent God's promise from being realized. But the Spirit of God used a Canaanite woman—a most unlikely choice—to bring Judah back to his father and his God and to preserve his line.

Since we are not told how much she understood about God's covenant with Abraham—and the role she was to play in it—the most we can confidently assume is that her desperate gamble stemmed from her determination not to let Judah cheat her out of the opportunity to have a child. But it required waiting, struggle, and pain.

Just as strenuous exercise—sweat and strain—are indispensable ingredients to building physical strength and endurance, barrenness and struggle are the indispensable ingredients in the development of fortitude. Waiting is preparation for challenges to come. We would err to concentrate solely on the brief flurries of action in Tamar's story even though they are the easiest parts of the story to see. If we pass over the periods of waiting without analyzing them, we will fail to see their effects and we will miss a significant message from God. Waiting, if handled correctly, can be useful in producing emotional resilience and endurance. Waiting is part of the process whereby God develops in us a different kind of strength—a strength that refuses to give up despite all of the clamoring suggestions of the enemy that life is hopeless, that it is only a matter of time before we will inevitably be crushed by overwhelming forces or sucked dry to slowly wither and die. The big question is: What must we do during periods of waiting for it to produce positive results in our lives?

The answer to this question is as varied as the people God has created. If you or I go to a doctor, we are seeking a diagnosis and prescription that is specifically targeted to our condition. We are not interested in the proverbial advice: "Take two aspirin, and call me if you don't feel better." Similarly, an athlete who goes to a trainer wanting to improve his or her performance in running, swimming, football, or basketball would not want an exercise program designed for a wrestler or a gymnast. God knows each of our shortcomings and the specific challenges He is preparing us for.

If we are sensitive to the leading of His Spirit, He will show us the things in our lives that are holding us back from being what we need to be to fulfill the purpose He has for our lives. Rest assured. To those who have ears to hear, God will speak clearly, be it with fire falling from heaven or in a still small voice or through the arrangement of the ordinary details of our lives.

And what will be the effect of these fallow periods of waiting and preparation on us? Here again the outcomes will be as varied as the persons God has created. What we must *not* do is try to dictate to God. In particular, many of us want to become something other than the way God made us.

God's intention, however, is not to change the personality that He gave us any more than it is His intention to change our height or our other features. Most of us want to be "super-Christian." But we may be disappointed to find that despite our trials and struggles, we remain quite ordinary.

The example of Moses provides some comfort in this regard. Even after tending sheep for 40 years on the back side of the desert, Moses did not come roaring out of that experience full of spiritual strength and ready to take on the world. In fact, when God told Moses that he was to go to Pharaoh, Moses' response was, "Who am I, that I should go unto Pharaoh?"[64] Then, despite one miracle after another, Moses continued to argue with God until the Bible tells us that God's anger was kindled against Moses.[65] Not a very auspicious start for someone God intended to make into a spiritual giant and use to lead His people out of slavery in Egypt!

While God is not going to let us dictate to Him or expropriate His power to sculpt ourselves into what we might like to be, He will be with us and will work in us that we may become "conformed to the image of His Son."[66] And if we cooperate with His grace at work within us, we can become all that He gave us the potential to be.

Perhaps you are facing a situation that seems nearly impossible—a challenge that you don't know whether you have the determination to conquer. We are responsible for doing the task that God sets before us and for making the right decisions in the situations we confront on a daily basis. As we seek His face, we can trust Him to lead us. God will give us the grace to handle whatever He calls us to do, *but* only He can determine the results.

The story of Tamar and Judah gives us the comfort of knowing that God accomplishes His purposes in spite of our human failures. But it is instructive, too, in how we must remain true to our convictions if we are to be women with a different kind of strength.

Coping with many of the challenges God allows into our lives will often seem impossible in terms of human strength and ability. Developing the courage and fortitude to be a different kind of woman in these days begins with this fundamental proposition from the Word of God: "I can do all things through Christ who strengthens me."[67]

When There's No Way Out

The Power of Wisdom
The Power of Boldness

Rahab

When There's No Way Out

It was springtime. Even though the early morning air had been cool, Rahab was hot and dusty from helping her father and brother haul bundles of flax up to the rooftop to dry. It was always such a special treat to have them visit. She wished they could have stayed longer, but she understood their hurried departure. There was always so much to do on the family farm. Even though the tiny farm was just a scrap of poor land at the far edge of the oasis of Jericho, it still took a lot of manpower to tend it. The fact that there was often not enough water for a good crop made the land undesirable, so no one else wanted it. Because the family was poor, they simply had to make do with what they could get.

Rahab lived for the times when someone from her family came to Jericho to bring the farm's meager output to market. During these occasional brief moments of reunion, Rahab experienced the only true happiness in her life. But when they had to leave, she felt her isolation all the more. The emptiness and embarrassment of her life threatened to overwhelm her.

Rahab knew a great many people in Jericho, but none of them knew her—not the real person inside. Sometimes she wondered if she even really knew herself. More often than ever before, she wondered who the real Rahab was.

In her work, she was the consummate actress. She had to be. Flattering egos and feigning interest. She was very good at it—good enough that she had developed a thriving business. In fact, she had prospered to the point she was able to have her own house.

And in the weeks when she had a lot of customers, she was able to give money to her family. She was always very happy when she could help them. But recently business had been so slow that she could barely support herself. She even had to ask the girl who helped with the cooking and cleaning not to come to work for a while.

She sighed heavily as she gazed at the thick, sturdy walls encircling Jericho, her home. The walls had been built to keep intruders at bay. They were erected primarily for safety. But to Rahab, these walls symbolized the prison her life had become. As she stood at the walls, she thought to herself, *If only there were a way out.*

Her eyes shifted out beyond the walls, and she took stock of the traffic entering the gates of the city. Because the Israelites had swept up from Moab into Gilead and then on north to Bashan, the big, rich caravans traveling to and from Ezion Geber were staying well to the east on the King's Highway in Ammonite country. The lack of men in and out of the city, of course, was bad for business. Even before the spring floods had made it difficult to cross the Jordan, only a few traders were turning west at Heshbon, or what was left of it, to ford the river just north of the Salt Sea for a stopover at Jericho. Before the Israelites moved in on the East Bank, traders stopping to rest and replenish supplies before continuing on north to Damacus or south to Ezion Geber had been a source of great income.

The few traders who did come through these days brought stories of terrible battles. A king of the Amorites, Sihon, had evidently tried to prevent the Israelites from passing north out of Moab. Sihon's attempt to stop the Israelites at Jahaz had ended in disaster. The Amorites in Gilead had been completely annihilated.[68] Rahab shuddered as she permitted herself a momentary thought of the Amorite men she had known.

Tales were that, further to the north in Bashan, King Og had fared no better. It seemed that the Israelites had destroyed him, along with his entire army, and taken control of all of his 60 cities.[69] The Israelites now controlled all of the land from the far bank of the Jordan eastward to the land of the Ammonites up in the hill country. The account was that thousands and thousands of Israelites were living in the plain across the Jordan from Jericho around Abel-Shittim, only a few days' march from Jericho. Evidently, not many of the large, heavily-loaded caravans wanted to risk an encounter with them.

The merchants in the market were complaining about poor business. Despite the king's assurances that the city could not be taken, people were wondering how long it would be before the Israelites crossed the Jordan and advanced on Jericho. Everyone was preparing for that day.

It was spring, and the Jordan River was flooding well out of its banks as the snow melted in the mountains. People said there was nothing to worry about for now, but Rahab wondered. What if the Israelite God, Yahweh, should part the Jordan the way He had parted the Red Sea when these same Israelites had fled from the Egyptians long ago?

Rahab knew that despite attempts at bravado, everyone was uneasy and disturbed. Even though the harvest was good this year, unless you went to the market on Saturday just after the farmers had brought in their produce, it was difficult to find food. The wealthy were buying up all of the grain and storing it. The poor were doing what little they could to prepare, but they would be the first to suffer if there were a long siege. Rahab had a little food stored, but she was worried about her family living outside the city walls. It did seem just a matter of time.

Looking out over the city that morning, her thoughts went back to the day she had first been sent from the farm to work in Jericho. Everything had been new and so exciting. Her father had arranged a job for her as a maid for one of the wealthy families, and their house had been large and clean. It was totally unlike the cramped and dirty little hovel she had grown up in. She didn't mind the work. It was certainly not as bad as doing farmwork, and it provided a little extra money to help the family.

She was a lovely young girl—a natural beauty. Even at the age of 13, she was aware that men's eyes lingered for a moment when they first saw her. She often imagined what it would be like to be grown-up—old enough to dress like a woman. She wondered, too, what it would be like to have the clothes and jewels her mistress wore. Then one day the mistress had given her one of her old dresses to wear. Rahab had promptly taken the dress completely apart and altered it to make it fit well.

When the mistress had seen how carefully she groomed herself and how quickly she learned any new task, she had begun to teach Rahab the manners needed to serve meals to the important guests who often visited in the home. Each new day had brought new things to learn. Rahab had been excited by every opportunity. It had seemed that her life was moving forward to better and better things.

But the new life which had seemed to be so full of promise had proved to be only a child's dream. She remembered bitterly now how much she had learned...too much, too fast. At first, getting attention and gifts had seemed wonderful. Men had found her extremely attractive. In the beginning, she had been intoxicated by her power over them. In her innocence and inexperience, it had seemed to her that she had found the road to freedom, independence, and success. In the end, she had learned that it was a road to emptiness and isolation. Her reality now.

Perhaps it was her father and brother's brief visit that prompted her reminiscence, she wasn't entirely sure. But whatever the reason, the memories of when she had first become a harlot came welling up—unbidden—as she stood on her rooftop overlooking the city that was now her home. The memories of the events that had plunged her into this life—this terrible existence of selling herself to one man after another—were so painful that she seldom let them rise to the surface.

Looking beyond the city again to the southeast, she could see the Salt Sea faintly in the distance over a half-day's journey away. Once she had visited that area during the spring floods. She had been surprised to see that the little river, which usually meandered its way along from the north, had turned into a wide, rushing current so swollen that its usual twisting banks were invisible. She had watched in amazement, and in her mind's eye she had seen all the little fish caught in the roiling waters of the Jordan as it swept down from the

Sea of Galilee during the flood tide. She had known that those not strong enough to swim against the current would suffocate in the briny waters of the Salt Sea. Tears began to stream down her cheeks now as she thought of how she had been swept into Jericho as a young girl…and as she realized anew what was becoming of her.

Early on, she had harbored the illusion that her life in the city was much finer than her mother's gritty life on the farm. Now she knew otherwise. She had no husband. She had no children. She was little better than a slave. She was looking desperately for some way out.

This was certainly not the life she had dreamed of as a beautiful young girl. Though it had been relatively easy for her to become a harlot, it now seemed impossible to find a means of escape. Every man in Jericho, and many beyond, knew her reputation. Sadly, she knew that each one saw her only as a woman to be bought. A beautiful woman—but a woman for sale to those who could afford the price. She knew that their true thought was: Once a harlot, always a harlot.

There had been a period of time when she had regularly gone to the temples of Baal and Ashtoreth, her Canaanite gods. On each visit, she had prayed for a miracle. But no miracle had come. She hadn't really expected one, but she had hoped. The prayers had been only the fruit of her desperation, her emotions overriding reason.

Rahab was no fool. She had learned the cost of ignorance the hard way. Her illusions had carried an enormous price. She had learned to look at life objectively—with clear-eyed realism. She had come to see how foolish it was to think that an idol created by a man could do anything for the man who had created it in the first place. Most perplexing of all, she had not been able to understand how any man…or woman…could ever sacrifice an infant to an impotent idol.

She knew better than to ever mention these thoughts about religion to anyone. If she gave up the gods of her people, she would be even more of an outsider. Just to survive her day-to-day existence, Rahab had learned to wear a mask, to be an actress, to keep her thoughts and feelings beyond anyone's reach. She had built a wall between the person that others knew and her inner self—the person no one knew. She had learned to be two people.

The air above the Salt Sea to the south was beginning to shimmer from the heat of the morning sun. Rahab knew that her gods were as dead and barren as that sea which watered nothing, quenched no one's thirst, and produced no life. Unlike Yahweh who helped the Israelites, the Canaanite gods helped no one.

Thoughts of the Israelites caused her to swing her gaze from the south to the east, toward the ford of the Jordan and the land of Shittim in the distance beyond. She could not actually see the Israelites camped among the acacia groves because the distance was too great for that. But at night, sometimes if the wind shifted and came out of the east, she thought she could smell the smoke of their campfires.

The image of smoke rising up to the sky made her think of prayers ascending into the heavens. She had heard stories about the miracles Yahweh had done in Egypt to deliver the Israelites out of slavery. It had been 40 years since He had opened the Red Sea to make a way for them to escape, and then closed it, drowning Pharaoh and his 600 chariots that were in pursuit. Still the story continued to be told and retold,[70] inspiring awe and a fear of the Israelites.

Their God was not at all like other gods. He was different in innumerable ways. He seemed to travel with them wherever they went. He had been with them in Egypt, in Sinai, and when they fought against the Amorites in Gilead. Then, when they had fought King Og at Edrei, Yahweh had given them victory in the land of Bashan as well. Not for the first time, Rahab wondered how one worshiped this powerful God, Yahweh.

Everyone in Jericho had heard these stories of the Israelites and their God. And despite the good harvest this year, the mood of the city was somber. People worried—and worried aloud—about how long it would be before Jericho would be under attack. Rahab closed her eyes and tried to imagine looking down from the walls to find a sea of fierce desert warriors surrounding them. And she knew she wasn't the only one thinking these thoughts. Everyone was terrified.

The leaders made brave-sounding speeches, and everyone cheered at the mention of the city's brave warriors and its impregnable high double walls. Rahab's house was a part of the wall, so she knew, more than some of the other residents of Jericho, its great strength. Still, she overheard the talk in the marketplace, and people were wondering if Jericho would fare any better than the cities of Gilead and Bashan, cities that also were fortified with high walls, gates, and bars.[71]

Rahab had no illusions. She knew full well that a siege lasting many months would make a prison out of the city for everyone—rich and poor alike. If the farmers whose property bordered Jericho were forced to come into the city for protection, the Israelites would take over the farms and pastures. Then there would be no fresh meat or other fresh food. The imprisoned people would exist on only grain, dried meat, and dried fruits...until they ran out. These desert nomads called Israelites were accustomed to living out in the open and could easily live off the rich land of the oasis. Even though the city had a good supply of fresh spring water coming from 'Ain es-Sultan, it wasn't hard for Rahab to see that the Israelites would fare a lot better than the people locked up inside Jericho's walls. She turned from scanning the horizon to look again on the city. Rahab was convinced Jericho was doomed.

As she worked that morning, spreading out the flax to dry on her rooftop, Rahab noted that there was a larger-than-usual amount of traffic coming into the city. Most appeared to be local farmers who were bringing in their harvested crops to sell, but there also appeared to be some strangers among the crowd—a few traders who might be looking for accommodations.

Rahab decided that it might be a good idea to bake some fresh bread. Perhaps, too, she should purchase some lamb to add to the stew, assuming she could find fresh meat in the market. If she could have done what she really wanted to do, she simply would have taken a bath. She decided the bath would have to wait until she got back from the market and put the stew on to cook.

If she worked quickly, she could get to the market, prepare the food, take her bath, and have everything in order by the time any customers arrived that evening. Rahab hurried down from the roof, splashed some water on her face to rinse off the sweat and dust, pulled her hair back, and put on the robe she usually wore to the market.

Whenever she went walking in the streets, Rahab turned heads. She had been taken by the elegance of the women she had served when she worked as a maid. She had watched how her mistress walked, held her head, and used her hands. A natural actress, Rahab had studied the movements and, almost without thinking about it, began to imitate them. Her adaptation wasn't much of an effort because she was naturally graceful in her own walk and movements.

As she matured, she became more than a match for the most elegant of women. Rahab's style and beauty had not gone unnoticed by the town's ladies. She soon became the object of their jealousy, scorn, and anger. The more attention the men paid to Rahab, the more difficult and isolated her life became. If they could have had their way, the women would have had her banished from Jericho.

In the early days when Rahab left her house on the wall to go to the market, the fact that she created a stir wherever she went had made her feel quite proud. The jealousy of the women in the streets and their snide remarks did not come as any surprise. She had, however, expected admiring looks from the merchants instead of the hostile glares she so often endured. She certainly had not been prepared for their biting remarks and cruel jokes. She was beautiful and had the clothes and manners of a wealthy woman, but the fact that she still came to the market marked her for what she was.

Rahab eventually saw that it angered the people in the streets to see a peasant dressed up and carrying herself like a wealthy woman. In their minds, it was an act of treason to their class, and it merited all the scorn and bile they could heap upon her. This they dished out in large quantities whenever she passed them in the market. If she were truly wealthy, she wouldn't be living on the wall. Everyone knew that, and they knew too that she was a harlot. Maybe she was beautiful, but she was simply an expensive harlot who put on airs.

Her natural reaction had been to return their scornful expressions with her own haughty looks of disdain. Rejected, Rahab consoled herself with the idea that she might not be wealthy but she was out of their price range. It had not taken her long, however, to get her fill of this diet. Subsequently, she had begun to dress as inconspicuously as possible and choose her route and time to market to ensure that she met as few people as possible.

This morning, however, she was in a hurry. So she decided to take the most direct route to the market. She would just have to put up with whatever harassment came her way. As she quickly moved through the city, she noted that the mood in the streets seemed quieter than usual. The children were playing as always, but the older people going about their daily business seemed preoccupied. Few of the townspeople were taking time to stop and talk as they ordinarily did.

Rahab had to pay an unusually high price for a small piece of lamb, but because there seemed to be some prospect of business, she decided it was worth it. She also purchased some figs, almonds, a melon, and one pomegranate. Instead of heading back home immediately, she made a complete tour of the area to see if she could spot any likely customers.

At one of the shops she occasionally frequented, the merchant caught sight of her and motioned her over. Because he was one of the few friendly faces in the market, she rewarded his greeting with one of her stunning smiles. The pudgy fellow wet his lips, swallowed, and took a deep breath. She noted with approval that her smile still had its usual effect on a man.

Finally finding his voice, he said to her, "No rich customers for you today, Rahab. The only strangers I've seen this morning were two scruffy Amorites from the East Bank who brought in a couple of goats to sell. Sorriest looking pair you ever saw." Pausing a second, he continued with a snicker, "The goats, that is."

For some reason that Rahab couldn't understand, he seemed inordinately pleased with his lame joke. "The Amorites didn't look like much either," he chuckled and slapped his thigh.

Rahab smiled politely, but she could not see what he found so funny. *Maybe he has been drinking,* she thought. But when he continued, he seemed quite sober. "Big, tough-looking guys, that's for sure. I'll tell you this much. I sure wouldn't want to run into those two alone on a dark night."

Curious, she looked up to see if they might be somewhere in sight. Noticing that she was surveying the market, he said, "You can forget about those two, Rahab. They certainly couldn't afford you. Besides, they left quite a while ago—just as soon as they sold the goats. You're not likely to see them. They headed that way." As he spoke, he motioned to the street leading out of the south side of the market, the opposite direction from her house on the north wall of the city.

Rahab started home at a leisurely pace. There was no need to hurry now. She knew that she could prepare the stew quickly enough and that in a couple of hour's time the aroma would fill the house. Plus, the bread was baked. Any customers she might have this evening would be wealthy men from Jericho. They wouldn't be in the market for food anyway—just some wine and her services would fill their needs.

As she walked, her mind kept drifting back to the merchant's remarks about the two Amorites from the East Bank. Curiosity gnawed at her. She would like to have talked to them to find out what was happening on the other side of the Jordan. She wondered if they were fleeing from the Israelites. She speculated about what it would be like to have no place to go home to.

It was late that afternoon before she stopped to get her bath and put on clean clothes. The bread she had baked earlier had filled the house with a wonderful smell that lingered still. She checked on the stew she had prepared and put on to cook as soon as she had arrived home. It would be a while yet before the lentils and lamb would be tender. She decided to prepare a plate of nuts and fruit to serve after the stew and bread. Even if she were dining alone, she wanted the meal to be nice.

Rahab decided to go up on the roof to watch the sun set behind the mountains. As the sun dropped closer to the mountaintops in the west, the long rays played across the towering, limestone cliffs to the north. Brilliant rosy hues contrasted with the shadows that were blanketing the slopes to the west. It was a sight of such incredible beauty that it took her breath away. Her spirits were sent soaring. Twilight was her favorite time of the day.

Movement on the street below caught her eye. Two men were coming in her direction. Strangers, from the look of them. Rahab noted the fluid athleticism with which they moved. She narrowed her eyes and looked closer. Their long strides did not seem hurried. They moved casually, like two men who had no place to go. Nevertheless, they were swiftly closing the distance to her house. They were obviously looking for something, someone, some place.

At this time of day, Rahab knew it was a good bet that they were hungry and looking for a place to eat. She hurried across the rooftop, taking care not to trip on the flax laid out to dry, and then descended the steps to the street. It was time for her to earn her living.

Joshua had handpicked these two himself. They were well-built young men with enormous strength in their arms and shoulders. They were stout hearted, and their courage in combat had been tested again and again in recent battles against the Amorites. They were not only fierce warriors; they were also swift runners. From his own experience as a spy, Joshua knew speed could be important for the mission ahead. His one concern was that they might be overconfident after their recent victories. He didn't want them spoiling for a fight. His decision in the end had hinged on one fact: They trusted Yahweh completely. Thus, Joshua concluded that he could count on them to obey his orders. They were to go on their mission and report back directly to him without talking to anyone else.[72] "No heroics," he had said to them sternly.

Joshua was confident that with the power of Yahweh strengthening them, Salmon and Abner had the quickness and endurance to outdistance any pursuers. If God did not see fit to keep them from an encounter with the enemy, Joshua also knew that they would put up a ferocious fight and would not be taken alive. For this reason, he had chosen unmarried men. He did not want men who might be distracted by worries about wives or children. Nor, God forbid, did he want this mission to produce any widows or orphans.

Rahab was a successful businesswoman partly because of her beauty. She was a graceful, statuesque, beguiling woman. But more importantly, she was a keen observer and knew how to take full advantage of her beauty to manipulate men. She was not just clever, though indeed she was extremely bright. She also had an ability to think quickly on her feet, to assess a situation, to make up her mind without hesitation, and to act decisively.

With her intelligence and skill as an observer, she could see a man's weakness and devise a way to exploit it. Given her combination of talents, few men were her equal when it came to bargaining. Many had been surprised to find that behind her demure, enchanting smile there was a very shrewd woman who had been a step ahead of them all the way. Those with generous dispositions found her quickness amusing. They thought it made her all the more entertaining. But others with thin skin and a pride that was easily wounded took offense and became angry when they found they had come up short in the negotiations. Painful experience had taught Rahab to take careful measure of potential customers.

In the beginning, Rahab's goal had been to attain by her own wits and efforts what had been denied her by her peasant birth. This determination required making money—and a great deal of it. Normally, she would not have considered these two in their hard-worn clothes as potential customers. They were obviously not rich. And two competitive young men together as customers at once was usually a recipe for trouble. She knew all this very well, yet she still hurried down from her rooftop to greet them. She was intensely curious to see if these were the two Amorites she had heard about in the market. If so, judging by the direction they were traveling, they had walked around the entire city to get there.

As they approached her door, she studied them carefully in the fading light. Their clothing appeared to be Amorite. But if they were traders, they were novices. Their expressions were too open for traders. They lacked the studious, blank look of professionals. Their faces were the faces of men who had spent long hours out-of-doors, faces that were used to sun and wind, strong faces that were bold, confident, and extremely alert. They reminded her a little of her brothers. She wouldn't have called either of them handsome exactly, but their obvious physical strength caught her eye. The older of the two was especially attractive. She estimated that he was two or three years older than the other man. The younger of the two seemed to be in his early twenties.

She had seen a great many men make a production out of appearing strong and manly, but she had never seen the likes of these two before. These men exuded rugged strength, but neither showed the slightest hint of self-consciousness or arrogance.

Experience warned her not to take the risk of allowing them to enter, but she told herself that she had stew cooking. Whether it was the thought of the stew going to waste, her curiosity about things on the East Bank, or ingrained habit taking over, she heard herself asking, "May I help you?"

The older of the two men smiled, patted his stomach, and said quietly, "We are very hungry."

Rahab returned his smile with a direct one of her own as she answered sweetly, "Very well. I have stew cooking and fresh bread. Do you have money?"

He replied by shaking the money pouch tied to his belt so that she could hear the clink of coins. At the same time, he gave her a devilish sort of grin. *He might be a poor novice trader,* she thought, *but he can certainly make a woman's heart skip a beat with that wicked grin of his.*

Ordinarily, she would have asked for payment in advance, but the faces of these two were so transparent that she nodded for them to follow her inside. Now, having set things in motion, Rahab automatically proceeded with the steps of her well-rehearsed routine. She was like a dancer moving to familiar music.

She stood in the doorway so that, as they stepped past her into the room, they would catch the scent of her perfume. The younger of the two entered first. Then, before the second man fully cleared the doorway, she reached behind him to close the door. This motion forced him to brush against her body in order to make room for the door to swing shut. She did this so naturally that only a professional would have recognized the practiced maneuver for what it was. At the same time that one hand reached for the door, she moved to let her other hand rest lightly against the flat of his belly—at least, that was all that it felt like to him.

To Rahab, it had been an opportunity to check the size of the money pouch tied to his belt. As she brushed seductively against him, not only had she felt his muscular body, she had also determined that he had a dagger strapped beneath his robe. He was a brave warrior, but he had never encountered an enemy as subtle as this woman.

Rahab had a woman's natural ability to keep track of things going on around her. With her peripheral vision, she caught the men's gaze upon her without losing her reserved, nonchalant look. She sensed these unsophisticated men drinking in the sight of her hair, her jewelry, and her fine linen gown, which was cinched tightly at her narrow waist, accentuating the curve of her hips and breasts.

But something else was evident as well. Most men who came to her house were totally focused either on her or on the food and drink, depending on which appetite was stronger at the moment. But not these two. Oddly, they seemed more interested in the house. She could see that they had quickly surveyed the location of every door and window. They seemed particularly alert to the sounds coming from the street. It almost appeared as if they were listening to hear if they had been followed. Something was amiss. But their open, honest-looking faces gave no clue to indicate that they might be thieves.

Rahab invited the men to sit down and rest while she checked to see if the stew was ready to eat. As she returned from stirring it for the last time, she saw that both men were standing by the front window looking up and down the street. She doubted they could see much more than shadows in the dim, lingering twilight. As she noted the gathering darkness, her apprehension about entertaining two strange men returned. Suddenly, she remembered the merchant's remark that morning, "Big, tough-looking guys, that's for sure. I'll tell you this much. I sure wouldn't want to run into those two alone on a dark night."

Even as she forced a smile to her lips, she was regretting her impulsive decision to open her door to them. She was determined not to let her nervousness show. And, in as even a tone as she could muster, she said, "The stew will be just a little longer. Would you like some wine while you wait?"

The older one replied, "No, thank you. Just some water, please."

As she returned with the water, she saw both of their heads jerk up at a sound in the distance. The scraping, creaking sound was so familiar to her that she would not have noticed it if had not been for their reaction.

"That's the city gate being closed for the night," she said.

She couldn't read the look that passed between them. It didn't seem like fear or even nervousness. Perhaps it was just one more thing to be catalogued along with the location of all the doors and windows of her house.

"With the gate closed, you'll have to find some place to spend the night in the city," she commented with a hint of nervous amusement in her voice. "If you're thinking of spending the night here, you'll have to pay for that in addition to the meal," she added firmly.

Then, after pausing deliberately, she said as calmly as she could manage, "You'll also have to hand over those daggers you're carrying. You'll not be sleeping in this house if you're armed."

It was not the first time she had demanded that a guest give her his dagger. In fact, many of her customers left them behind as a gift to her. Most she sold, but a few of the more beautiful ones she had kept.

Despite her experience with this maneuver, she was extremely nervous when confronting these two men. She was trying to stay ahead of things. Better to confront the problem now while the neighbors were still up to hear her if she screamed than to wait until everyone was asleep.

It helped restore her equilibrium a bit to see the surprised looks in their eyes. But that feeling lasted only long enough for her to take a single breath. The next few moments seemed like an eternity to Rahab. She saw them both tense like lions preparing to spring. In that instant, all of the pieces of the puzzle she had been working on dropped into place. These men weren't Amorites. Their clothes were, but they certainly weren't. She could picture in her imagination these two Israelites surveying the city from all sides. They would have noted the steady flow of traffic bringing food and other goods into the city. It was the same traffic that she herself often studied from her rooftop, noting the various incoming pack trains and their masters.

She guessed that after some deliberation they had decided to try to pass themselves off as traders in order to get a closer look at the fortified buildings inside the city's wall. She thought what a bitter irony it was that they could not know just how easily their open, honest faces had given them away. She knew only too well that the merchants in the market, with their years of experience, could count the coins in your purse from ten paces away. They would not have been long in figuring out that these muscular young men dressed as poor traders were anything but.

Now the fact that they had walked around the entire city to get to her house made perfect sense. She also understood why they had stayed near the front window. They *were* listening to see if they were being followed.

As the younger man started to reach for his dagger, she saw the older one lay a hand on his arm and growl something she couldn't understand. The younger man nodded with a thin half-smile. She guessed they were going to force her into the back of the house and then...

Images exploded in her mind. She envisioned them, daggers in hand, hurling themselves at her before she could make a sound. She wanted to scream and run out the door. And scream she would...if only she could have! But her heart was stuck in her throat. She felt her head start to swim. She tried to run for the door, but when she moved her knees buckled. She would have collapsed to the floor in a heap except for the strong hands that flashed out to catch her.

Through a swirling gray haze, she felt herself being lifted, cradled like a child, and then gently laid on the couch. She felt a blanket being tucked around her. Then she became aware of rough hands gently rubbing warmth back into her numb fingers. She thought she heard one of them ask the other if she was pregnant, but the voice seemed so distant she could not be certain of the question. Pregnant? Why would he care if she were pregnant? She felt a large hand on her stomach. Would they spare her life if they thought she was carrying a child?

Her head was lifted and a cup of water pressed to her lips. She opened her eyes and took a small sip. Then she took a larger sip. The water helped clear both her mind and her vision. She heard their sighs of relief when her eyes fluttered open. Squinting to force her eyes to focus, she saw concerned smiles on their faces.

"What is your name?" the elder one asked.

Her head was still swimming...what difference did it make what her name was?

"Rahab," she answered weakly.

"Are you ill, Rahab?"

"No," she replied, "I'll be all right. I'm just a little tired, I guess." It wasn't fatigue she knew, but she needed time to lie there and figure out what to do next.

Strangely, their expressions reminded her of the relieved looks she had seen so often on her brothers' faces when they realized that she had survived yet another of their reckless pranks and that she was not going to run off in tears to tell their mother.

But reality quickly set in, and she reminded herself that these men were not her brothers. These were Israelite warriors who had come here to plan an attack on Jericho—an attack that would destroy her, her family, and her home.

They saw her shudder. Their smiles changed back to looks of concern. They were clearly worried about her, which made no sense. She
wanted to run, to get away, but her legs were too weak to carry her—
even if these men would let her go.

To buy time, she asked them their names.

"I'm Salmon," said the older of the two. "And he's Abner," he added,
nodding at his younger companion.

She asked for more water, and Abner, who was on his feet, moved
quickly to refill her cup. She gulped it down hoping it would restart
her brain, which seemed to have quit working.

Maybe they were not going to kill her. If they had wanted her dead,
they certainly could have carried her to the back of the house and
killed her without a sound when she fainted. *Perhaps that is still to
come. Maybe they have other "business" they wanted to attend to first. Is
that why they seem so eager to make me comfortable? But that doesn't make
sense either,* thought Rahab. She was too familiar with the leer of a
rapist. These men didn't look at her in the way her other customers
usually did.

It was not that they hadn't noticed her or that they had avoided
contact with her. Indeed, one of her small hands still rested in the
large, rough hands of Salmon. His hands were huge by comparison to
hers. He had been careful to be gentle and not bruise her as he rubbed
her hands to get the blood circulating.

Gentle hands or not, she thought, returning to her predicament, *they
are here on a spying mission.* She had no idea how she fit into their
plans—dead or alive. Rather than just lie there and wait to see what
their next step was going to be, Rahab decided it was time for her to
take the initiative.

"You must be hungry from your travels. I'm sure the stew is done,
and there is fresh bread in the kitchen," she said, starting to get up.

But Salmon's big hands restrained her. When Abner returned from
the kitchen carrying the bread and pot of stew, Salmon, who had continued to rub Rahab's hands, reached into the bag tied to his belt and
extracted a coin that he offered her. It was a small gesture in the grand
scheme of things, but under these circumstances it was an extremely
significant one. It was a clue of some sort, but Rahab just could not get
all the clues to add up. Why would these men, whom she was expecting
to kill her at any moment, offer to pay her for the meal?

It startled her when she saw Salmon reach beneath his robe and pull out the dagger she knew was concealed there. As she watched him, he carved the melon that was already sitting on the table, and Rahab managed to force her heart back down out of her throat. She noted that the dagger was extremely sharp, and he handled it as skillfully as if he had been born with it in his hand. Abner, meanwhile, was stirring the stew.

With everything in place for their meal, they bowed their heads and silently said a prayer of thanksgiving to their God. Though she could not hear their words, she was certain that they were praying in Hebrew to the same God who had parted the Red Sea so far away in Egypt.

Is their God everywhere? she wondered to herself.

She was helped to her feet and escorted to the table, where the food was placed in the center for all three to reach. To her surprise, she was ravenously hungry. Even the plate of figs and nuts was in its place. They all ate quickly, dipping their bread into the stew, until both bread and stew were consumed.

As she ate, she felt her strength returning. Her mind kicked into action and started sifting through the pieces furiously. As the meal was finished off with the beautiful red melon and with the figs and nuts being passed around, she added up all of the facts. She could see now that her fear of these men had been the product of her overheated imagination. The spies had been clearly distressed when she had collapsed. Plus, they had paid her for the meal. Even though they were not versed in the fine arts of seduction as were some of the more sophisticated men of Jericho, she could see from the open looks of admiration on their faces that they were clearly struck by her beauty.

Lust she understood, but their simple appreciation of her beauty was unfamiliar and disconcerting. She had learned to steel herself against the assault of leering looks that "took," to inwardly parry the message that she was only a toy—only a desirable plaything, only a "thing" to be bought for a few minutes of pleasure. To her amazement, she found herself blushing like a schoolgirl under the worshipful gazes of these Israelites. These were looks that "gave," looks that made her feel like a whole person. These looks seemed to liberate her from the need to act a part, to seduce, to play the harlot. She found the freedom to be just herself so exhilarating that she felt slightly out of control.

Now she felt lightheaded, not from fear, but with a heady elation.

She had heard nothing, but in an instant Salmon was on his feet and moving to the front window. As he stood watching and listening, Rahab spoke softly to Abner, "What did Salmon whisper to you when I asked for your daggers?"

A faint smile creased his rugged features, and he replied softly, "'She sounds just like Miriam.'"

"Miriam? His mother or his wife?" she asked hesitantly.

"She was his wife," he said flatly.

Rahab heard the "was" and eyed him intently.

"She died in childbirth a little over a year ago. And the baby, he died too."

A little boy, she thought. *His firstborn son.*

Even though the light from the oil lamp was dim, the pain behind the stoic look on his face was palpable. *There must be a deep bond between these two men,* she thought. There was complete silence as Rahab and Abner stared at the back of Salmon's rugged shoulders while he leaned against the edge of the window, looking first one way and then the other.

"Did you know her?" The question startled her. She was shocked to hear the sound of her own voice. The question was in her mind, but she hadn't intended to ask it. She couldn't believe that it had crossed her lips. She was even more shocked when she saw the look on his face as he turned to her and replied, "Miriam was my sister."

Rahab groaned and turned away in shame for having exposed his grief. At that moment, Salmon returned. The nod of his head indicated that he had seen nothing on the street. He pulled up a stool and sat down beside the couch she was sitting on.

They had not yet had a chance to give her their daggers. But now, Salmon cleaned his and laid it on the couch beside her. Abner unsheathed his dagger and put it beside Salmon's. Their peace offering.

She was already perturbed at herself for the question she had asked Abner. Now she was perturbed at them. Presenting her with the daggers in this way told her that they knew she had fainted from fear. She knew it was true, but she was piqued that they knew it too. She wanted to tell them that she wasn't the kind of woman who went around fainting all the time. She wanted them to know that she had never fainted before in her whole life…that she could remember. But she had already heard herself say enough impulsive things for one evening, and she decided that silence was the wiser course.

She was not used to feeling so muddled and indecisive, but she wasn't sure where this encounter was headed. But what if, just maybe…could it be possible? Would this provide her a way out?

Pondering that thought, she reached over and fingered the daggers pensively. Salmon's dagger was stunning. As she studied it carefully, she saw the royal seal of Sihon, king of the Amorites, on top of the handle. The sight of the steel made a shiver crawl up her spine, for she pictured Salmon locked in bloody, hand-to-hand combat with Sihon. She had heard brutal stories of that duel to the death.

He saw her examining the dagger. He reached to pick it up and hand it to her. As he extended his arm, she saw the bright pink line of a new scar running up his arm. She took the dagger from him with her right hand. The fingers of her left hand moved to touch the scar.

"Does the wound still bother you?" she asked tentatively.

"Not really. I just don't have quite as strong a grip in that hand as I did before," he replied. Then he added with the same impish grin she had seen earlier, "I got the dagger from the same guy who gave me the scar."

Men! she thought in exasperation. Men talk about nearly getting themselves killed like it was a joke. The brave ones go off cheerfully to die in battle, leaving their widows behind to grieve forever. He didn't realize, of course, that she had recognized the royal seal, that she knew exactly to whom the dagger had originally belonged, or that she knew the story of what had become of King Sihon.

"Put that thing away," she ordered crossly as she handed it back to him.

"But I thought you told me I had to give it to you if I planned to stay the night," he replied with surprise.

"A lot of good that would do," she said, building up steam as she went. "I'm not a fool. Do you think I don't know you have another one on the other hip?"

Salmon's eyes met hers. It was plain, even to Abner, that something passed between them. Suddenly her confusion cleared as she chose sides. Seeing the path before her, she moved forward with her characteristic decisiveness.

"Anyway," she added, "you can't stay down here. I've got to get you two out of the house. Someone else could come along any minute now and recognize you. Those Amorite robes you're wearing are about the worst disguise you could have chosen."

With that, the wheels in her mind started turning furiously as she tried to decide the best thing to do under the circumstances. She was aggravated with herself for how long it had taken her to figure out who they were and what they were up to. All of Jericho had heard the story of how the Israelites had left no survivors in their war with the Amorites.[73] The merchant who had told her that two Amorites from the East Bank had come to Jericho had been pulling her leg, and, stupidly, she had fallen for it.

The merchant's strange laughter, so puzzling at the time, now made complete sense. It did not tax her imagination to see that Salmon and Abner's Amorite disguises had left a trail that eventually would lead the king's men straight to her house. She couldn't picture either Salmon or Abner meekly surrendering. It shocked her to realize how desperately she wanted to protect them.

She didn't know how long it would take for word about the spies to reach the king, but she imagined that his officers had already been combing the city for hours. Now that the gates were closed and no one could leave, she knew that before long the king's men would come to her house to check and see if she had any overnight "guests." In fact, she knew that they could arrive at her door at any moment.

"Follow me," she demanded as she headed toward the back of the house.

Salmon and Abner exchanged amused glances, but she noted with satisfaction that they immediately fell in behind her without a word. Being in motion gave her back a sense of being back in control of her life, and that helped settle her nerves a little. She was moving into new territory—territory that promised even more uncertainty than the considerable risk she was used to facing daily. Instead of a sense of dread, however, she felt a tingle of excitement—a sense of newness and wholeness. She felt more alive than she had felt since her first days in Jericho.

Rahab worried about who might have seen the spies come to her house earlier. If they had been seen, she certainly didn't want anyone to see them again. Even though it was dark now, someone in the street might notice if she took the men out the front door and around to the steps on the side of the house that led up to the roof. She couldn't take that chance.

There was only one other option. They would have to go up through the ceiling. When they stepped into the kitchen, she motioned for them to move the table under the hole that served as a skylight and provided ventilation. Rahab grabbed a stool and placed it on top of the table.

She talked quickly and with determination. "If you can get your shoulders through that hole, you're on the roof. Once you are through, stay low on your bellies and out of sight. I'll go outside and come up the stairs as soon as I move the table back in place. I have a load of flax drying up there that I can use to cover you so that none of the neighbors can see you from their rooftops."

As soon as they had each wiggled their way through the opening and disappeared, she pulled the table back to where it belonged. She grabbed the bowls and pot from their meal, put them in a basket, and covered it with the robe she wore to market. With a few swipes of her broom, she swept the floor to erase the telltale marks from where she had moved the table and to remove the debris the men had knocked loose from the ceiling as they squeezed through the hole. There was so much trash that she looked up to see that the opening was now half again as large as it had been originally!

As she moved through the door and around to the steps leading to the roof, she heard the sound of a troop of men clattering through the streets. She had not the least doubt that it was the king's men headed her way. She forced herself to walk slowly in case someone might be watching. Once she climbed the steps and reached the roof, she began to gather armloads of flax and cover the men who were lying down. No sooner had she finished covering Abner than she heard one of the king's officers knocking on her door. He was demanding in a loud voice that she bring out her "guests."

Rahab looked down from the rooftop and waved to the big man. "You're looking for someone?" she asked ever so politely.

"Bring out the two men you're entertaining," sneered a man whom she knew well. "They're spies, and the king has sent us to arrest them."

It took all the self-restraint Rahab could summon not to say, "If you want them, you big coward, why don't you go in and get them yourself instead of telling me to bring them out to you." Instead, she smiled wickedly and said, "Spies, Simon? Well, I wish there were that much excitement around here...send them my way!"

As the crowd of men roared with bawdy laughter, she saw that one of Salmon's feet was still showing. She reached down and tried to be casual as she strategically rearranged the bundles of flax.

"Are you talking about the two big foreigners?" she asked, straightening back up.

"Yes!" Simon bellowed.

Heads were popping out of windows up and down the street at all the commotion.

"Just a minute," she said, making her tone as nonchalant as possible. "I'll be right down."

As she headed across the roof to the top of the stairs, the flax crunched under her feet. Seeing a slight movement in one of the mounds of flax, she leaned over and whispered softly in a scolding tone, "Lie still, you simpleton." She thought she heard a muffled chuckle, but she saw no more movement. From the head of the stairs, she glanced to the east and saw a full moon beginning to peek over the ridges behind Abel-Shittim.[74]

It was going to be a beautiful night...if she lived through it, she thought. By now it no longer surprised her to realize that she was just as concerned about whether the spies would live through this night to make it back to Shittim.

As she climbed down the steps, she smiled to herself as she thought again of how ludicrous it was to order a woman to drag two armed warriors the size of Salmon and Abner out of her house and into the waiting arms of the king's men. When she reached the officer, she gave him one of her practiced smiles. She hoped in the dim light he couldn't see that the smile didn't quite reach her eyes.

"Are you sure you're looking for strangers?" she said with another sly smile.

Irritated, he again growled his command for her to bring out the two spies.

She tilted her head and looked at him intently. All of her senses were on high alert. She worked to bring all of her gifts of performance into focused control. "But as you can see, Simon, I'm all alone," she looked down and then back up at him seductively. "Come on in...check for yourself...and stay awhile," she invited brazenly, hoping fervently that he would do no such thing.

The men all laughed again. They had relaxed a bit as they watched her spar with their leader. Unconsciously, she reached up to run her hands through her hair to remove stray pieces of flax. The movement lifted her breasts, and she was pleased to see that she had managed to distract the men without intending to.

"The foreigners, Rahab. Where are they?" insisted the soldier.

"Right, right, the two strangers," she murmured. She paused and flashed a brilliant smile at the group of men grinning back at her from behind him. "Let's see. They got here right about sunset. I can't tell you who they were. Never saw them before. Complete strangers. They only wanted to buy some food. Just as well, I guess. They didn't look like they had enough money between them to pay for one bed for the night, let alone two."

The soldiers guffawed.

Rahab was gaining momentum, enjoying her audience. She continued, "They seemed to be in something of a hurry. I noticed that one of them kept looking out the window as if to see if anyone was following them. It did seem strange. They didn't take the time to eat. Just paid for the food and took it with them."

She fished around in her pocket and produced the coin Salmon had given her. The officer took it from her and squinted at it in the flickering light of the torch one of his men was carrying.

"I didn't hear them say which way they were headed. About the only thing they did say was to be quick about fixing the food because they needed to get going. Rude ones, they were. Said they had to make it out of the city before the gate closed for the night. One of them mentioned to the other that there would be a harvest moon tonight and they'd certainly have enough light to travel by. They didn't leave here that long ago. Shouldn't be that hard to catch them…if you hurry."

Rahab ran her hands through her hair again. She could see that the men were doing as much looking as they were listening. She yawned and turned slightly to look back over her shoulder at the moon. Then, she stretched her arms high over her head to stretch in a well-rehearsed move that gave them an eyeful of her curves under her soft linen robe.

"Beautiful moon tonight," she said in a tone intended to convey to them that they had just enjoyed the grand finale. From the way they had stared at her every move, she felt there was a good chance that about all they would remember was, "They left before the gate closed."

As they headed down the street, Rahab sat down wearily on her doorstep. Though she was exhausted, her mind continued to whirl furiously, replaying the scene of the last few minutes. She had just given the performance of her life.

But had it been good enough? Had she completely convinced them? What if some of them came back and decided to go inside and search the house? What if they saw the damage to the roof in the kitchen and went up to search the rooftop?

If they did come back, she decided she would have to slip away. Not that she could escape for they would, of course, eventually find and kill her. But at least she would not be there to hear the sounds of the bloody battle that would occur when the king's officers found Salmon and Abner.

She sat quietly with the tears welling up in her eyes. She listened intently for any sound of the men returning. She wished she could have a really good cry, but she knew that this certainly was not the time nor the place. Presently, she heard the creaks and groans of the city gates being opened, and then after a short while the same noise indicated they were being closed again.

At first the cool air of the evening felt good. It helped her to relax a little. But after sitting for a while, she started to shiver. It took all the strength she could muster to stand up and go into the house. Walking stiffly inside, she found a shawl to wrap around her shoulders. She went to the kitchen and drank a cup of cool water. Then she dragged the table back under the skylight, put a stool on top, and climbed up so that the top of her head stuck through the hole.

Softly she whispered, "Can you hear me?"

"Yes," came an equally soft reply.

"It will be me that you hear coming up the steps in a moment. Okay?"

"Okay." After a moment's pause, Salmon added, "Rahab, you are..." then his voice trailed off.

Rahab opened the front door quietly and slowly walked around the house to the steps that led up to the roof. To anyone looking out a window, she appeared calm and indifferent to the world around her. On the inside, however, her stomach was in knots. After all the commotion this evening, if any of her neighbors looked out a window and saw her looking at all suspicious, they might very well get word to the king's officers that something was wrong.

The steps were in the shadows, so she was careful about her footing. She tiptoed quietly up the darkened stairs. When she reached the top, she emerged into the startlingly bright moonlight. She stooped over and took off her sandals so that she could move as quietly as possible across the flax-strewn rooftop to the corner where the spies were hidden.

Quietly, she spoke their names and was relieved when they showed the good sense not to sit up but to merely poke their heads up through the flax...just enough for her to see them. Relieved, she reasoned that they may be bold and daring but at least they were starting to show some sense. Even so, she scolded them with a curt command to stay down.

She heard a muffled response, but she couldn't tell if it was a sarcastic, "Yes, Mother" or "Yes, Miriam."

❦

Here she was facing the most dangerous moments of her life, and these two were making jokes. She let it pass because she had serious matters she wanted to get settled. Kneeling down to be as close as possible, she whispered, "Listen carefully. I told the king's men that you left Jericho in a hurry before the city gate was closed. I told them that I didn't know where you were going."

Abner said quietly, "Yes, we heard."

Rahab ignored him and continued, "They will head toward the Jordan River. Since the road is downhill in that direction and they think that you are on the run, they will want to take advantage of the moonlight to get down to the ford quickly and cut off your escape route. This will also give them an excuse to stay together. I am sure none of them wants to run into the two of you in the dark alone.

"Everyone in Jericho, including the soldiers, is terrified by what we've heard about you. No one has any courage left. We heard how your God divided the water of the Red Sea for you when you came out of Egypt long ago. Then we heard how you completely destroyed all the cities of the Amorites—even the fortified ones—and that even King Sihon and King Og perished.

"When we heard these things, everyone gave up hope. There have been some brave speeches, but no one actually believes them. After what we know about you, there isn't anyone left in Jericho with any hope that the city will survive. People say it's because there are too many of you for us to fight.[75] But I know it's really because your God has given you the land." She paused to catch her breath and scan the housetops to make sure no one was in sight. Neither of the men said anything as they watched her face bathed in moonlight.

She went on, her voice becoming more urgent with each word. "So, I beg you to swear to me by Yahweh that since I have showed you kindness you will also show kindness unto my father's house. I want you to give me your solemn word, as God is your witness, that you will save the lives of my father, my mother, my brothers, my sisters, and all their children."

Rahab paused again. When she did, she heard her heart pounding in her ears. Then, she heard the faint sounds of the two men quietly easing themselves further up on their elbows. She wanted desperately to see their faces, but their backs were to the moon. In the hushed silence of the moonlight, she heard one of them cough gently to clear his throat. When he spoke, Rahab's heart began to sing. She couldn't be certain, but she thought it was Salmon who said the most wonderful words she had ever heard in her life, "Our lives for your lives."

She buried her face in her hands as tears of hope and joy began to roll down her cheeks. The words echoed in her mind, "Our lives for your lives. Our lives for your lives." When she looked up into the shadowed faces again, she heard him continue, "As God is our witness, we promise faithfully that we will remember what you've done for us and we will treat you kindly when the Lord gives us the land. But there is one condition. You can't tell anyone about this."

"Certainly, I understand," Rahab said. "But I will have to warn my family to come into the city. When should I do that?" she asked.

Salmon—this time she was sure it was him speaking—gave her a reassuring nod and said, "Rahab, when we get ready to cross the Jordan, we'll be coming with an army of 40,000 fighting men.[76] That's a column of men five abreast stretching from here all the way to the Jordan.[77] It will take several days to get everyone ready to travel. We'll raise a cloud of dust that you should be able to see as far away as from here to the Salt Sea. You're not going to have any problem knowing that we are coming. You'll see signs that we are on the move even before we cross the Jordan. You'll know when it is time to send word to your family. Just make sure they are here with you before the king orders the gates closed."

Rahab looked up at the moon and noted its course.

"The moon is about over Pisgah now. By the middle of the night, it will be over the Salt Sea," she said softly pointing across the city to the southeast.[78] "At that time, the moon will be casting a deep shadow on the wall below us here," she said softly, pointing to the city's north wall that formed the back wall of her house.[79] "When that happens, you must come back down through the skylight into the kitchen.

"I'll hang a rope out of the kitchen window for you to use to get down the wall. When you leave here, go to the mountains to the west back behind the city. That route will ensure you'll be heading in the opposite direction from where they are expecting. Then you won't run into any of the search parties between here and the river. The mountains are full of caves, and you shouldn't have any difficulty finding water this time of year. Find someplace to hide for three days. By the end of three days, the search parties will have given up and come back to the city. After that time, you shouldn't have any problems making your way back to Shittim."

Her knees were getting sore from kneeling, and she knew it was time for her to leave. She was reluctant to go, but she could think of nothing further to say to postpone her departure. Slowly, she rose to her feet. Her legs were stiff and aching.

"I'm a light sleeper," she added. "I'll hear you when you drop down into the kitchen. The table is back under the skylight, so you won't have far to drop. Just be careful you don't twist your ankle. You've got a lot of ground to cover before daybreak."

As she headed down the stairs, she heard a bemused chuckle that she was pretty sure had come from Salmon.

Rahab lit a lamp and went into the kitchen. She began selecting food to send with Salmon and Abner from the stores she had been collecting to prepare for the coming siege. As her thoughts rambled about in her head, she looked for items that would travel well. She settled on dates, almonds, cheese, and some parched corn. She also included the pomegranate she had selected so carefully just today. Was it possible that her visit to the market had actually been this morning? How could all of the events she had just experienced have happened in one day? She refocused and studied for a few moments, wondering how they could carry the supplies.

The best thing, she decided, would be to roll the supplies up in long sheets of cloth and then tie the ends together in a knot. With the rolls slung over their shoulders, they would have their hands free to climb down the rope. For a moment she fingered the fine linen robe she was wearing. Then, without hesitation, she swiftly stripped it off. Seizing a knife, she cut it in half from hem to neck and then cut away all of the embroidery. She spread one of the pieces on the table and rolled up as much food in it as it would safely hold. Then, she tied the two ends together and slung it over her shoulder to test whether it made a secure bundle. Satisfied that it was travel-worthy, she did the same with the other piece and then headed off to bed.

Rahab lay awake, sleepless, replaying the events of the evening over and over in her mind. What was it that had made her decide to hide the spies and lie to the king's officers when they came to arrest them? Why had she taken her life into her hands? She didn't have a satisfactory answer before she dropped into a deep sleep. She was exhausted by the strain of the last few hours.

She sat up with a start when she felt a hand on her shoulder. She was embarrassed to have to be awakened after her confident assertion that she would hear them when they dropped down through the skylight. She got to her feet and started to the back of the house shaking her head and yawning.

The moonlight pouring through the front window shed enough light so that she didn't bother to light a lamp. She poured herself some water and offered some to the men as well. Abner had climbed up on the table and was busy tying the rope to one of the ceiling beams.

Salmon turned to her and said, "Rahab, you made us swear an oath to you by the Lord our God. Now listen to me very carefully. For us to fulfill our promise to spare you and your household when we cross over and take possession of this land, we will have to be able to tell all of our fighting men which house to stay away from. As a clear sign of which house is yours, you must keep this scarlet cord tied in the window. If you don't do that, we will be released from our oath. All of your family must be in this house, not in the house next door, not anywhere else."

She nodded vigorously. He paused and took a drink of water.

Then, he took her hands in his and gazed at her directly, "There is no room for even the slightest error, Rahab. If anyone in your family leaves this house during the battle and goes out into the street, they are going to get themselves killed. It will be their own fault. However, if anyone who stays in the house is harmed, their blood will be on our heads for failing to keep the promise we made to you before God. One last thing. Remember what I told you to begin with. If you tell anyone about this, that will release us from our oath."

Again, she nodded vigorously and murmured, "It will be just as you say."

"Our lives for yours," he said intently.

Fervently she echoed, "Our lives for yours."

As Salmon finished speaking, Abner moved over to the window and was ready to climb out when Rahab interrupted him.

"Hold on. I've packed some dates and other things for you to eat. You can move faster if you don't have to look for food."

Abner looked at Salmon, who nodded a yes.

Rahab slung the first bundle over Salmon's left shoulder and under his right arm with the food riding between his shoulder blades.

"Okay?" she asked.

Salmon gave her a broad affirmative smile.

As she was slinging the bundle over Abner's shoulder, he muttered affectionately, "You're right, Salmon. She is like Miriam."

"Don't just stand there, slowpoke," she smarted back, giving him a playful shove. "Get moving and don't wake up the neighbors, or I'll drop a pot on your head."

With that Abner was out the window and silently lowering himself hand-over-hand to the bottom of the wall.

Salmon stood at the window watching Abner descend. When it was his turn, he turned to Rahab and said softly, "Don't think we don't know how much you've risked for us. Don't take any more chances." Unconsciously, he fingered the linen around his chest, looked at her searchingly one last moment with his direct gaze, and whispered solemnly, "Rahab, take care of yourself. I'll be back." With that, he disappeared and started his descent.

Rahab stood at the window for a long time. She nervously watched for any sign that the watchmen on the wall might have noticed any movement. But the spies used the shadows as cover so skillfully that Rahab neither saw nor heard anything. It pleased her to see that the only thing clumsy about them had been their disguise.

"So, Mommy," the little boy said intently, "Tell us what happened next?"

"Boaz," Rahab said, smiling indulgently, "you know what happened next. I've told you this story a hundred times before. And besides, it's time for you to go to sleep. There isn't time for the rest of the story tonight."

No matter how many times she told four-year-old Boaz and six-year-old Miriam the story, they always listened as if they had never heard it before. Unless, of course, she left out any details. When that happened, they would always remind her of her own omission, trying to delay sleep as long as possible.

Their chorus of "*please*, Mommy" won out, partly because of their persistence and partly because of the joy that reliving the moment brought. She continued, "I didn't see your father again until the Israelites started marching around Jericho on the first day of the siege. Your father was at the front of the advance guard that went before the priests and the ark when they started marching around the city. When the news came that the city was being surrounded, I went up on the rooftop, along with Grandfather Sidon, to see what was happening."

"But, Mommy, you promised Father that you wouldn't go out in the street. How did you get up on the roof?"

"Now, Boaz, you know I wouldn't break a promise, least of all one to your father. It was simple. Grandfather got up on the table and climbed up through the skylight—just like your father had done—then he pulled me up after him.

"I wasn't sure whether I would be able to pick out your father from all the rest, but it turned out to be fairly easy. He was carrying his spear and tied to it was a long linen banner."

This was Miriam's favorite part, "Your dress..." she murmured.

Rahab smiled and continued, "When he saw the red cord hanging from my window on the north wall, he raised his spear high over his head and waved the banner back and forth."

"Did you wave back, Mommy?" Boaz asked right on cue.

"Oh, no. It was very important that no one learn that I helped your father and Uncle Abner escape from Jericho."

"And then what happened?"

"What happened next was the most incredible week in my life. Everyone braced for the attack. But the Israelites just kept marching. Day after day. They would circle the city once, *without making a sound*. Finally, after marching around the city once a day for six days, on the seventh day, the army and the priests carrying the ark marched around Jericho seven times in a row. Then, the priests blew their trumpets, and Joshua commanded all the people to shout.

"When I heard the noise, I tried to run to the window to see what was going on, but the house started shaking so hard I couldn't stand up. I was so frightened! I thought the house was going to collapse on top of us. We could hear it groaning and cracking, and the air was full of noise and sand. When I was finally able to crawl to the window, I looked out and there was a tall plume of dust. I realized that the walls of the city were tumbling down...all except for where my house was."

Again, on the cue he had been waiting for, Boaz asked, "Why didn't the wall fall down where *your* house was, Mommy?"

"Because," she said reverently, "the Lord, who is our God, who rules the heavens and the earth, who parted the Red Sea and the Jordan River, kept us safely in His hand."

"Tell us the ending, Mommy, please, tell us," he urged breathlessly.

"Well, at first when the noise of the walls tumbling down stopped, there was a moment or two of quiet. Everyone was stunned. The dust was so thick it was hard to see what had happened. When the dust started to clear a little, I saw your father and Uncle Abner climbing over the tumbled-down pieces of the wall. They were leading a dozen, handpicked warriors. I wanted to run out to meet them, but I had promised your father that I wouldn't leave the house. I thought about climbing up through the skylight to the roof where I could see what was going on, but I was afraid it might collapse. I did, however, peek out the front window from time to time to see if I could see him coming down the street."

"How did you know he was headed for your house, Mommy?"

"Oh, I just guessed." she said with a mischievous smile.

"Boaz," Miriam scolded, "Father told her he was coming back!"

"That's right," laughed Rahab. "The last thing he had said before he left was, 'I'll be back.' I knew even then he was a man of his word."

She continued, "Soon I heard the sounds of men making their way along the street. I peeked out of the window again and saw some of the king's men running away towards the king's castle. Then, coming from the other direction, I could see your father leading his men at a dead-run up what was left of the street. They were jumping over all sorts of fallen rubble.

"When they reached the house, both your father and Uncle Abner started calling out, 'Rahab, Rahab, are you all right? Joshua has commanded us to come and take you to safety just as we promised before God.'

"I shouted that I was okay and that everyone in the house was safe. Then I yelled that the front door was stuck and that I couldn't get it open."

"Mommy, you know what?" asked Boaz. "I think God shut the door so you would be safe, just like He closed the door when Noah went into the ark."

"You know what, Boaz?" asked Salmon, who had entered the room so quietly that no one had heard him. For all his size, he could move as silently as a cat.

"Oh, my, Salmon! I wish you wouldn't do that. You startled me," sighed Rahab.

Salmon chuckled gently, turned toward Boaz, and continued, "Young man, I think you have it just right. And, of course, God had it all arranged so that I could rescue your mother. He knew that I needed the chance to repay her for hiding me and Uncle Abner."

"Please finish the ending," pleaded Boaz.

"But you know the rest," said Salmon, who didn't quite understand all the finer points of ritual storytelling.

Rahab resumed the story with increased animation now that Salmon was part of her audience. "When I couldn't get the door open, your father shouted at me to stand back. He and Uncle Abner put their shoulders to the door and with a couple of shoves pushed it open."

"And then what, Mother?" asked Miriam, her dark eyes sparkling with eagerness.

"Your father," said Rahab, her eyes misting, "took my hands in his, and looked into my eyes. I was so excited to see him that I could hardly breathe. Then he gave me that mischievous grin that had melted my heart the first time I saw it, and said..." her voice caught.

"He said simply," she continued, softly, looking up at Salmon, "'I'm back.'"

Salmon smiled at her.

"I was so happy I didn't know what to do," Rahab continued, still looking into his eyes.

"I turned and looked at your grandfather and grandmother, and I'll never forget the way they were looking at us. They recognized what they saw on our faces—Grandmother more so than Grandfather—but they couldn't quite believe it.

"Uncle Abner broke the silence and said that we needed to get everyone out of the house and out of harm's way. Your father and the other men took us all safely out of the city. In the spot next to where the Israelites were camped, they made a place for us.

"When the battle was over, your father returned and talked with my father. He explained that Grandfather Nahshon was dead, and so he himself had come to pay the bride price. My father gave his blessing, and together your grandmother and I sewed my wedding dress. That's the end of the story, and now it is time to go to sleep."

Boaz was already asleep, but Miriam had one last question.

"Mother, is Uncle Abner your brother or Father's brother?"

"Well," said Rahab, "he's your father's brother by marriage. You are named for Uncle Abner's sister. And she was named for the prophetess Miriam, who was the sister of Moses. You should ask Uncle Abner to tell you about both of them one day soon. Good night, my precious."

Salmon added, "May the Lord God, the Almighty, watch over you as you sleep."

And Rahab said, "Amen."

And the Lord said to Joshua:
"See! I have given Jericho into your hand,
its king, and the mighty men of valor..."
And on the seventh day, Joshua said to the people:
"Shout, for the Lord has given you the city!"
"Now the city shall be doomed by the Lord to destruction,
it and all who are in it.
*Only **Rahab** the harlot shall live,*
she and all who are with her in the house,
*because she hid the **messengers** that we sent..."*
And they utterly destroyed all that was in the city...
But Joshua had said to the two men who had spied out the country,

*"Go into the harlot's house, and from there bring out the **woman**
and all that she has, as you swore to her."*
*And the **young men** who had been spies went in
and brought out **Rahab**, her father, her mother, her brothers,
and all that she had.*
*So they brought out all her relatives and
left them outside the camp of Israel…*
*And Joshua spared **Rahab** the harlot,
her father's household, and all that she had.*
*So she dwells in Israel to this day,
because she hid the **messengers** whom
Joshua sent to spy out Jericho…*
JOSHUA 6:2,16-25

Salmon begot **Boaz**
by Rahab,
Boaz begot Obed
by Ruth,
*Obed begot Jesse,
and Jesse begot David
the king.*

The Power of Wisdom

The fear of the Lord is the beginning of wisdom.
PSALM 111:10

Though poets and sages have valued wisdom throughout time, wisdom doesn't sell for what it is worth in everyday affairs. It doesn't have a quantifiable dimension. It is such a humble virtue that often it is only visible in a crisis when its presence or absence makes the difference between tragedy averted or not. Sadly, it is most often noticed by virtue of the pain and loss caused by its absence. Yet Scripture tells us that wisdom is supreme.[80]

In the book of Proverbs, wisdom is described as better than rubies.[81] But the Bible is also a realistic book, and it quickly points out that great people are not always wise.[82] In fact, human beings, as Francis Bacon noted long ago, are usually more foolish than wise.[83] Perhaps we value wisdom so highly because it is so rare.

One of the remarkable instances of wisdom in Scripture is Rahab's change of allegiance. Rahab, even in the midst of pagan Jericho, recognized the greatness of the God of the Israelites, and she was wise enough to side with the men of God. God, in His graciousness, used her life as a demonstration of His forgiveness and of His healing power by giving her a special place in the genealogy of Christ.

God's purposes are often not the same as ours—they are better! They are always good and they are always wise. And they are also always greater than the plans we design.

Joshua thought he was sending the spies out for one purpose—to prepare his people to conquer the land. But God had something altogether different in mind. When the dust settled from the earthquake God used to destroy the walls of Jericho, two things had been revealed: First, there was no doubt that God was not going to be hemmed in by traditional battle plans. Second, He demonstrated that He was not only a God of judgment but of mercy as well—One who was willing to accept even pagans who turn to Him with all their hearts.

It was obvious that the victory at Jericho had nothing to do with a brilliant military strategy! Although Joshua had planned on using the critical information his spies brought back from their foray to ensure their success, God had a different idea in mind for Jericho. Instead of military force to lead the people to victory, God revealed that His ways are higher—and far more wondrous. The ultimate victory had everything to do with the fact that the people of Israel faithfully obeyed the instructions given to Joshua by the captain of the Lord's host.[84]

Instead of using a direct assault, which had been the tactic when going up against the Amorites on the East Bank, God terrified the defenders of Jericho by shaking the walls down right out from under their feet. Jericho's impregnable walls lay in rubble. In the confusion that ensued, the spies fully performed the oath that they had sworn to a lowly Canaanite woman.

When Joshua sent the spies to Jericho, God put in motion His plan to save a woman who had come to faith in Him against all odds. How amazing! A prostitute living in the midst of pagans. How utterly amazing that Rahab had come to believe that Yahweh—the God of the Israelites, an enemy to her people—was the one true God! Oh, the magnitude of His love and forgiveness. He provided for the salvation of a single, solitary person. And not just any person, but an outcast woman who was not even one of the chosen seed of Abraham.

The Truth Shall Set You Free

Rahab's conversion from paganism to faith in the one true God is one of the most miraculous stories recorded in all of Scripture. The story is so incredible that it is celebrated not only in the Old Testament book of Joshua but twice in the New Testament as well by both James in his epistle[85] and by the writer of the book of Hebrews.[86] (Though some writers have suggested that Rahab was not a harlot, but merely an innkeeper, we note that both of the New Testament writers refer to her as a harlot.) Given her circumstances, it staggers the imagination that this pagan woman could come to accept the God of the Israelites as the "God in heaven above, and in earth beneath."[87] Note that she didn't view Yahweh as just another local deity or the god of a particular people. She declared Him the Lord of all—of heaven above and earth beneath. Rahab did not consider the looming battle to be a contest between the gods of her people against the God of the Israelites. Amazingly, she saw Yahweh as God over *all* of heaven and earth.

The wisdom of this "outsider" from Jericho brings to mind the wisdom of another outsider. Recall that one day Jesus was in Capernaum when a Roman centurion requested that Christ heal his servant who was sick. When Jesus offered to come and heal him, the centurion objected saying, "Lord, I am not worthy that thou shouldest come under my roof: but speak the word only, and my servant shall be healed. For I am a man under authority, having soldiers under me: and I say to this man, Go, and he goeth; and to another, Come, and he cometh; and to my servant, Do this, and he doeth it." Jesus marveled at the man's words and said to His followers, "Verily I say unto you, I have not found so great faith, no, not in Israel."[88] Just as He had rewarded Rahab's faith without regard for the fact that she was not an Israelite but a Canaanite, the Lord rewarded the centurion's faith though he was a Roman. Scripture records the fact that Christ spoke and the servant was healed.

What was it about these two outsiders that set them apart and made them candidates for God's mercy and blessing? One obvious characteristic they shared was the clarity with which they saw the truth. Though many in Jericho and Capernaum were hearing and seeing the same events as Rahab and the centurion, these two saw beyond the specifics of the incidences to the deeper truths those events revealed about God. Two persons, separated by hundreds of years and vastly different circumstances, developed a capacity to see the true meaning of the evidence about God that He brought into their pathways in the day-to-day events of their lives. What fantastic displays of wisdom they each exhibited—life-changing, life-preserving wisdom.

The path to life is learning to see the truth in the events of our lives and to believe it. The sterling quality of the wisdom of Rahab the harlot and of the Roman centurion shines all the more brilliantly when we contrast it with the faltering faith of the disciples who had so much more opportunity to learn than they. Recall that Thomas' reply to Christ's assurance that He was going to prepare a place for them was to say, "We don't know where you are going, so how can we know the way?" This brought from Christ one of His most awesome, mind-bending statements: "I am the way, the truth, and the life."[89] Couple this statement of Christ's with the one He had made earlier to His disciples—"And ye shall know the truth, and the truth shall make you free"[90]—and we know the secret to Rahab's survival.

What Blinds Us to Truth?

The question, of course, is what made Rahab different from all of the others in Jericho? How is it that she could see the life-giving truth that none of the others in her city saw? Though the answer is not recorded, we have a lot of information about what those differences had to have been from the universal principles about life we learn from Scripture and confirm in our life experiences. First of all, we are all born with a fallen nature.[91] This reality means that though the image of God remains in us, it is marred by selfishness, pride, fear, anger, greed, lust, and other base motives that cause us to sin. But because God made us with an inclination to do good, we feel conflicted and guilty when we give in to temptation and do that which is evil.

The propensity for selfishness in us struggles against the imperative to do what is right. It forces us to grapple with the issue of who we are and what is good. It is as children that we first stub our toes on the truth that we are not the center of the universe (contrary to what our experience as infants seemed to teach us). Sooner or later when we cry over not getting our way, we all hear the words, "Stop being a baby!" The second truth we learn as children is that we are not autonomous. As created beings we are accountable and also dependent. Both realizations rankle our pride.

Beginning as very small children, when we disobey our parents, we find that we have also disobeyed the law written on our hearts that commands us to do good. Thus, we find ourselves not only in trouble with the first authority figures of our life to whom we are accountable, but we also must contend with our conscience that fills us with fear and guilt. And what do we do to resolve both the external and internal conflicts we have created? We try to escape by denying the truth about our actions, to our parents as well as to ourselves.

We deny truth in several ways. First, we often say that what we did or said was not really evil because of "special" circumstances: For example, the actions of others forced us to do what we would otherwise not have done. Or, if that alibi won't work, we say that though the deed was evil, our motives and intentions were good—even though our actions turned out otherwise through no fault of our own. (The boldest among us these days even argue that good and evil are self-defined by every individual, that there is no absolute standard of good to which everyone is accountable. Until, of course, someone else happens to violate what they consider to be one of their rights, and then they suddenly feel differently about the question of each person being totally autonomous and answerable only to their own ideas about what is right and wrong.)

In short, we make excuses, and we rationalize. We offer excuses to escape punishment or embarrassment or to try to quiet the accusing voice of conscience within us. Deceiving others damages our relationship to them. This understanding is extremely important because so much of our humanity is wrapped up in our relationships with others. But even greater damage is done when we lie to ourselves. Each time we do that—even if it is only in a small matter—we sever some of the slender threads of truth that connect us to reality. Cut enough of these threads, and we are set adrift without any mooring in a troubled sea of unreality. If we call good evil and evil good often enough, we end up in a world of illusions peopled by the demons of our imagination. Unable to bear looking truthfully at our moral nakedness when we have broken His laws about doing good, we, like Adam and Eve, are afraid to stand in the illuminating presence of the God who is truth.

The Role of Empathy

Hollywood plays and replays the threadbare myth of the generous, big-hearted, good-natured "lady of the evening," even though the facts generally give lie to the myth. Most prostitutes end up being very dysfunctional, because both their bodies and spirits are shattered by the physical and emotional abuse they experience. A high percentage die at an early age. Their lives are shortened by the alcohol or drugs that numb them to the realities of their lives. But strange as it may seem, there is a biblical precedent for the myth...and her name is Rahab!

This woman is a source of many surprises, but none is more unexpected—given her profession—than her great capacity for empathy.

We see her genuine regard for others in two respects. First, seeing the spies as threatened human beings, Rahab acts decisively and effectively to protect them at tremendous risk to herself. Second, though she found a way to personally escape the impending destruction of Jericho, she immediately set about to ensure the safety of her family as well.

At its core, empathy consists of seeing others as of equal value to ourselves—a natural corollary to the truth that we are all created and loved by God. Only infants and totally depraved individuals see others merely as a means to satisfy their own needs and desires. When we see others as important, in and of themselves, we see their hurts and pain as of equal importance to our own. Given our fallen nature, however, the self desires to be preeminent. It is human for us to put ourselves first. It is as natural as breathing—and just as subconscious. But an empathetic person has developed a true picture of the worth of others and sees the needs of others as similar to their own. So we see then that empathy and truthfulness are closely related.

Because God made us in His image, there remains, despite the fall, a part of us that inclines to the good. As a consequence of this propensity to do good, we must first formulate excuses to resolve our inner conflict before we can take advantage of another person. We have to rationalize our evil behavior. If we lie to ourselves by fabricating a reason why the other person is of less value, if we convince ourselves that their needs are not as important or as urgent as our own, we have an alibi. We have a way out of our dilemma. Such thoughts serve to trump our sense of guilt, making it easier for us to act selfishly and hurtfully. But these are counterfeit permission slips—fake IDs admitting us to a land of guilt-free self-absorption. God's truth is plain: Selfishness and dishonesty go together in the same way as empathy and truthfulness.

One thing is abundantly clear about Rahab: She saw things very clearly. With all of the pain she experienced as a prostitute, it is amazing that she did not withdraw within a protective shell of self-delusion just to survive. Somehow, despite all the hurts she had endured, she continued to see the needs of others as equal to her own.

Holding on to this truthful view of others, she preserved her capacity for empathy and preserved her God-given humanity.

"Looking Out" for Reality

Unlike many others in Jericho, Rahab did not delude herself with wishful thinking. Nor was she close-minded. She looked at the evidence that Yahweh had done a great miracle to deliver the people of Israel from Pharaoh. She doubtless compared the impotence of her own people's gods to help her with the real miracles performed by the God of Israel. She had never seen the gods of the Canaanites perform miracles, and she was honest enough not to dodge that truth or its implications. She, like others in Jericho, had heard that Yahweh had given the Israelites victories in battle against the Amorites. She, no doubt, saw that these events clearly foretold the truth about Jericho's impending destruction—Jericho was doomed. While other people in Jericho might delude themselves, Rahab did not. She was too honest for that. The facts spoke the truth, and she listened. She learned. She lived.

Self-absorption, at its root, is a denial of the truth about who and what we are and about what this denial means in terms of our relationships with others. Self-absorption and dishonesty are barriers not only in our relationships with other human beings, but they are major roadblocks to our relationship with God. As we conclude our attempt to understand how Rahab came to believe in the God of the Israelites, it may be helpful if we link the words of Christ with those of John.

Christ, in answer to the question of which is the greatest commandment, replied, "Thou shalt love the Lord thy God with all thy heart, and with all thy soul, and with all thy strength, and with all thy mind; and thy neighbour as thyself."[92] John then expands our understanding of Christ's message by posing the question, "If a man say, I love God, and hateth his brother, he is a liar: for he that loveth not his brother whom he hath seen, how can he love God whom he hath not seen?"[93]

Because of her honesty, Rahab had a true picture of where she stood in relation to others. Thereby, she was that much closer to Him who called Himself the truth, the way, and the life. She was a pagan, but she was not an atheist—for the most part, atheism is a modern development of "educated" persons. The step she had to take, as a "truth-lover," was to come to an understanding of the nature of God—who He was and how to follow Him. As a wise and honest pagan, Rahab looked outside of herself and her own feelings. She weighed the evidence and discovered that the miracle-working God of the Israelites was the one true God over *all*. Seeing this truth and embracing it set her free!

The Path to Wisdom

"Who is wise and understanding among you? Let him show it by his good life, by deeds done in the humility that comes from wisdom. But if you harbor bitter envy and selfish ambition in your hearts, do not boast about it or deny the truth. Such 'wisdom' does not come down from heaven, but is earthly, unspiritual, of the devil. For where you have envy and selfish ambition, there you find disorder and every evil practice. But the wisdom that comes from heaven is first of all pure, then peace loving, considerate, submissive, full of mercy and good fruit, impartial and sincere. Peacemakers who sow in peace raise a harvest of righteousness."

The early chapters of Proverbs encourage us to develop wisdom. As modern women seeking to be wise, we can learn much from these chapters: Listen to your father's instruction and do not forsake your mother's teaching (see Proverbs 23:22). The first chapter warns us about rejecting wisdom, "Since they would not accept my advice and spurned my rebuke, they will eat the fruit of their ways and be filled with the fruit of their schemes" (1:30,31). The second chapter, verse 6, proclaims, "For the LORD gives wisdom, and from his mouth come knowledge and understanding." It promises, "Wisdom will save you from the ways of wicked men, from men whose words are perverse…" (verse 12). Chapter 3 continues to list the benefits of wisdom: It will prolong life, bring prosperity, bring you favor and a good name. It warns us, "Do not be wise in your own eyes," and declares, "Blessed is the man who finds wisdom" (verses 7,13).

We need to take special notice of how wisdom is described in Proverbs 4, for there we see reiterated the theme that wisdom is supreme. "Get wisdom though it cost you all you have…Esteem her and she will honor you…I will guide you in the way of wisdom and lead you along straight paths. When you walk, your steps will not be hampered; when you run, you will not stumble" (see verses 7-14).

So how does a modern woman become wise? Wisdom is not one of the freebies of life. Those who would be wise must be willing to exercise the mental, emotional, physical, and spiritual disciplines that are required. In fact, the Bible warns that our lack of discipline—which is pictured as the opposite of wisdom—will lead to heartbreak and ruin.

Knowledge alone is not enough. We must move beyond the mere accumulation of knowledge. We must develop our capacity for insights by learning the *whats* and *whens* and seeing the *whys* and *hows* of life. Chapter 5 of Proverbs challenges us, "Listen well to my words of insight, that you may maintain discretion and your lips may preserve knowledge." It is all too easy, with the pressure and distractions of daily living, to go through life without observing and analyzing the cause-and-effect relationships that link our decision making and actions to consequences.

The tone of Proverbs is humility, fear, and respect before the Lord God Almighty. Only when we abandon our pride can we begin to acknowledge that "the fear of the LORD is the beginning of wisdom: and the knowledge of the holy is understanding."[94]

Clearly, those who are wise, like Rahab, will find themselves amazed by the wonderful ways of God, who goes before us with plans and strategies that we can scarcely imagine. If we listen carefully for His command and move forward to follow His orders, it won't be long before we find ourselves experiencing the miracle of victory. What an adventure to experience true wisdom! What a joy and privilege to find ourselves on the path to a different kind of strength.

The Power of Boldness

According to my earnest expectation and my hope,
that in nothing I shall be ashamed,
but that with all boldness as always,
so now also Christ shall be magnified in my body,
whether it be by life or by death.
For me to live is Christ, and to die is gain.
PHILIPPIANS 1:20,21

What are we to learn about boldness from the remarkable story of Rahab? None of us in contemporary culture will find ourselves in circumstances quite like hers, but each of us will, at some point in our lives, face situations requiring boldness in the face of uncertainty.

Billy Graham once declared, "Those who stand by the cross are those who change the course of history." What an endorsement for being bold and taking a stand! Dr. Graham's comment is also a signpost. Only those willing to go the way of the cross will change the course of history redemptively!

The story of Rahab reverberates with energy and adventure. Rahab gives us a beautiful picture of the power of boldness in the life of a woman who faces life with courage, with dignity, and with strength— even in the face of impossible odds. If you or I had been in her shoes, would we have believed we had any reason to have hope or faith? To the human eye, Rahab seemed doomed, along with all of the rest of the people in Jericho. No way out! She could see destruction coming, but she could never have envisioned that Jericho's desolation would mean her deliverance. When the two spies arrived at her door, she could not possibly have imagined the incredible plan God had set in motion.

The Riddle of the Flax

The story of Rahab poses many fascinating questions about her motivations and methods. What convinced her that the magnificent city of Jericho with its seemingly impregnable double walls was doomed? How did Rahab learn the identity of the spies? After all, spies don't normally march up and present a business card listing their profession as "Intelligence Officer for the Enemy," particularly deep in the heart of hostile territory. Why did this clever woman, when she detected who they were, decide to protect them from her own people? In addition to these questions and others—like a message in a bottle lying half-buried in the sand—a riddle lies half-buried in the story of Rahab and her spies...the riddle of the drying flax.

Just as God had a different purpose for sending the spies to Jericho than Joshua had intended, God had a different purpose for the flax than Rahab ever imagined when she spread it on the roof to dry. The spies thought they were going to Jericho to learn about the city's fortifications, but God intended for them to learn about a woman's faith. Rahab thought she was going to use the flax to make cloth, but God intended for her to use it to conceal the spies.

With her keen, logical mind, Rahab saw the clear implications of God's miracles in delivering the children of Israel from bondage to Pharaoh. Likewise, she saw that God was going to deliver Jericho into the hands of the Israelites—just as He had all the fortified cities of the Amorites on the east side of the Jordan. When the decisive moment finally arrived, she quickly devised a detour for the spies that took them to the mountains west of Jericho. Thus, they avoided their pursuers who were searching for them to the east along the banks of the Jordan River.

Why would this woman with the mind of a military strategist, a woman who understood that Jericho was doomed, undertake a long-range task like making cloth out of flax? Why would she obtain a load of flax and put it on her roof to dry when she was convinced Jericho was soon to be attacked and probably destroyed? Drying the flax was but the first step in the lengthy process of converting it into linen cloth.[95]

The riddle of the flax may boil down to a matter of plain habit. Making linen may have been an important means of therapy for Rahab.

It could have been a way to keep her emotional equilibrium, given her occupation. The honest, hard work could have served as a creative outlet as well as an emotional safety valve. Viewed with this eye, the contradiction of starting anew on the cycle of cloth production, despite all the evidence that time was running out for Jericho, may be resolved by viewing the work as such a habitual part of her life that she continued it without giving it any thought. It could be that she saw the contradiction but chose to continue working in order to occupy herself as a means of coping with the uncertainty and the sense of impending doom. She could well have been practicing the same principle that someone facing a health crisis follows—say someone diagnosed with cancer who copes by following the principle of "just do the next thing." Putting one foot in front of the other is sometimes all we can do in the face of overwhelming crisis...and, sometimes, it is exactly the right thing to do.

Another alternative that may explain the seeming contradiction is the premise that she was deliberately maintaining her ordinary routines in order to disguise her intentions. It could be that she was looking to find a means of escape from Jericho, and she knew that if her intentions became apparent her neighbors might attack and rob her or that authorities of the city might detain her. There is no doubt that Rahab was intelligent enough and farsighted enough to have formulated such a plan. In this scenario, she would have been looking for any opportunity for contact with someone from outside of Jericho whose assistance she might enlist to help her leave the city. This explanation would also be consistent with the fact that she recognized the spies very quickly and set about to hide them from the king's men.

Whatever the true explanation of the riddle of the flax may be, God was working through Rahab's plan to accomplish His own purpose: He equipped her with the means to hide the spies. As we saw in the last chapter, God's plans are different from ours: They are better!

At some point later in her life, perhaps in the quiet of the midnight hour as little Boaz lay nursing at her breast, Rahab may have been able to look back and marvel at the intricate beauty of God's plan. As a person experienced in working with flax, Rahab knew that in order to get at the strong inner fibers that can be used to produce beautiful linen cloth, the outer layer of the stalk must first be beaten and crushed. She would have known how to carefully hammer the rotted outer layer to expose what was of value underneath. Perhaps she marveled to see how the hardship of her life had been designed, not to destroy her, but to lay bare the strong fiber in her and to weave it into a grand and glorious design.

Seizing the Moment

So, what was there about Rahab—what streak of raw truthfulness and integrity could be seen in the expression of this prostitute—to convince those spies that she was dealing honestly with them? Given her profession and intelligence, it is almost certain that she was an accomplished actress. What was there about Rahab that made the spies follow her instructions to hide on her rooftop under the flax? What made them believe she wasn't just laying a trap,[96] that she wouldn't turn around and lead the king's men to their hiding place—either from fear or loyalty to her own people? It's quite amazing that the spies trusted her at all!

Somehow, the changes God was making in her were so miraculous that they were evident to two complete strangers—but not just any strangers. The spies were more than just two foreigners. They were two of God's chosen people being led by Him on a mission—a mission they could never have predicted! The salvation of a Canaanite woman!

Of course, the other side of this coin is the question: What was there about the spies that made Rahab think that she could make a deal with them? What was there in their manner that signaled these were men of their word? What did she see in their faces, their eyes, their treatment of her that told Rahab they would deal fairly with her and repay her for the risk she took in hiding them? Could she see the evidence of their belief in God even in the way they played the role of spies? Was the strength of their character so transparently obvious that Rahab believed they would keep their word and hold up their end of the bargain?

Finally, what kind of deal did she think she was making? What kind of life did she think she would have if she escaped the destruction of Jericho? Being a prostitute, what kind of life did Rahab think she would have living among these fierce people from the desert? How would they treat her? Did she face slavery and abuse? What were her hopes for the future in those circumstances?

In our fictionalized account of Rahab's meeting with the spies, we have tried to imagine ways in which these questions might have been answered in a natural fashion. As we noted earlier in Tamar's story, God often—though by no means always—works in the ordinary affairs of our lives to accomplish His purposes. For example, it seems likely that the spies went to Rahab's establishment to find food and lodging because going there was the best way to avoid looking suspicious.

But there are times when God speaks directly to His people. There are times when He gives directions by direct revelation. We should not rule out direct revelation from God as the answer to many of the questions we are puzzling over. But in Rahab's case, the author of the book of Joshua says nothing to indicate there was a direct revelation, even though he does record that the Lord specifically instructed Joshua to circumcise all of the men of Israel after they crossed the Jordan.[97] In addition he tells of Joshua's encounter with the captain of the Lord's host where he receives detailed instructions about how to take the city of Jericho.[98]

What we do know is that when opportunity knocked, Rahab broke down the door in her haste to answer. Though she was frightened, along with everyone else in Jericho, she did not give in to her fears. Had Rahab given herself over to despair, she could have been immobilized by depression and missed her opportunity to act. Though she didn't know what to do, she kept putting one foot in front of the other. She kept on doing the next thing—preparing the flax to make linen.

The Voice of Wisdom

Rahab is one of those people in the Old Testament who possessed an arresting voice of wisdom. Even though she was a woman and a harlot, what Rahab said made so much sense to the spies that they followed her instructions without question or hesitation.

Another notable woman of the Bible, Deborah, also had a commanding voice, but she had the advantage of being a prophetess. It seems a little strange, in a time when mostly men occupied leadership roles, that God raised up this woman to be a prophetess and a judge in Israel. It is all the more extraordinary in light of the fact that the period in which she lived was a dark and violent one. It was not the sort of time and circumstances in which we would expect to see a woman rise to leadership. Ehud, the leader who had preceded her, had been a daring warrior.[99] But when the people heard the words that Deborah spoke, they recognized that they were hearing the voice of the Lord. Because her words were wise and true, the people came to her to arbitrate their disputes. To fully comprehend the awe in which this woman was held, we have to also know the warrior-leader Barak's response when Deborah told him that the Lord had commanded that he should go to war against Sisera. He said in reply, "If you go with me, I will go; but if you don't go with me, I won't go."[100] God dispenses talents upon whom He will, and He works through whomever He chooses, whether it be prostitute or prophetess.

What made Rahab so different from all of the others in Jericho? How is it that she, among all of the rest, heard the stories of God's miraculous provision for the Israelites and understood what they meant? Was it because she was more intelligent? Certainly, we can see that she was highly intelligent, but she was not unique in that regard. And anyway, intelligence is not the same thing as wisdom. The notion of the "intelligent fool" is legendary.

First, let us reckon that for an intelligent person to be wise they must also be honest. In particular, they must be honest before God—not making excuses for having violated His law. Before this is possible, it is necessary to admit that we are His workmanship and that we are accountable to Him.

In Job, Psalms, and Proverbs, we find the proposition that "the fear of the Lord is the beginning of wisdom."[101] The knowledge that God created the universe and all that is wonderful and beautiful gives us cause to fear His awesome power and majesty. Recognizing Him as the good Creator carries with it the necessity of acknowledging Him as Lord of all, as the one whose word we must obey. Job amplifies his fear-of-the-Lord statement by adding "to depart from evil is understanding" (Job 28:28). The psalmist echoes this same note by adding "a good understanding have all those who do His commandments..." Because God's creation shows us that He is great and good, logic tells us that it is foolish and evil to disobey the law He has put in our hearts to incline us to do good.[102] Wisdom involves both knowing and doing that which is good.

Rahab's knowledge about the God of the Israelites and her ability to recount the details of His miracles are remarkable, but knowing—even savoring—the details of a multitude of stories only makes a person a good student of history and literature, not a believer. Rahab listened and learned. She honestly faced the fact that the gods of her people did not do miracles to help them the way Yahweh performed for the Israelites.

Rahab's occupation may have played a role in her identification with the Israelites and their miracle-working God. It may be that the bondage she felt in her life as a prostitute made the stories of the Israelites' deliverance all the more appealing to her, all the more a source of hope and longing. Everyone in Jericho had heard about the Israelites, but not everyone was ready to make the changes in their lives that Rahab was willing to make to have a new life.

She did not know what a new life amongst these people would be, but Rahab knew choosing Yahweh meant life, not death. She was not there to hear Moses say to the Israelites, "I call heaven and earth to record this day against you, that I have set before you life and death, blessing and cursing: therefore choose life, that both thou and thy seed may live."[103] Still Rahab heard the message in her heart, and she answered...life.

A Heart Prepared to Risk

God's plan to deliver Rahab from her bondage shows some interesting parallels with that of His deliverance of the Israelites. They both had to make a move. Neither she nor they could become free if they remained where they were. They both had to make a move out of their old circumstances. Their old lives had to be left behind. Now this kind of full-scale change is not easy. In fact, it is so hard that we have to be highly motivated before we can contemplate the uncertainty of such a change. But before we can be motivated, we have to be honest enough to admit the need for change.

The Rahab we meet in the story was already far along the road to deliverance from her sinful life. We know that she had faced the fact that her people's gods were not good or powerful like Yahweh, and, without a doubt, she had much more to learn about living a life of obedience to His will. But here we do well to remember the words the Lord spoke to Samuel when he was searching for the right son of Jesse to anoint as the second king of Israel (a man who according to God's plan would turn out to be the great-great-grandson of Rahab), "Look not on his countenance...for the LORD seeth not as man seeth; for man looketh on the outward appearance, but the LORD looketh on the heart."[104]

When we begin to understand who God is, we begin to see more clearly who we are. Viewing ourselves in the mirror of God's greatness makes us, like Adam and Eve, feel naked and ashamed. Seeing ourselves in the light of His truth forces us to confront the things in our lives that are not good, but evil. Still, God takes us, as He did Rahab, where we are. Then He starts us on the road to becoming what He intended us to be when He created us. That Rahab changed is clear, even though we do not know a great deal about the process. The writer of the book of Joshua provides us with mere glimpses of the remainder of Rahab's story. He writes: "And Joshua saved Rahab the harlot alive, and her father's household, and all that she had; and she dwelleth in Israel even unto this day..."[105] In the book of Ruth, we read: "And Salmon begat Boaz, and Boaz begat Obed, and Obed begat Jesse, and Jesse begat David."[106] The book of Matthew gives us the final missing piece: Salmon was the father of Boaz, and his mother was Rahab![107] Honesty, wisdom, and obedience led to the fulfillment of God's purpose.

The Path to Boldness

Will Rogers once said, "Even if you are on the right track, you'll get run over if you just sit there." Sitting there is not an option for a Christian. In a pulsing outburst of extravagant exuberance, the apostle Paul boldly proclaimed to the Corinthians, "God is able to make *all* grace *abound* to you, so that *always* having *all* suffering in *everything*, you may have an *abundance* for *every* good deed" (2 Corinthians 9:8 NASB, emphasis added).

Christ came to give us life. He will supply all the grace that we need to be fearless in the face of any challenge before us. Our problem is being willing to let Him take charge. The bold souls who change the world are empowered by the force of God's presence. They are standing by the cross.

Sam Shoemaker tried to put into words what it would take for Christians to boldly proclaim the power of God:

Drop the old pictures of yourself, either as unable to do anything for Him, or as merely ambitious to do great things. If we are to channel His power, something in us must break. Christ does not break us cruelly as events sometimes do (though, remember, He may be in the event for good); He breaks the pride and will-fulness in us by letting us see as much of ourselves as we can "take," and then surrendering as much of ourselves as we see.[108]

Christ's bold warriors always have tackled problems that no one else would touch and made advances others considered impossible. There are circumstances, almost daily, where we must each overcome our fears and stand by the cross. It is certainly more than calling forth ephemeral New Age angels to empower and embolden us. It is more than possessing specific personality traits. It is truly possessing a different kind of strength. For we have access to the Holy Spirit who came to fulfill Christ's promise. And He is available to all of us to give us the spiritual power to do what we are called by God to do.

When Life Seems Empty

The Power of Devotion
The Power of Obedience

Ruth

When Life Seems Empty

R̸uth hurried to fill the basket with food for the grieving Israelite family, the Ephrathites from Bethlehem. *How sad,* she thought. They had barely arrived before tragedy struck. After their tiring journey from Bethlehem in the Judean hill country west of the Jordan, they needed to find food and safely establish a home in Moab. But a peaceful life was not to be. Elimelech,[109] the husband, had died.

Now the poor wife, Naomi, and her two young sons faced the daunting task of trying to settle in a new village among strangers without a man at the head of their home.

Ruth tried to imagine the woman's feelings. What would it be like to endure all that she had suffered? To be hammered by one blow after another? Because of the famine in her land, Naomi had left behind all that was dear to her. She had traveled many miles over dusty roads to a distant village on the far side of the Salt Sea to live among strangers. And then her husband had died! Though a Moabitess and not from the widow's tribe, Ruth still grieved to think of the pain and loss of this foreign mother. It was bad enough that Naomi had to face life as a widow. Now she also had to raise two sons who would have to grow up without a father to teach them how to be a man.

What anguish this mother must be feeling! Ruth's eyes burned from unshed tears as she imagined the distress these Israelites were experiencing. She quickly blotted her eyes and joined her family as they left to pay their respects to the newcomers in their grief.

When they entered the newly occupied home, Ruth was startled. The two sons whom she had pictured as little boys were, in fact, nearly grown men. And quite handsome ones at that! She moved toward her friend, Orpah, who was removing empty cups from the table.

"What are they like?" she asked.

"Quiet. Devout. Their father's name meant 'my God is King.' Ruth, do you know anything about their God?"

"Not a lot. I know that the God of Israel is named Yahweh. And I know that He is so powerful that King Balak was afraid to attack the Israelites. You remember that the Israelites are the ones who took the Plains of Moab north of the Arnon from King Sihon. All of the Amorites on the east side of the Jordan were annihilated."[110]

"Oh, so they're the ones who conquered the Amorites?"

"Yes, and they say that the Israelite God is invisible. You can't see Him like you can our god, Chemosh."[111]

Why is this family so different? Ruth wondered, as she looked over at the mother, Naomi. Ruth had expected her to be devastated, inconsolable. As their eyes met briefly across the room, Ruth was mystified by the strength she saw reflected in Naomi's eyes. Although her face was clearly etched in grief, Naomi still moved around the room with dignity and calm as she greeted her visitors. Ruth felt inexplicably drawn to this woman who exuded such a peaceful, yet authoritative, presence in the room.

Ruth turned back to Orpah, and the two girls quietly moved on with their duties. They became increasingly aware that the two young Hebrews, Mahlon and Kilion, who had their mother's solemn eyes, were equally aware of them.

Later that year, when the period of grieving was over, Ruth was not at all surprised to learn that Mahlon[112] had called on her father and asked for her in marriage. And she was thrilled to hear that Kilion had asked for Orpah. They would be sisters!

Over the next ten years,[113] Ruth came to respect and love both her mother-in-law and the God whom Naomi served. Though she never conceived the grandchild she knew her mother-in-law longed for, there was never a time when Ruth felt condemned by Naomi. Instead, Ruth found that she could freely share her tears of disappointment with her mother-in-law and always felt loved, encouraged, and accepted. When Ruth was most discouraged, Naomi would put her arms around her and say, "Ruth, God knows what is best for us. It is for Him to decide when a woman should have a child."

Though Naomi's words comforted Ruth, her gentle assurances did not erase Ruth's longing. In the pain of her barrenness, she marveled at Naomi's faith through all of her own suffering. Ruth often wondered how Naomi could speak such sincere encouragement when her God had allowed her family to be driven from their home by famine and then had allowed Elimelech to die and leave Naomi alone in a strange land. When Mahlon and Kilion both died unexpectedly, Ruth and Orpah experienced the same tragic loss they had seen Naomi, Mahlon, and Kilion confront years earlier.

Ruth grieved her husband's death and missed him terribly. With neither child nor husband, her life was empty. Ruth often wept in the wee hours of the night, longing for things to be as she and Mahlon once dreamed they would be. As heavy as her own grief was, she also ached terribly for Naomi. Dear Naomi had become a real mother to her! Naomi, first bereft of her husband, now had lost both of her sons as well! Ruth knew that Naomi, despite her losses, continued to believe in her God. As far as Ruth could see, however, He seemed to have turned His back on her.[114]

Ruth worried about Naomi even though she seemed strong and assured in her faith. She had been through so much. Everything she had when she came to Moab was gone. She was left with nothing.

Now she was an aging widow, childless, and living in a foreign land alone. She had gained two Moabite daughters-in-law, but both of them, like her, were childless.[115] What a bitter irony! The three of them had no husbands and no children. Totally barren—all of them! Ruth was frightened to think of the years ahead. What would they do now? What was left of their lives?

One day word arrived that "the Lord had come to the aid of his people" and was "providing food for them" in Judah.[116] Thoughts of home brought memories of happier times flooding back to Naomi.

Ruth saw the quickening in Naomi's spirit and was elated to see her smile again. There had been so few occasions for smiles of late. Ruth wondered if finally Naomi's God had answered their prayers! She threw her arms around her and joyfully danced her mother-in-law around in circles. They both wept. "Now we can return to my home and my people," said Naomi with a wistful sigh of relief.

"Yes," Ruth responded, deeply moved by Naomi's jubilant tears, "let's start preparing for the trip. If we work quickly, we might even be able to set out on our journey tomorrow." No sooner were the words out of her mouth than Ruth began to wonder at the enormity of what she had set in motion. It was a hard thing indeed to bury a husband, even in your own homeland. If she left the land of her birth, she would have nothing left. What would life hold for her in another land?

Orpah and Ruth worked all day selecting the few items they would be able to take with them on their journey to Bethlehem. That evening they said their farewells to family and friends.

The next morning they left the place where they were living "and set out on the road that would take them back to the land of Judah."[117] The journey would not be an easy one. They would spend days covering perilous miles, two major rivers, and dangerous terrain. And, if they arrived safely, Ruth and Orpah, as Moabite women, would likely face suspicion, possibly even scorn and hatred. They would be foreigners from a despised, and sometimes, enemy nation.[118]

When they reached the ford of the Arnon River, Naomi stopped the little caravan and turned to her daughters-in-law. "You must go back to your mothers' homes. I don't know what I was thinking. I should not be taking you away from your homes and your families. You must go back where you belong, and I will pray that God will watch over you. I will ask Him to show you kindness just as you have shown kindness to my sons and to me. You have honored your husbands, my sons, in their deaths. Now, may God give you each rest and peace and bring you in to the home of another husband in your own land."[119]

Ruth and Orpah were deeply moved by Naomi's unselfish love. They were amazed at her deep concern for their welfare and her willingness to continue on the long, hazardous journey alone. The two younger women couldn't help but weep with Naomi. It was obvious to Ruth that Naomi was worried about returning home empty-handed, that she would have nothing to offer them when they reached Bethlehem.

"Naomi," they both protested, "we wouldn't dream of going back." The picture of Naomi making the journey alone was too much to bear. They were determined to continue on with her as she returned to her people and her land.[120]

"You sweet, wonderful, foolish girls, you must return home," said Naomi. "I have no more sons to become your husbands." With a pensive sigh, she added, "I am too old to get another husband. And even if I married again and could have more sons, they would be too young for you." Turning her hands upward in an empty gesture, Naomi asked the question that needed no answer, "Would you wait for my baby sons to become men?" Stating the obvious, she added, "By then, you would be too old."

She hugged the two young women close to her heart. Slowly, she released them and stepped back. "No, my dear daughters, you must go back. God has given me a bitter cup; He is against me." Shooing them away with her hands, she urged, "Go. Go home. Go back to your people. Go now, before you are hurt more than you already have been."[121]

Orpah kissed Naomi, said a muffled goodbye through her tears, then turned dejectedly to head back the way they had come. She walked a few steps and then paused to give Ruth time to join her. But after Ruth kissed Naomi, Ruth waved to Orpah to go. Orpah was puzzled. She hesitated and watched Ruth as she continued to talk to Naomi.

Orpah saw Naomi give Ruth another gentle nudge as she said, "Go back with her. You must go back to your people." Then seeing Ruth's determination not to leave her alone, Naomi said more urgently, "You can't throw your life away like this."[122]

But Ruth clung to her mother-in-law with tears streaming down her face. "Don't ask that of me," she begged. "I can't leave you all alone like this. I can't turn my back on you. You know I could never do that," she said with emotion. Orpah hesitated only a moment longer. Then, although she felt torn, she turned sadly and headed back down the road toward home...alone.

Naomi looked intently into Ruth's face. Her eyes pled with Ruth to do what was best. Naomi struggled to find a way to help Ruth see what it would be like to return to her kinsmen in Bethlehem with nothing but the clothes on their backs and the few things they were carrying. But Ruth's expression told Naomi that further words would be futile. Ruth had made her decision. She would not return to the old place where her husband and the past lay buried. And she couldn't leave the mother and counselor whose faith and conviction had shown her the true and living God.[123] Ruth was turning her back forever on the idols of Moab, on the human sacrifices of Chemosh.

With quiet determination, Ruth took Naomi's hands and solemnly announced, "Where you go I will go, and where you stay I will stay. Your people will be my people and your God my God. Where you die I will die, and there I will be buried. May the LORD deal with me, be it ever so severely, if anything but death separates you and me."[124]

The two women stood brushing away their tears. Both were too emotionally drained to move. Finally Naomi smiled through her tears and took Ruth's arm. The two women turned and together resumed their long journey. Side by side, they continued on to Bethlehem, pressing toward their uncertain future.[125]

The journey was full of bittersweet memories for Naomi. She relived the days she had trekked this same road journeying in the opposite direction with her husband and sons. To crowd out her wistful thoughts, she began telling Ruth stories of when the Israelites had come up out of the desert along this route. When they passed by Pisgah, where God showed Moses the Promised Land, Naomi told Ruth the story of the awesome way that God delivered the Israelites from Pharaoh. It pleased Naomi that Ruth showed so much interest and asked so many questions. Ruth wanted to know everything about Moses and why he didn't go into the Promised Land.

To answer her questions, Naomi decided to start at the very beginning. She told how God watched over Joseph after he was sold as a slave, and how He blessed him until Pharaoh made him his second-in-command. She told how Jacob and his sons were forced to move to Egypt by a famine—just as she and Elimelech had been forced to move to the land of Moab. Naomi looked at Ruth to see if she was still interested in hearing more.

Ruth nodded and listened gravely as Naomi continued the long story of how the Israelites grew in numbers until the Egyptians feared them so much that a new ruler, who did not know about Joseph, ordered the midwives to kill all of the Hebrew baby boys. She told Ruth how Moses' mother had hidden him for three months, then cradled him safely in a basket and floated him in the Nile. She explained that he was found by Pharaoh's daughter and raised in the palace as her son. She told how, as a young man, Moses killed an Egyptian who was mistreating a Hebrew slave.

Naomi omitted no detail as she recounted God's amazing provision for His people. She talked about the burning bush, of the power God granted to Moses to do signs and wonders, of His love for the Israelites, and of all the plagues God brought against Egypt. Naomi's voice began to grow in strength and energy as she built to the climax of the story. She richly described the scene of the Red Sea rolling back to form a wall on each side of the people who crossed on dry land. From her vivid description of the towering waters, Ruth could picture the Egyptian army mindlessly chasing after the children of Israel, only to be swallowed by the sea as they pursued the chosen ones!

While they were stopped for a rest, Ruth studied all that Naomi had told her. "But, Naomi," she said at last, "you still haven't explained why Moses had to go to the top of Pisgah for his only glimpse of the Promised Land."

"I know, my child," Naomi said, "I was coming to that." Then she told Ruth about the giving of the law and some of the stories of the wanderings in the wilderness. At last she told of how one day Moses became so impatient with the people's complaining that he failed to follow God's instructions at the waters of Meribah.[126] Ruth thought of all she was learning about Naomi's God, of His mighty power to deliver, of His commandments, and of His judgment.

When they arrived at the Jordan River, Naomi had a chance to catch her breath. As they bathed their tired feet in the river, she began again to recount the story of how God raised up Joshua to take Moses' place. She told how God directed Joshua to lead the people across that very river during the spring floods. Ruth's mind wandered as she listened to Naomi's voice telling about episodes that revealed how great and powerful her God was.

Ruth wondered what her new home would be like, what these people she was hearing so much about would think of her—a foreigner—coming to live among them. All of a sudden, Ruth realized that Naomi had stopped talking. They stood looking at the river, still somewhat swollen from the spring floods. Ruth commented that it would be nice if they didn't have to ford the river that day. Naomi nodded. Then, they walked in silence for a while.

When the two women reached Gilgal on the West Bank, Naomi pointed out the monument of twelve stones that had been taken from the middle of the Jordan River when God held back the flood. She told Ruth the story of how those stones commemorated the miracle God performed to bring His people into the Promised Land.

Then they saw the ruins of Jericho in the distance, and Naomi began yet another story. This time, she told Ruth about how God had destroyed the walls when the children of Israel marched around the city at the Lord's instructions. Ruth noticed, though, that Naomi seemed distracted and that now her stories lacked the detail that had made the earlier stories so interesting. Finally, conversation ceased altogether as the climb up out of the Jordan Valley into the Judean hill country required all their energy.

But Ruth sensed that there was more to Naomi's silence than mere fatigue. From the apprehensive look on her face, Ruth surmised that Naomi was growing a bit nervous about what she would find when they reached her old home. Ruth realized many things were bound to have changed in the years Naomi had been away. She thought of the many friends and relatives who likely would be gone. Perhaps Naomi was wondering about those who remained. She wondered if Naomi might not be anxious about what kind of reception she would receive from her friends and relatives.

As they drew closer to their destination, Naomi's spirits began to lift a little. As the town came into view, she saw that the barley fields were ready for harvest. Naomi picked up her pace. Ruth marveled at her sudden burst of energy.

As people in the town saw Naomi, many dropped their work and ran out to welcome the two women. The relatives and friends were excited to see Naomi, but they were obviously very curious to see her traveling with only a young Moabite woman. Ruth could see that they were wondering what had become of Elimelech, Mahlon, and Kilion. News of their arrival traveled quickly throughout the town.

"Can this be Naomi?" they exclaimed.

"Yes," she replied solemnly, "but do not call me by that name."

"Why not?" a cousin asked. "Did you change your name in that far-off country?"

"No, but I am different. I left young and full. I return old and empty. God has taken everything away."

Her friends and neighbors would have interrupted, but Naomi raised her hand to silence them. Then she continued, "God has brought misfortune to me. He has afflicted me. Call me Mara because my life is bitter."[127]

Ruth was very relieved by the way the people of Judah received her. Since she was not an Israelite, she had wondered if she would be despised—just as all Moabites were by those of Abraham's seed. Yet because she acknowledged their God and was devoted to Naomi they seemed to accept her as one of them.

It was harvesting time, and there was ample opportunity to obtain free grain for those willing to work the fields. Naomi explained to Ruth that Moses had established a practice that enabled the poor and aliens to work for their grain. It was a way for the richer landowners to share their bounty with those less fortunate.[128]

Ruth insisted on gleaning the fields behind the harvesters. Naomi hated for Ruth to have to do such hard, backbreaking labor. Plus, only those in desperate need pursued such humbling work. But both Ruth and Naomi recognized the necessity. So Naomi gave permission, and Ruth set out to find a good field.[129]

Although she didn't know the owners of the various fields, Ruth chose one that seemed to offer a good situation. Without knowing the connection, she ended up in a field owned by one of Naomi's kinsmen, Boaz, a man from the same family clan as Elimelech. Boaz was a man of high standing and wealth.

Ruth began working and diligently labored, except for a brief break under the shelter to escape the heat. She looked up from her work only once when a very distinguished man arrived at the field mid-morning. She couldn't help but see him as he strode across the field greeting the harvesters. He was an obvious leader who carried himself with dignity and confidence.

He called out to them, "The LORD be with you."

"The LORD bless you!"[130] they responded.

Ruth stood watching the exchange. She found the man captivating. He was impressive in his command of the men, and he was obviously respected.

One of the servant girls nearby whispered, "That is the owner, Boaz. He's just returned from Bethlehem."

Ruth was embarrassed to have been caught staring and quickly returned to her work.

But Boaz had noticed her, too. She stood out among the girls who were trailing along behind the harvesters. He could see she was a for-eigner—unattended and unprotected. He asked the foreman, "Who is that young woman?"

The foreman quickly told Boaz all about the Moabitess who had so politely asked if she could glean and who had worked so hard all morning, taking only a short rest in the shelter.

Boaz, a middle-aged man well past the age of flirtation, laughed indulgently at the man's enthusiasm for the young woman. "I think I'd better go over and meet this paragon of virtue. What is her name?" Boaz inquired.

"Ruth," he replied. "Her name is Ruth."

Boaz walked over and said to Ruth, "Welcome, my daughter. Please stay in these fields with my servant girls where you will be safe. I have instructed my men not to touch you, and they will treat you well. You may also help yourself to water from the jars that the men keep filled" (see Ruth 2:8,9).

Ruth was deeply affected by the kindness shown to her. She bowed down to the ground before this striking man. "Why have I found favor in your sight…since I am a foreigner?" she asked.

Boaz stepped back as Ruth came to her feet. He explained, "I have heard about all that you have endured—the loss of your husband and leaving your homeland to come live with a people you do not know. I've also heard how you have cared for your mother-in-law."

Ruth started to interrupt, to say that she had done nothing special.

But Boaz continued, "May the LORD repay you for what you have done. May you be richly rewarded by the LORD, the God of Israel, under whose wings you have come to take refuge."[131]

"Oh, sir," Ruth said, "you have been very kind even though I have less standing than your servant girls. Your words have comforted me. I pray that I will continue to find favor in your eyes."

At noon, Boaz again made his way over to the girl, who had continued working diligently even though she was obviously weary from the heat. He offered her bread and wine. When she sat down with the harvesters, Boaz made a point of insisting that she take some of the roasted grain. His offer was a signal to the others of how he wanted her to be treated.

After the meal, he turned to his workers and instructed them, "See that there are plenty of stalks for her to gather, but don't embarrass her by being obvious about it."

At the day's end, Ruth had an ephah of grain, an extraordinary accumulation for one day's efforts. She rushed home proudly to show Naomi the results of her labor.

Naomi was thrilled. "Where did you work? You have done so well!"

Ruth told her about Boaz and of his kindnesses to her.

"Boaz!" exclaimed Naomi. "May the Lord bless him!" Then, she explained to Ruth, "He is a kinsman-redeemer."[132]

As Ruth washed up and prepared for bed, Naomi was deep in thought. The beginning of a plan was taking shape in her mind.

During the weeks until the harvest was finished, Ruth obeyed Boaz and remained in his fields. All the while, Boaz noted how hard she worked. Her gentle kindness to those around her was especially noticed. They saw that Ruth did as she was advised and stayed close to the servant girls for protection as Boaz had instructed her.

Naomi, too, observed with pleasure that Ruth was settling into a harmonious schedule as they lived together. She was overwhelmed with gratitude that Ruth was helping her reestablish roots in her homeland.[133]

As the harvest season drew to a close, Naomi's plan was formulated in her mind. She called Ruth to her side and said, "It is time for me to find you a permanent home. I won't always be here. Plus, you are too young to spend all your time with me. You need a husband and children. Now listen carefully, and follow my instructions exactly."

Ruth smiled and listened indulgently as Naomi laid out her strategy. As Naomi talked, Ruth thought about how she had come to value the older woman's wisdom and judgment. *How like Naomi to be worried about me.* Still, it seemed clear to her that God was providing for them. Ruth began to pray a silent prayer of thanksgiving in her heart as she reflected on how Naomi's God had now become her God, too.

What was Naomi saying? Ruth's mind snapped back to attention as she realized that Naomi was laying out the details of what she was to do. As Naomi finished, Ruth's heart was racing at the daring plan she had laid out. It was a plan for her to go and speak with Boaz! She tried to sound steady as she replied, "I will do what you have said."[134]

That evening Ruth drew water and bathed carefully. She perfumed her body and chose her finest garments. Then she slipped out and went down to the threshing floor. She was quite nervous because she knew women were not supposed to be anywhere near the threshing floor after dark. She wished she knew the customs better. There were so many things that were not allowed. She didn't want to embarrass Naomi, and she definitely didn't want to spoil the plans that Naomi had laid out so meticulously.

Ruth crept over to where she could see what was happening without being seen. As Naomi had cautioned, she waited until Boaz finished eating and drinking. She couldn't help but be amazed at her demure mother-in-law's wily strategy. This plan had revealed a side of Naomi that she had never seen before. She recalled that Naomi had warned, "It is very important that you wait until he has eaten and had a drink. Then he will be in good spirits and will sleep soundly."

Boaz did exactly as Naomi had predicted. He ate. He drank. He laughed and joked with the men, slapped them on the back, and talked until late in the evening. Then, when conversation dwindled down, he walked back to the far end of the grain pile and settled down for the night.

Ruth watched and waited until she was certain he was sound asleep. Then she approached quietly, uncovered his feet, and curled on her side there. She lay very still. But unable to sleep, she remained wide-awake, waiting…and wondering.[135]

Several hours later, Boaz turned over and was instantly awake and alarmed. Something was different. What was amiss? Cautiously, he eased up, trying to see without being seen. If there were thieves at work he wanted to locate their position without giving away his own. He knew how to fight if he needed to and was ready to defend his crops. Instead of thieves, what he discovered was someone lying at his feet. From the small build and the scent of perfume he knew it was a woman.

"Who are you?" he whispered softly.

"Ruth," she replied. Then she said exactly what she had practiced with Naomi. Naomi had explained that Ruth's actions would be a request for marriage and that, as an honorable man, Boaz would do the right thing. She spoke in a low voice barely above a whisper, "Sir, spread the corner of your garment over me, since you are a kinsman-redeemer."

Boaz blinked, swallowed, and then spoke solemnly, but with confidence and determination, "You honor me. This kindness is greater than that you showed to others earlier. Do not be afraid, dear girl. I will do what you ask. Everyone in Bethlehem knows you are a woman of noble character; you have not run after men—young or old, rich or poor." Then Boaz paused.

Ruth could feel her heart pounding as she waited and listened intently.

Boaz's slow, measured response finally resumed, "There is one problem with what you have asked." He continued, "There is another kinsman who is a nearer kin. Stay the night, and tomorrow I will see what he wants to do. If he is not willing, I will do it."

Ruth woke before daylight the next morning. Although she tried not to make a sound, Boaz sat up and whispered to her, "You must be very quiet. It is important that no one else know you were here on the threshing room floor."

Embarrassed by his admonition, she started to slip away. But then she felt his large hand on her shoulder and heard him whisper. "Wait. Hold out your shawl." Quickly, Boaz filled her shawl with barley and then lifted it up and set it on her shoulder.[136]

Naomi was waiting when she returned and immediately asked, "How did it go, my daughter?"

Ruth showed her the six measures of barley and answered, "I don't know. I did exactly what you told me to do. But when I asked him to marry me, he said there was a problem."

"What problem?" Naomi asked quickly.

"There is a nearer kinsman. He said that he would have to go and talk with him first. And he didn't want anyone to know that I had come to the threshing floor. I'm afraid the whole thing was a mistake, Naomi. I think I may not have carried out your plan very well. I'm sorry. I'm not sure he really wants to marry me." Ruth paused, and then added thoughtfully, "But he did stop me as I was leaving and insisted that I bring a gift of barley back to you. He said it wouldn't do for me to come back to you empty-handed."

Hearing this, Naomi smiled broadly and put her arms around Ruth, "Sweet child. Just you wait. It won't take long. He will take care of everything! Today. The man will not rest until this matter is settled!"[137]

"But what if he doesn't want to marry me? I think it embarrassed him for me to come to the threshing floor. And to ask him so boldly! I spoiled everything. Oh, Naomi, I could have died when he told me that I was not to let anyone know that I had been there." Ruth lamented. Then she exclaimed, "I was leaving already when he said that!" Ruth was almost in tears at discussing such an embarrassing incident—especially one in which she thought she had failed.

"Ruth, dear," replied Naomi, "Trust me. Boaz is at the town gate right now negotiating. He doesn't really want my husband's land. He has more than enough land already. It is you he wants. Just relax. God will take care of the problem with the other kinsman. Now come with me. There is a lot about Boaz I haven't told you yet. Let's get you something to eat and a hot drink. There is another story you need to hear."

As they ate Naomi began to tell Ruth more of the details of the story about the fall of Jericho that she had been too weary to include on their journey from Moab. This time, she included everything about Rahab the harlot and the spies.

At first Ruth only listened halfheartedly, too weary and distracted to be very curious. Her mind kept drifting back to the events of the night before. But when Naomi came to the part about the arguments in the clan over whether Salmon should have married someone who was not an Israelite, Ruth's attention suddenly snapped into sharp focus. By the time Naomi got to the part about Rahab having a son, Ruth's mind was racing ahead and she exclaimed, "You mean Boaz is the son of Rahab the harlot!"

"Exactly," replied Naomi. "I could have told you all of this earlier, but I wanted you to be free to be yourself. I didn't want to burden you with the knowledge that Boaz grew up with a mother who was a foreigner. I felt certain he would be sympathetic to your situation as a foreigner here in Bethlehem, and I was right. I could see that he was interested in you from the very first day at his fields.

"But there's much more that you need to know, too." She knew she had Ruth's full attention now and continued, "Salmon, Boaz's father, had fought alongside of Othniel, the nephew of Caleb, to capture Kiriath Sepher.[138] In this battle, Salmon was as daring as ever and was gravely wounded. They carried him back to his home where Rahab tenderly nursed and cared for him. But Salmon never fully recovered.

"Life was hard for Rahab. She had to manage all the land that Salmon had been given for the many battles he had fought in. It was good land, and Rahab turned out to be a skilled manager. The family prospered even though Salmon was unable to work because of his injuries. Rahab also developed a highly profitable trade in linen. Because her cloth was of such fine quality, traders from as far away as Egypt came to purchase her fabric. In time, her linen trade became even more profitable than the land. After a few years, I think it was when Boaz was about 12 years old, Salmon died.

"Following Salmon's death, some relatives tried to take over his land. They felt that a woman couldn't properly take care of and defend the land. Plus, they argued that with her linen trade Rahab didn't need the land. Rahab, though, went straight to Othniel—the judge that the Lord raised up to deliver us from the king of Aram.[139] Othniel heard her protest that Boaz's claim to the land should be preserved. When Othniel learned that Boaz was Salmon's son, he was enraged that relatives would try to take away land from such a noble warrior's son. He ruled that anyone who trespassed on Boaz's land would be executed. That ended that. But it left a lot of bitter feelings.

"When the famine came, Rahab had more than enough wealth to buy food for her family and some to spare. When we ran out, Rahab gave us food and offered Elimelech a job." Naomi paused and shook her head wearily. She paused a moment and then added, "My husband was too proud to work for a woman—let alone one who was not born an Israelite. That's why we left and moved to Moab.

"All of this was happening about the time Boaz became a grown man and would have married. If I remember correctly, he was born about five years before my Mahlon. I doubt any young woman around here would have been happy to go into Rahab's home after all of the unkind things that had been said about her.

"So, you see, Ruth," Naomi said, "although Boaz has earned everyone's respect now and all of this happened long ago, it left an impression on him. He was but a boy then and was deeply affected by the criticism of his mother. I thought my plan would get you and Boaz past several hurdles." Ruth smiled indulgently at her mother-in-law, impressed once again at her insight. Naomi continued, "Did you notice that Boaz commented about the fact that you had shown no interest in any of the younger men? Mark you well, he is sensitive about not being married at his age." Ruth acknowledged Naomi's counsel and waited for the rest of the story.

"Rahab became a devout believer in Yahweh. But you know how people are. There were some who would never let others in Bethlehem forget where she had come from and who she had been." Ruth started to express her indignation that anyone would malign Rahab. But Naomi stilled her with a nod and added, "Ruth, you are not a part of all that ugliness. That is one of the reasons that I believe you and Boaz will be perfect for each other. Boaz is justifiably proud of his mother. He takes after her, you know, with his business skills and farming success."

Naomi watched Ruth's reactions and was reassured by what she saw. "Now you understand why Boaz insisted that you leave the threshing room floor. He wanted to protect you from unkind gossip. That kind of talk can hurt, and Boaz would not want you to go through the kind of difficult days his mother had to endure. I'm very sorry, dear. I should have thought about that," Naomi said, eyeing Ruth intently to see if she understood.

Naomi was quiet for a few moments and seemed deep in thought. Ruth wondered if she had finished their conversation. Then Naomi looked up and slowly nodded, "It was risky, but my plan was right. It was the only thing that would have worked." Then she continued, "Don't you see, Ruth, my dear, Boaz needed to see that, in addition to all of your other virtues, you want the same things he wants. He needed to see that you desperately want marriage and children. Sometimes deeds speak far clearer than words." Pausing a moment, Naomi concluded with a satisfied smile, "I believe that the barley Boaz sent will provide me with just enough to pay for the coming wedding celebration."

Naomi could tell from Ruth's knitted brow that she was not totally convinced. She gave Ruth a reassuring smile and said, "Ruth, everything you told me about what Boaz said and did indicates that he has wanted to marry you almost from the very beginning. He's just been cautious because of his mother's experience. He knows that there could be some difficult times ahead for you if you marry him. So he needed to be certain that you wanted to marry him. Why, Ruth, the man had already checked out the facts regarding my nearest kinsman! He didn't do that because he wants more land. Don't you see? It is because of you! He has seen what a virtuous woman you are. I assure you that he is at the town gate this very moment negotiating with the other kinsman. And I can tell you how that's going to come out, too. He inherited every bit of his mother's skill.

"Have you finished that drink? I have a surprise for you," Naomi said mischievously. Ruth looked up in amazement. "A surprise?" she questioned with wonder. Naomi took Ruth's hand and pulled her over to a basket hidden in the corner. "I purchased some of Rahab's finest linen from a friend who bought it years ago. It is perfect for a wedding dress. Come, let's get it out and begin working on your dress. I know you will look lovely in it." Naomi could hardly contain her excitement.

The minute Ruth was gone that morning, Boaz headed back to town and made his way to the town gate where the men conducted their business. He sat there—waiting and watching—until he spotted Naomi's nearest kinsman and called him over. He also asked ten elders to join them as witnesses. All the men settled down to consider the business Boaz was intent on conducting. He wasted no time with preliminaries. He told them about Naomi's return from Moab, her need for money, and her desire to sell the land that her husband had owned.

He turned to the kinsman and said, "You have the right to first choice on the property. If you want it, it is yours. But if you do not take it, I will."[140]

The kinsman quickly said, "I'll redeem it."

"Fine," said Boaz. "But on the day you buy the land, you also acquire the dead man's widow so that the man's name remains with the property."[141]

"Oh, I can't do that," said the kinsman. "That would endanger my own property. You'll have to buy it yourself," he concluded. The other kinsman then took off his sandal and handed it to Boaz. This action signaled the finalizing of the deal and the legalizing of the transaction in Israel.

Though he was very pleased, Boaz studiously kept his face grave and otherwise expressionless as he turned to the ten elders. "Today," he said, "you are witnesses that I have bought Naomi's property and that I have obtained Ruth the Moabitess, Mahlon's widow, as my wife. Now, the name of the dead will remain with the land and will not disappear from the family or from the town records."[142]

The elders joined together with all who were at the town gate to wish Boaz well. "May the Lord make the woman who is coming into your home like Rachel and Leah, who together built up the house of Israel. May you have standing in Ephathah and be famous in

Bethlehem. Through the offspring the Lord gives you by this young woman may your family be like that of Perez, whom Tamar bore to Judah."[143]

*So **Boaz** took **Ruth** and she became his wife;*
*and when he went in to her, the L*ORD* gave her conception,*
and she bore a son.
Then the women said to Naomi,
*"Blessed be the L*ORD*, who has not left you this day*
without a close relative;
and may his name be famous in Israel!
And may he be to you a restorer of life and a nourisher of your old age;
for your daughter-in-law, who loves you,
who is better to you than seven sons, has borne him."
Then Naomi took the child and laid him on her bosom,
and became a nurse to him....
*And they called his name **Obed**.*
*He is the father of **Jesse**,*
*the father of **David**.*
RUTH 4:13-17

The Power of Devotion

Well done, good and faithful servant!
You have been faithful with a few things;
I will put you in charge of many things.
Come and share your master's happiness!
MATTHEW 25:21

"Where you go, I will go, and where you stay I will stay. Your people will be my people, and your God, my God."[144] This powerful pledge of devotion, often recited or sung at weddings, has touched the hearts of lovers throughout the centuries. However, these poignant words—so often assumed to be romantic by those not familiar with their origin—were spoken by a daughter-in-law to her mother-in-law.

The love and loyalty between Ruth and Naomi contradicts the common assumption that this unique and demanding relationship must lie inevitably in the spectrum from wary to abusive, from contentious to hostile. Though Ruth had been barren for many years, when she finally conceived and bore a son, Obed, she graciously shared him with Naomi. Her unselfishness was so remarkable that the women of Bethlehem said, "Naomi has a son."[145]

Ruth and Naomi were both admirable women who exemplified godliness in numerous aspects of their character and behavior. The veneration of Ruth in this Hebrew story is all the more remarkable since she was a foreigner and not of Abraham's lineage. Yet, even though Ruth was not a Hebrew, not only is she included in Christ's genealogy, she is one of only two women for whom books of the Bible are named. Certainly, she is a special, powerful woman—biblically and historically.

While Tamar's courage surprises us and Rahab's wisdom astonishes us, Ruth's loyalty is a delight. The Ruth of the Bible is like a deep, clear pool. She is a rare and priceless discovery. In Ruth we see the affirmation of womanhood at its finest. She is pure in devotion, pure in obedience.

The Journey to Destiny

Down through the centuries, Ruth has come to personify qualities we all want to emulate. Ruth's love is trustworthy and tender, reliable and dependable. Her loyalty is unshakable, sturdy as an oak. She is devoted, faithful, and obedient.

We may think of those qualities as resident only in the personality of one who is quiet and unassuming. And, too often, in our celebrity-crazed society, we attribute negative connotations to these virtues that we see exemplified in Ruth's character. Boring, uninteresting, unimaginative are some of the adjectives our culture often assigns to these qualities.

However, while the idea of loyalty may seem dull, Ruth's life certainly was not. In fact, her life is a testimony that devotion and loyalty can lead to a life of challenging and stirring surprises.

The famine in Israel drove Elimelech and his family to Moab. Here, Ruth married one of Naomi's sons and was nurtured and mentored to faith in the God of the Israelites. After the deaths of her husband and sons, and with relief from the famine, Naomi desired to return to the land of Judah. As we know from the story, Ruth would not turn back from Naomi. When they settled at last in Bethlehem, the new homeland for Ruth, she allowed Naomi to instruct and guide her in the customs of the land.

In this new environment, Ruth did not "fade into the woodwork." She faithfully and obediently stood by her mother-in-law, and in the process, we see her even slipping into a place women did not frequent. Not boring!

In the face of life's challenges, Ruth also had staying power. When she said something, she meant it. She was single-minded. She was the direct opposite of the double-minded person described by the apostle James as "unstable in all his ways."[146] In more psychological terms, we might say that she had a well-integrated personality. She was not an adult one minute and a self-absorbed child the next.

Out of 66 books in the Bible, the only two that bear the names of women are: the book of Ruth and the book of Esther. Both Ruth and

Esther were strong women whom God used to accomplish His highest purposes. However, Ruth's inner beauty stands in contrast to the external, physical beauty that Scripture credits to Esther.

Esther was a beautiful woman, and her beauty is instrumental in her rise to the position of queen. As queen, God used Esther to save the Jewish people. Esther became a woman of the heroic model.

Ruth, in contrast, was a humble woman about whose appearance the Bible says nothing. Yet, she is a shining example of many of the strong virtues of womanhood—gentle, yet tough as steel. Diligent and devoted. Like Christ who set His face like a flint to go to the cross,[147] Ruth would not be deterred from going with Naomi.

Just as Joseph of the Old Testament is considered by many Bible scholars to be an archetypal forgiving redeemer and, thus, a precursor of Christ, so, Ruth, in her devotion and obedience toward Naomi, is a precursor to Mary—a humble, devoted servant who was willing to offer her life on the altar of God's will.

When Ruth, out of loyal devotion, chose to accompany Naomi, she took a momentous step. She began a journey that would lead her to her destiny—a destiny that would make her the great-grandmother of the mighty King David and one of the five named women in Matthew's genealogy of the Lord Jesus.

Widowed and Barren

Ruth lived in a dark period, historically speaking, yet her story is not about broad, national problems. It is not about war and disunity. The story does not wander into the challenges which confronted the Israelites during the period of the judges or focus on the hostilities between the Judahites and the Moabites. The story is, instead, a record of personal relationships and the roles the central characters play in fulfilling God's plan.

Author Leo G. Perdue writes that in ancient Israel "the household was the theological lens, the ethical paradigm, the human context for understanding the character and activity of God and for living out moral responsibilities to others."[148] In that sense, the book of Ruth in the Old Testament provides a template for thinking about God and God's relationship to His people. Ruth's story is an intimate family picture. It is also a poetic masterpiece. One author describes it as "an exquisitely wrought jewel of Hebrew narrative art."[149]

In the story of Ruth, two important themes that run throughout the lives of the women of biblical times are highlighted: The necessity for a woman to bear a child to carry on her husband's family line, and the desolate hopelessness of those who are barren or who have lost their husbands and have no prospects for another.

The drama of Ruth's story illustrates the truth that the circumstances of our lives are not accidents or coincidences. The death of her husband and her uncertain future play themselves out in ways that are clear evidence that the events of her life—and ours—are not mere happenstances without purpose or meaning. Instead, the ins and outs of Ruth's life were divinely orchestrated to bring about God's purposes.[150] Our lives are a part of the mystery of God's omniscience. He even weaves together the seemingly hopeless tragedies of our lives to create a design of poignant beauty and texture that will bring His plans to completion.

How was Ruth able to exhibit such remarkable devotion to her mother-in-law? How was it possible that this "common" person could possess such an uncommon degree of moral virtue? Often we do not recognize the purity and depth of character of such individuals in ordinary circumstances. Something has to happen for us to see them from the proper point of view. For us to fully appreciate their true value, we must see them in unique circumstances—in the same way that placing a gem at the correct angle allows it to catch the light and reveal its true magnificence. While it may appear to be tragic to us, the opportunity for hidden character to be revealed often comes at a very high price, but it is the only way that this true magnificence can be revealed.

The Shattering Blow

A geode is a sphere-shaped rock whose rough, often-ugly exterior gives no indication of the secrets that may lie within its core. Some geodes contain rare, amethyst crystals that sparkle and glitter like rippling water shimmering in sunshine when exposed to the light. But for these crystals to be exposed, the geode must first be struck with a shattering blow. Only after this awful impact can the beauty, long-hidden inside, be seen. The blow is not only an end, but a beginning. It is the end of something ordinary...and the beginning of something quite extraordinary. Before the blow is struck, only the outside of a nondescript, ordinary-looking rock is visible to the human eye. Afterwards, when the broken pieces of the rock are exposed to the light, we marvel at the intricate beauty of its glittering, crystal formations that were hidden deep at its center.

Some blows of life merely shatter a small hope or dream. Others are totally devastating and seem to leave life broken beyond all repair. Consider Tamar who was sent away childless under a cloud of suspicion. Or Ruth and Orpah who buried their young husbands. Or the women who stood at the foot of the cross and watched the life ebb from Christ's broken body. When struck with a devastating blow, we may feel as they did—that all we believe in and dreamed of has been shattered. At the time of impact, it may seem as though there is absolutely nothing left of our lives, but it is this blow that will reveal whether there is anything of value inside. Had Ruth not been struck with the shattering blow of her husband's death, millions of believers would never have seen the beauty of her character or been inspired by her devotion to Naomi.

God, in His grace and mercy, chose Ruth, a Moabitess, to be the great-grandmother of David. The people of Moab were descendants of the drunken, incestuous union of Lot with his two daughters. Though the people of Moab were scorned by the Israelites, God demonstrates anew in this instance that He chooses unlikely people to accomplish His purposes. How astonishing! How unlikely! This important point is worth our serious reflection, for it is one that God makes repeatedly throughout Scripture. Inheritance may be important, but ultimately God looks at the heart. The choices that issue out of the heart are the most important factors in determining our character.

God's choice of Ruth to be the wife of Boaz and the mother of Obed, the grandmother of Jesse and the great-grandmother of David, indicated that character means far more than inheritance. Hundreds of years later, when God surveyed all of Israel to choose a virgin to bear His son, He used the same criterion in choosing Mary that He used in choosing Ruth—purity of character. The prophet Micah describes the requirements of character in these terms: "He has showed you, O man, what is good; and what does the Lord require of you but to do justice, and to love kindness, and to walk humbly with your God?"[151] Character counts.

Millions of women have been dealt tragic blows that left them forever bitter and empty. What was there about Ruth's habits that formed in her a character of such pure and priceless beauty? What aspect of her character enabled her to endure, to go on, and "do the next thing"? From our study of Scripture, we believe that Ruth avoided two common traps that destroy devotion: self-pity and self-deception.

The Trap of Self-Pity

Even though she was a relatively young woman when her husband died, Ruth was mature enough to bear her own grief and share Naomi's grief as well. Though her pain and grief were real, she didn't try to escape from them by lashing out at Naomi. Nor did she try to escape her grief by indulging in the "if only" game: "If only the Israelite family had never come here, I wouldn't have married Mahlon and ended up a young, childless widow. If only Mahlon had given me a child before he died, people wouldn't think I was infertile. If only..."

There is no mention of Ruth being angry that Mahlon died, leaving her alone. Instead, the evidence indicates that she did not give herself over to "if only" escapism. Self-pity would have choked her capacity to share Naomi's grief and to grow in the tender, steadfast relationship with her mother-in-law that we see displayed.

Because of the "pure" way in which she faced her loss, Ruth's grief was not contaminated by destructive emotions that would have prevented her from sharing her loss and bonding with Naomi. Her grief was real, and it was painful. But it was a clean wound. Because she did not add further self-inflicted damage, it was possible to heal without complications—individually and in her relationship with Naomi.

Job's companions tried to get him to play the "if only" game when disaster struck. Job described his circumstances this way: "For the thing which I greatly feared is come upon me, and that which I was afraid of is come unto me."[152]

Despite this admission, Job refused to give in to his companions' pressure to anesthetize his pain by saying, "If only I had not sinned, this wouldn't have happened to me." That response might have resolved the dilemma he felt in that it would have removed the frustration of unexplained suffering. But it would have been false. God Himself had said of Job, "There is none like him in the earth, a perfect and an upright man, one that feareth God and escheweth evil...."[153]

Here was a "perfect" man experiencing incredible suffering. And for what cause? We want life to make sense. In fact, we demand that it make sense. But sometimes in this fallen world, things simply do not make sense. It would have been false for Job to say, "I brought this on myself. If only I hadn't sinned, I would not be in this awful condition." This approach would have offered some explanation for his predicament...it would have eased the torment he felt over the inexplicability of all that was happening to him, but it would have been a lie! He had not sinned, yet he suffered.

All of us will, at one time or another, experience bitter disappointment, sorrow, or grief. And ever since disobedience brought death into this world, women like Naomi, Ruth, and Orpah have had to bury their husbands, their children, their mothers, and fathers. Mercifully, few of us will be called upon to endure as many blows as Job, but we all face the possibility of hearing a grim-faced figure clad in a physician's garb solemnly intoning those awful words, "I am so sorry. We did everything we could." It is a reality we must face. Life is precious and over too soon.

If you haven't yet experienced the death of a loved one, then certainly separation of some degree has touched your life or that of someone you know. Alienated relationships and the pain of divorce are increasingly common in American culture—even among Christians. Brokenness is a fact of life.

The remnants of shattered relationships are all around us. In the end, godly devotion can help empower us to repair frayed relationships when possible or to rise above the disappointments of broken relationships and the "if onlys" of life. The strength that springs from devotion is one of the truest expressions of Christian character.

The Trap of Self-Deception

Most of us have had arguments that started off as discussions about something that happened, some problem that arose, something said or done. After a few exchanges, however, the discussion moves beyond what happened to involve opinions and statements about what we "think" or reactions to and interpretations about what happened. There is an almost inevitable progression from events to the meanings of those events.

We should remember Eve's experience and realize that the "evil one" will encourage us to pity ourselves and convince us that whatever has happened to us is not right and not fair. He will lead us down the primrose path to a welcomed, comforting conclusion—that we are victims! Excuses are always treacherous, so we must be alert to the fact that the "deceiver" will provide a positive spin for our selfish and self-centered actions *every time*. Such rationalizations are pitfalls to be avoided. They are dangerous because they jeopardize our true understanding of the events in our lives. The thin threads of truth are our links to reality.

When we cut away those threads of truth, our position becomes as perilous as a person driving down the highway in the dark without headlights. What we say to ourselves about the things that happen to us can be far more important than the experiences themselves.

Paul, in his second letter to the Corinthians, tells us to be wise and "take captive every thought to make it obedient to Christ." Then he underscores the danger posed by undisciplined thoughts: "I am afraid," Paul wrote, "that just as Eve was deceived by the serpent's cunning, your minds may somehow be led astray from your sincere and pure devotion to Christ" (2 Corinthians 11:3).

We are accustomed to hearing, "The facts speak for themselves." This dictum is so popular that it is accepted as a truism. However, facts are but the bare bones of truth. Our interpretation of the facts is the meat on those bones. We must use wisdom in interpreting life's events, and we must use logic and imagination to see the linkages between things (possible cause-and-effect relationships), to figure out what to make of things, and then to understand how they relate to one another. Facts must be interpreted if we are to understand them, know their significance, and attach meaning to them.

When circumstances come to bear upon us, we perceive the situation and try to catalogue it—as to its nature and its meaning. For example, when crossing a street, we look to see if anything is coming. If we see a vehicle, we try to determine its distance and speed based on the skill we have developed from our past experience. Then we make a decision whether to wait, walk across the street, or run for it! In more complex and significant experiences, the mechanics by which we process our experiences are, of course, more difficult to specify.

Thoughts connect to events, and the events of our lives are not stand-alone experiences. All that touches our life is recorded in our memory and wrapped in layers of interpretation—in much the same way a bird adds a layer of shell to envelop her egg.

Each time we recall an event to reassess it, we add to the outside layer of interpretation, making it thicker. If we repeat the process often enough, we may build up so thick a layer of interpretation that we essentially lose the essence of the event itself. This reassessment that causes us to lose the essence is like an argument that ceases to be about what was originally done or said and becomes focused instead upon beliefs about the meaning of what was done or said.

What did Ruth tell herself when both her husband and Orpah's died? We don't know. The author doesn't tell us directly. But we do know what she *didn't* say to herself. As we have pointed out already, she didn't blame Naomi or Naomi's God. This fact can be easily deduced from her actions. She also didn't tell herself that she wished she had never met Mahlon or his mother. She may have deeply considered her situation, but regardless of what she thought, what is most evident is what she did. Ruth acted with confidence. Instead of telling herself that her life was over, she did her best to move forward and remain engaged with life. She didn't become mired in her own pain. She avoided self-absorption by reaching out to Naomi. Ruth stepped out in devotion. She embraced her circumstances in faith. And if we are to experience the joy and strength of devotion, so must we.

We must come to the point in our faith where we are willing to say, "God alone understands this. I don't. I can't. But I am going to trust Him anyway!" The fact is that some mysteries can never be resolved in this life, and we accomplish nothing by giving in to the temptation to hold God hostage to our demand for answers that our logic can comprehend.

The enemy wants us to say to God: If You don't give me answers that I find agreeable, I refuse to believe You are good; if You don't solve my problem the way I think You should, I won't believe You are great; if You won't be accountable to me by preventing bad things from happening to me or my loved ones, I won't be accountable to You!

Notice how quickly our normal human quest for understanding the meaning of pain can degenerate into a debilitating and depraved refrain of "it's all about me."

Why did Ruth continue on with Naomi while Orpah was persuaded to return to her parents? What Orpah did was sensible, and it conformed to the logic of Naomi's argument. Ruth's choice, on the other hand, defies all logic. God's plans frequently do!

The Path to Devotion

Sacrificial devotion such as Ruth gave to Naomi defies our fallen self-centeredness. Likewise, the cross is the greatest contradiction in all of human history. We deserved justice…God gave us mercy. We deserved rejection and abandonment…God gave us His unconditional love and grace.

"Let the wicked forsake his way, and the unrighteous man his thoughts: and let him return unto the LORD, and he will have mercy upon him; and to our God, for he will abundantly pardon. For my thoughts are not your thoughts, neither are your ways my ways, saith the LORD. For as the heavens are higher than the earth, so are my ways higher than your ways, and my thoughts than your thoughts" (Isaiah 55:7-9).

Carl F. H. Henry, founder and former editor of *Christianity Today*, warned us that we must "purify our priorities" and "reinforce the imperatives" of our faith. "Purifying our priorities" means doing the right thing for the right reason regardless of the cost. It means choosing devotion over denial, righteousness over rebellion. "Reinforcing the imperatives" of our faith includes strengthening our willingness to obey.

When we set our priority on developing our capacity for sacrificial devotion, we draw closest to God. It is then that we breathe in His Spirit.

The Power of Obedience

I will not sacrifice to the LORD my God
burnt offerings that cost me nothing.
2 SAMUEL 24:24 NIV

We sometimes say that time is of the essence. And it certainly is. A dandelion may spring up overnight, but God uses hundreds of years to produce a giant redwood. In the life of Ruth, as in the lives of Tamar and Rahab, we have to remind ourselves to look beyond the immediate actions of the characters who occupy the foreground and not to miss the fact that God is patiently and with endless persistence at work in the background. Though the writer of the book of Ruth does not give us the details, we can clearly see that God was at work in Ruth's life all along to cultivate in her habits of devotion and obedience. He was developing within her a different kind of strength.

How could a woman as virtuous as Ruth come from the pagan background of Moab? We can no more explain Ruth than we can explain Tamar and Rahab—two other women in Christ's genealogy who come from outside of known religious traditions—other than to say that God chose them along with Abraham and his seed to be examples of His grace. We can only marvel that God produced this woman in such an alien environment to accomplish His divine purposes. Ruth's character did not spring up overnight, of course. God had been working in her life for years—probably since early childhood.

In our postmodern and materialistic age, God's principles are not in vogue. But even though they are not considered "cutting edge," those principles work—including the principle of obedience. If we obey God's laws, we will live joyous and fulfilling lives. If we choose to disobey, our lives will be futile. Jesus' simple words are recorded in

Luke 11:28 (NIV): "Blessed rather are those who hear the word of God and obey it." The laws of God apply equally to all cultures and in every period of history. God does not exempt any race, people, or time. The imperative for obedience must be respected even in our technologically advanced, but morally bankrupt, culture.

As women living in the postmodern world, our lives—even as Christian women—are shaped by what we see, read, and hear in the popular culture. Rather than focusing on obeying God's call on our lives and obeying the disciplines He mandates for happy, harmonious, holy living, we are saturated too often with the foolishness of trendy, avant-garde thinking.

It's easy to understand why we are so influenced when we consider that modern media and entertainment often portray those who are obedient to moral principle as weak and passive nonentities. It is true that rebellion and disobedience are often associated with strong-willed people, but sometimes these individuals are actually weak and are passively conforming to peer pressure. At the same time, we cannot assume that those who obey are always meek or weak.

One of the hallmarks of Ruth's character was obedience. Her obedience, however, was a result, not of weakness, but of strength. Ruth was anything but passive when Naomi advised her two daughters-in-law to return to their homes. Orpah meekly followed Naomi's advice, but Ruth resisted all of Naomi's arguments. She insisted on staying with Naomi to the point that Naomi—seeing Ruth's determination to act according to her view of what was right—simply gave up.

When they reached Bethlehem, Ruth's strength was again evident. She initiated the idea of going into the grain fields to glean behind the harvesters in order to provide for their physical needs. It is instructive to see how Ruth handled herself in her new environment as the daughter-in-law of a woman who returned home impoverished, widowed, and childless.

Rather than announce to Naomi that she had decided to go to the grain fields to provide for their needs, Ruth conferred with Naomi and requested her permission before proceeding. Ruth tempered her strength and initiative with deference to Naomi's experience, wisdom, and senior position. Ruth's esteem for Naomi and her willingness to take a subordinate position were yet other beautiful facets of her character. Ruth was generous, not only in wanting to help provide for

Naomi's needs, but also in the respect she gave to Naomi and the deference that she showed her.

"Better than Seven Sons"

There is an unheralded law of life that obedience will, inevitably, call for sacrifice. We know that if tulip or daffodil bulbs lie in a warm, dry, safe place, they remain sterile. But if they are planted in the fall and spend the winter in the cold, wet, dark ground, when the spring sunshine warms the soil, the bulbs will put out roots and a shoot will sprout out and strain upward toward the light. Soon we are blessed by a parade of color quite unlike anything one might think of when looking at the bulb that was buried long before in the dirt. Christ admonished His disciples, "Unless a kernel of wheat falls to the ground and dies, it remains only a single seed. But if it dies, it produces many seeds."[154] In another instance He said to them, "Whosoever will come after me, let him deny himself, and take up his cross, and follow me."[155] The result of such radical obedience is not death, but renewed life.

Certainly Ruth's life illustrates Christ's words. Ruth practiced sacrifice—first by refusing to leave Naomi to make the hazardous journey home alone and then by providing for her needs once they were in Bethlehem. She also exemplified obedience by deferring to Naomi's experience and knowledge about her new community. Ruth's love and commitment to Naomi caused the townspeople to speak of her as, "your daughter-in-law, who loves you and who is better than seven sons" (Ruth 4:15).

In a wonderful passage of Scripture David declares, "I will not sacrifice to the LORD my God burnt offerings that cost me nothing" (2 Samuel 24:24 NIV). In our contemporary culture, we have little understanding of the concept of sacrifice. Sacrifice in order to provide better opportunities for our children, or to provide comfort and security for our parents during their declining years, is becoming more and more rare. Sacrifices offered to the Lord are even less understood. Giving up soft drinks or chocolate for Lent is a major accomplishment in our overly affluent world. The cost of our modern sacrifices is minimal. At a time when charitable giving is down and tithing is becoming rare even for regular churchgoers, our homes are overflowing with stuff. We are building bigger and bigger closets in our houses to hold all of our accumulated material goods, and most towns can hardly keep up with the demand for storage units by those who need extra space to keep their treasures.

Today there is much we can learn from looking at Ruth's life as an illustration of both the costs and the rewards of sacrifice. By giving up the security of her home to follow her mother-in-law and see to Naomi's comfort and well-being, Ruth opened the door to a new and different life and, thus, held a pivotal place in the lineage of Christ. Interesting, isn't it? *We sacrifice one way or the other.* If Ruth had not sacrificed for Naomi, she undoubtedly would never have had the opportunity to be in the lineage of Christ and have her life celebrated for all time. Orpah's decision to turn back and take the easy road back to the familiar meant that she was never heard of again.

Another form of sacrifice is giving up our "control" in preference to another person's good judgment or advice. In that sense, Ruth "sacrificed" her own comfort zone to follow Naomi's instructions to go to the threshing floor to sleep at Boaz's feet. Ruth obeyed Naomi, though it meant going into uncharted territory and, certainly, feeling ill at ease in a strange and uncomfortable situation. But, because she obeyed, Ruth married Boaz and had the son who brought so much joy to her...and to Naomi as well.

The Security of God's Omniscience

The problem we have with obedience, of course, is that it inevitably calls for faith—faith to respond to God's command even when we cannot discern His purpose. And from where does our faith issue? Faith begins with an understanding of the appropriate relationship between us, as human beings, and God, the almighty King of the universe.

When situations arise where we can't see why God is asking us to do something, we are tempted to agree with the enemy's suggestion that if God really cared about our needs, He wouldn't treat us that way...He wouldn't make unrealistic demands on us. Of course, the voice planting those thoughts in our mind is the same one that Eve heard that fateful day in the garden.

God, the all-wise and loving heavenly Father, does care about our needs which—having made us—He understands far better than we do ourselves. If we always knew what God's purposes were, we could always walk by sight and would never have to rely on faith. But since we are not omniscient, walking by faith comes down to our willingness to resist the temptation to question God's goodness and to obey Him even when we don't understand.

Sooner or later something happens in our lives where God is asking us to do or endure more than we think we can handle. Overwhelmed and frightened, we struggle to understand what good could possibly be accomplished by this burden. Not understanding and not being able to see what the point is, we plead with God to deliver us. Even Christ in Gethsemane prayed, "Father, if it be possible, let this cup pass from me" (Matthew 26:39 RSV).

We have no difficulty with the first half of this prayer, but then we come to the really hard part: "Nevertheless, not as I will, but as You will" (Matthew 26:39 NKJV). At some point in our struggles, we can expect a warm "comforting" hand on the shoulder—too warm to belong to anyone but our adversary—and sugarcoated words of sympathy, "If God really cared about you, He wouldn't be putting you through this." Or, "It's not fair." Or, "It's unreasonable to expect..."

The story of Ruth spotlights the issue of God's omniscience. If Ruth could follow Naomi's instructions even though she couldn't fully understand all the reasons why, then shouldn't we follow the leading of the infinite Creator of the universe when He directs us to do something that is beyond our limited understanding? Shouldn't we, at the same time, acknowledge that in the end—either in time or eternity—whatever He requires of us will turn out to be good and wonderful? Naomi knew what the circumstances required; Ruth did not. As a stranger, Ruth couldn't know the situation as well as Naomi—for Naomi, Bethlehem's culture was second nature.

In our story, Naomi didn't think it served a useful purpose to explain her strategy. Perhaps she didn't want to burden Ruth with too much information beforehand because Ruth might have become distracted and self-conscious in her interactions with Boaz. Obviously, Ruth had already proved to be a diligent worker and showed she wasn't looking for a romantic fling with a young man. Now Naomi wanted Ruth to establish that she was ready for marriage to a man who could provide children. In her wisdom, Naomi apparently gave Ruth only the information that she needed to know. To Ruth's credit, she trusted Naomi's counsel and followed her direction.

Knowing the family history and the culture, Naomi also knew and understood Boaz—understanding that was impossible for Ruth at that point. Naomi asked Ruth to do a difficult thing. She asked her to surmount important obstacles and to move far out of her comfort zone. Naomi's instructions, though difficult, sprang purely from her love for Ruth and from her desire for Ruth to have the very best.

Ruth provides us with an example of what it means to trust and be obedient. Indeed, Ruth illustrates what it means to sacrifice—to give up control. Though she didn't understand the full implications of what Naomi was asking, Ruth nevertheless followed Naomi's instructions to the letter.

Ruth's obedience is all the more remarkable when compared to some of those whom God had blessed abundantly. Moses was one of the greatest spiritual giants in Scripture. We are told that he was the most humble man on the face of the earth.[156] God said He spoke to other prophets only in visions and dreams, but He spoke to Moses face-to-face.[157] Of such a man, we might expect an unblemished record of obedience. But as it turns out, Moses, like us, on at least one occasion, had a problem handling his emotions, and his lack of control caused him to disobey God's instructions.

The High Cost of Disobedience

The people of Israel grumbled and complained about their hard life in the wilderness. When the people couldn't find water and became hostile toward Moses, he cried out to God, seeking deliverance both from thirst and from the people's wrath.[158] God responded by telling Moses to take his staff and "strike the rock, and water will come out of it for the people to drink."[159] Moses obeyed, and God provided water. Many years later on a second occasion much like the first, God told Moses to "speak" to the rock so that it could pour out its water.[160] In his anger with the people, Moses did not speak to the rock as God commanded. Instead, he struck the rock with his rod. In fact, Scripture records that Moses struck the rock twice! Unlike the episode recorded in Exodus, where we are told merely that Moses did as the Lord instructed him, the author of Numbers, for an important reason, wants us to know that Moses had to strike the rock twice to get the water to come forth.[161]

Imagine Moses' consternation. Before, when he struck the rock as God had commanded, water gushed forth. But this time, nothing happened. Perhaps God didn't let the water flow after the first blow was struck in order to give Moses a second chance—a chance to "speak."

It was almost as though God were saying, "Moses, stop and think about this a moment. Do you realize what you are doing? Are you sure you want to go down this road?" Moses, it appears, wasn't in a listening mood, and he struck the rock a second time. We can imagine the savage blow Moses delivered the second time in his frustration and fear when God didn't provide water the first time! But, the second time despite Moses' failure to follow His instructions, God was gracious and provided the water the people needed just as He had promised Moses He would do. Was that the end of story? Hardly!

The book of Exodus explains that God told Moses to strike the rock. Forty years later, in Numbers, God told Moses just to speak to the rock. Outwardly, it looks like the same situation and logic would dictate that the same method would produce the same response. No big deal, right? Yes, it was a big deal! There was an important difference.

Plan A was for the first situation. But God told Moses to follow Plan B the second time around. Similar situations, but slightly different instructions. Why? We don't know. What was God up to? We don't know. The text simply does not explain what the difference was between the first and second times. But whatever it was, God gave specific instructions, and He expected Moses to obey.

When Moses did not do as he was told, God punished him. Moses' seemingly minor disobedience kept him from crossing the Jordan and entering the Promised Land.[162] Moses could only view the land from atop Mount Pisgah before he died.[163]

If God did not exempt the man He called "My servant" from the consequences of his disobedience, shouldn't you and I be wary of the consequences of ignoring God's commands? When Moses disobeyed, God considered it a serious matter and exacted a heavy price. Moses' experience illustrates the trouble we can bring upon ourselves when we fail to obey in things small as well as large.

Saul, too, learned that lesson in an even more disastrous way. He was the central figure in an incident that today we might consider minor disobedience. Like Moses, Saul did things his own way, even though on several occasions he had been given specific instructions from God's prophet Samuel regarding exactly how he should proceed.[164]

We can track King Saul's path to disaster from the point where he started rationalizing his disobedience. For instance, God commanded him to completely destroy the Amalekites for their wickedness—including all of their possessions. When Saul met Samuel after the battle, he announced, "I have obeyed God's command." Samuel asked, "Oh, why do I hear sheep bleating?" Saul replied, "But we're going to sacrifice them." Saul claimed that his men had saved the best livestock in order to offer them as a sacrifice "to the Lord your God."[165]

Samuel pressed him about his failure to destroy everything. A second time Saul excused his actions by blaming his men for taking the sheep and cattle. Samuel's response is very familiar, "Obedience is far better than sacrifice."[166] The third time Saul tried to talk his way out of things, he admitted that he had sinned and violated the Lord's command, but he added that he was "afraid of the people" and that his fear had caused him to give in to them.[167]

Like Saul, we learn to twist and distort things—just slightly—to put ourselves in a better light, to excuse ourselves, to talk ourselves into doing something we know in our hearts we shouldn't do. These examples of Moses and Saul send an important message for us today: God considers even minor disobedience a serious matter, for He understands the consequences far more clearly than do we.

The Beauty of Sacrificial Love

Ruth is a shining example to us precisely because God considers obedience such an important issue. We sometimes fall into the temptation of responding to God as if He were some tyrannical ruler who derives satisfaction from controlling His subjects. It is one thing for immature little children to react like this to their parents. But as adults we should be ashamed to let the enemy trick us into having such feelings. There is nothing more foolish than the notion that the omnipotent Creator has any need to force His will upon us. Even though we are only flawed, fallible human beings, as parents we nevertheless love our children and want only the best for them. How can we then do God the injustice of ever thinking about Him as other than an all-wise, patient, tender-loving Father whose only desire is our good?

The commands of God are given so that we might prosper. Because He created us, He knows what it takes for that to happen. That is why in His wisdom He holds so steadfastly to His prerogative to set boundaries and lay down demands. It is God's plan that we learn obedience in small matters so that we will be prepared for His call to duty and sacrifice in the large matters of our lives. And the purpose of all of this? It is God's plan to make our lives richer and more meaningful than we could ever dream. Ask Ruth.

God calls us to sacrificially tend to the needs of others, not because our own needs have no value, but because He knows that obedience to the call of sacrificial love makes our lives rich, complete, and full of meaning—as the case of Ruth so vividly demonstrates. The priceless quality of sacrificial mother-love has been justly celebrated in poetry and song. A mother who gives of herself for her children forges a bond of incredible strength and value. The bride and groom who lovingly subordinate their own needs to serve one another find a love so fine that Scripture uses the image of the church as the bride of Christ to help us see what we mean to God. In Ruth's story, we see one of the most improbable examples of sacrificial love: The love of a woman for the mother of her dead husband.

Over the long dreary trail from Moab to Bethlehem and in the long backbreaking days of gleaning in the fields, God was preparing Ruth to assume her place in the lineage of Christ. Ruth's life serves to remind us today that God sometimes requires us to labor in what might be long, dull, wearying, and seemingly fruitless duty. Often, in that process, He uses the labor of our hands to heal our souls.

As moderns, we have been sold the notion that self-actualization lies in the pursuit of self-interest. Nothing could be further from the truth! Self-actualization is to be found in caring for the needs of others. This reality does not dictate that we should despise ourselves as though we have no value or as though our needs are not important. Our own growth, development, and fulfillment are paramount in God's concern when He calls us to the duty of sacrificial love of others. Note that Christ did not say, "Love your neighbor and hate yourself." Instead, He said, "Love your neighbor as yourself."

In the quest for power today, sacrificial obedience is anathema to many women. Sadly, like Eve, some Christian women have been taken in by the desire to be independent and answerable to no one. The unwillingness to be subject to the authority of God is the crux of the modern tendency to eschew obedience.

In his book *The Last Word*, Thomas Nagel wrote, "It isn't just that I don't believe in God and, naturally, hope that I'm right in my belief. It's that I hope there is no God! I don't want there to be a God. I don't want the universe to be like that."[168] Gilbert Meilaender, in reviewing Nagel's book, commented, "Relativism and subjectivism are not then simply philosophical problems. They are also, and perhaps primarily, moral problems. We do not want to bend the knee."[169]

Postmodern women prefer to be characterized as strong, dominant, and competitive. But God calls us to a different kind of strength. He calls us to the kind of self-confident power that is not afraid to "bend the knee" when it is appropriate. One of the common threads of radical feminism and other postmodern ideologies is rebellion against authority and boundaries. These allow a self-centeredness that is disrespectful of others—especially those who should be closest and dearest to us. A philosophy based on hatred, anger, and rebellion is a corrosive, not a constructive, program for power. One of the basic problems with postmodern thinking is its emphasis on self-fulfillment. That focus leads to self-centeredness—a deceitful vice that is ultimately self-destructive.

Facing the Truth

As we ponder the importance of the path to obedience, the examples of Saul and David are insightful. Our commonly used expression "standing head and shoulders" above the rest, is a biblical expression first used to describe Saul (1 Samuel 9:2). At one point in his life, Saul was referred to as the "most handsome" person in all of Israel. In spite of, or perhaps because of, that description, Saul struggled with obedience. If someone so highly esteemed had difficulty with obedience, it will not be as easy for us.

Scripture gives honest accounts of people's struggles. The Bible doesn't sugarcoat reality. The wages of sin are clearly spelled out. Both Saul and David were tempted and their lives provide a pointed lesson about disobedience. The way the two leaders handled their sin, however, is distinctly different. And that difference is significant. Obedience is where the parallels between these two kings of Israel diverged.

When confronted by the prophet Samuel, Saul didn't repent. He tried to talk his way out of his disobedience. He rationalized. He lied. He blamed the people. He made a show of repenting, but his life didn't back it up. Eventually, his unwillingness to "bend the knee" led to his destruction.

King David also had to face up to his sin. Nathan told a story of a terrible, hateful sin that had been committed. David angrily demanded to know who would do such a thing. Nathan grimly told him, "Thou art the man." His sin was every bit as serious as Saul's, but David's response was entirely different. Saul rationalized. David repented. David's response was to promptly admit his guilt. He repented, was sorely punished, and was finally redeemed. His house was established. It is through David that we trace Christ's lineage.

Notice, too, that prophets, "truth-tellers," confronted both Saul and David and laid out right and wrong for them. In these confrontational moments, each of them had to decide what to do with that truth. God is very generous with us. If we are willing to listen, He will see to it that we are given the opportunity to confront the truth.

We must be aware though that, more often than not, the truth will come from a still small voice that can be drowned out by the clamoring of praise and adulation. We must be wise enough to provide openings for the voice of truth and welcome it when it comes. If we do not do so, we suffer the consequences. The voice of truth is the bedrock upon which we must build our obedience.

Nothing is a clearer example of this principle than Eve's temptation in the Garden of Eden. Eve wanted to escape the boundaries of God's commandment. What was the boundary? God's admonition that she should not eat of the fruit of the tree of the knowledge of good and evil or even touch it was the boundary God set. God had defined what was good and stated what was true.

Just like Eve, the rebel in us—the adventurous spirit within us, the desire to explore and discover what is on the other side of that fence that God labels "not good"—wants the power to decide truth for itself. That part of us wants the power to be disobedient and go our own way.

As a result, when Eve disobeyed and went exploring the territory God said was out of bounds, she experienced alienation from God and from Adam. She refused to accept God's boundaries, and her rebellion led to disobedience and her fall from grace. Nothing about the story has changed: When we listen to the lies of the enemy and do what God forbids, we sow seeds of disaster.

Originally, Saul was humble. But when he became king, he became stiff-necked and proud. With the prerogatives of power, he became jealous and tried to kill David numerous times. He refused to listen to wise counsel and obey God's commands. Instead, his disobedience destroyed the harmony in his family, and he became alienated from both his daughter Michal, David's wife, and from his son, Jonathan. Disobedience carries a very high price.

The Path to Obedience

Recently, some friends of ours had a rather graphic demonstration of how destructive disobedience can be in our lives and how important it is to guard our hearts. One Sunday morning as they left for church, they noticed the flowering ornamental tree in their front yard was at last in glorious, full bloom. It was literally aglow in the sunshine!

To their utter astonishment, upon their return home only a few hours later, the tree had been stripped of almost all flowers and greenery. It looked like a skeleton. They were completely shocked by the rapidity with which it had gone from vibrancy to violation.

The explanation came several days later when a gardener diagnosed the problem. The tree was strong and had survived, but the source of the problem was Japanese beetles, with which that beautiful tree will always be plagued.

During the winter, the beetle larvae burrow into the ground under the tree where they are virtually untouchable and certainly unseen. Then, in the spring, they emerge to feast on the blossoms and leaves. Without constant vigilance on the owner's part, the beetles will eat at the roots of the tree and eventually destroy it. What a perfect picture of the effects of disobedience.

Unfortunately, our propensity to disobey is nurtured by the relativism of our culture. Unrecognized, the false prophets of compromise, tolerance, and ease burrow into our very souls and weaken our resolve to obey. They are diligently at work and then, periodically and sometimes when we least expect it, they strip the visible growth of our lives. But the real danger is deep within where disobedience eats away at the roots, where lack of diligence will allow our faith to deteriorate and eventually rot. In this state, the roots are no longer able to nourish and sustain us to act in obedience and with sacrificial love.

Like a severe pruning, obedience can be painful. But it is an essential discipline. It strengthens our commitment and builds the qualities of godliness in our lives. Paul exhorts us in the path to obedience with these instructive words: "Do not let sin reign in your mortal body so that you obey its evil desires. Do not offer the parts of your body to sin, as instruments of wickedness, but rather offer yourselves to God, as those who have been brought from death to life; and offer the parts of your body to him as instruments of righteousness."[170]

For women of strength, obedience begins with offering ourselves to the one true God as those who have been brought from death to life. Then, like Ruth, we will sing the praises of our Kinsman-Redeemer as we love and serve Him with our lives.

When Your Dreams Have Died

The Power of Beauty
The Power of Endurance

Bathsheba
When Your Dreams Have Died

$\mathcal{I}$t was unseasonably warm for early spring. A week of regular late-afternoon showers had turned the air oppressively damp. Bathsheba lay tossing and turning in the clammy bed linens. Thankfully, her monthly period of impurity was over. It had been several hours since she had lain down, but sleep wouldn't come. She decided to get up for a drink and found the cool water to be delicious and soothing to her throat. It made her wonder if a bath might help her sleep. A few moments later she headed up the stairs with a large pitcher of water, hoping there might be some breeze, however slight, on the upper level.

When she had first lain down, the moon had not yet risen. Bathsheba thought the night's shadows would still be dark enough for her to bathe where she could enjoy the evening air. But as she stepped out onto the roof, she discovered a milky harvest moon climbing into the heavens in a perfectly cloudless sky. With the light from the moon so bright, she hesitated a moment, glanced around, and reconsidered her plan.

Perhaps it is too risky, she thought. But as she looked down on deserted streets below and saw only shadows blanketing the house all directions, she relaxed. Most of the men were gone to

Jerusalem was nearly empty and still as a tomb. It was late and, except for a dog barking far in the distance, there was no sound. The city lay cloaked in sleep.

She was as eager to complete the ritual bathing that would mark the end of her uncleanness[171] as she was for some respite from the humidity that made her linen gown cling to her skin. Assured now in her own mind that everyone nearby was sleeping, Bathsheba tipped the pitcher of water she'd brought with her and began pouring it slowly into the basin.

As the cool water splashed in the night's silence, her thoughts turned to Uriah, her husband. Might he also be awake on this beautiful night? Reports from the battlefield were infrequent. It had been days since she last had word of her husband. The account had been that Uriah and the rest of the king's men had destroyed the Ammonites, besieged Rabbah, and were camped in open fields preparing to renew battle.[172] She sighed wistfully. There would be no bath for Uriah camping out in the open fields.

Bathsheba longed for her husband to return home. They had been married only a short time, and she was eager to have a child—Uriah's child. But this would not happen any time soon...not with Uriah away at war. As she performed the familiar ritual marking the passage of another month, she felt the sting of tears and watched as they dropped and mingled with the water she had poured. Her heart was troubled, and her mind was distracted. Otherwise, she would have better guarded her privacy.

Instead, she slowly undraped her body, lowered her hair, and dipped her hands into the basin. Her thoughts tumbled from one troubling idea to another. Yet despite the turmoil of her mind, her movements were languid and graceful as she bathed. Lost in thought and preoccupied, Bathsheba was totally unaware that someone, transfixed by her womanly form and captivated by the beauty of her movements, was observing her every move.

Unable to sleep in the muggy air, David also sought escape in the cool, fresh air of the quiet night. He turned at the far end of the palace roof and slowly walked back to the other side. David brooded as he paced like a caged lion.[173] He would normally have gone off to war with his army, but this spring he had remained behind. In his place he had sent his sister Zeruiah's son, Joab, to lead the Israelite army. He could never think of Joab without being troubled. He was a great warrior, but he was ruthless. He had murdered Abner in cold blood to avenge the death of his younger brother Asahel.[174]

David partly understood Joab's feelings. Abner had killed Asahel. But Asahel had died in battle because he refused to break off hot pursuit when Abner was already in retreat. Word had come back to David that Abner—not wanting to start a blood feud with Joab—had tried to avoid the fight, but young Asahel's tremendous speed and endurance had left him no choice. Asahel's dogged pursuit of Abner had made it a matter of kill or be killed.

David had denounced Joab's treachery and buried Abner with a great ceremony.[175] But the matter was far from over. Remembering these details, David wasn't entirely sure that the only thing motivating Joab to kill Abner had been revenge. Without a doubt Joab had known that Abner was negotiating with David to end the war with the house of Saul, and that he was very close to brokering a peace where the elders of Israel recognized David as their king instead of Saul's son, Ish-Bosheth.[176] David wondered if Joab hadn't been concerned that Abner would replace him as David's second in command.

Abner was now dead and buried, but David didn't know quite what to do with Joab and his brother Abishai. *It would have simplified things,* David thought, *if Joab had been killed in the last round of battles against the Ammonites and Syrians.* Thinking like that made David uncomfortable, but he could not help but wonder why God had not meted out justice upon the man. However, instead of falling in battle, Joab and Abishai, though they were trapped between two armies, had fought like lions. Joab had attacked and defeated the Syrians, and Abishai had chased the Ammonites back into their fortified city.[177]

Have I done the right thing? David wondered. *Maybe it is pointless to keep sending Joab off to battle to keep him occupied and out of sight.* Suddenly, a slight movement caught the corner of his eye. His eyes quickly swept the scene of the sleeping city below him trying to pinpoint what he had glimpsed momentarily. Then he saw her. He was mesmerized by the sight of a woman's body etched by the moonlight. The gracefulness of her movements and the ethereal beauty of her form held his gaze and banished all thoughts of Joab. Her loveliness was breathtaking. Each aspect of her was perfect. She was as graceful as a young fawn with its head held high, watchful in the moonlight; her hair was shining; her skin translucent; her waist, hips, and thighs perfectly shaped. She raised her hands and arms like a hawk riding the wind. When she turned or straightened, her movement was as lovely as a cloud gently stirred by the breeze.

He soaked in the scene as she completed her bath and poured the remaining water through her hair. His gaze was transfixed as she luxuriated in the coolness of the water streaming over her and then as she toweled herself dry. When she reached for the empty water pitcher, he leaned forward...willing her not to leave...yearning to hold onto her image.

David waited for a long moment after the woman vanished from sight...staring, hoping that she might return. Then he saw the flickering light of a lamp briefly lit and then extinguished. When the darkness reclaimed the night, he knew there was no chance she would return to the roof. He resumed his pacing, but he did not return to plans for war or building his kingdom. His mind replayed the scenes from his neighbor's roof.

With her image filling his thoughts, David began to consider what would be the least noticeable way to learn the identity of this woman who had so thoroughly invaded his imagination. When he finally went back inside, he found that his dreams, too, had been taken over by the vision he had seen from his roof.

The next morning David told his servants to bring his breakfast to the rooftop. After they had spread out the meal, he pointed to the house where he had seen the woman the night before and asked, "Who is the strange woman who has moved into that house? Who gave permission for her to live there, only a stone's throw from the palace?"

"I do not know, my lord," answered a servant. "I don't see anyone."

"I can see that there is no one there now," said David testily, "but there was someone there last night. Go and find out who she is... immediately!"

The servant returned shortly, breathing heavily. He had obviously run all the way, "Sir, the woman is Eliam's daughter. She is Uriah the Hittite's new wife."

"Uriah the Hittite?" David mused and recalled that it had been Joab who had asked him to give Uriah the house near his palace. It was a reward for his role in the battle against the Syrians. Joab had said Uriah had been at his side during the ferocious attack in the center of the Syrian battle line, the attack that had broken the Syrian ranks and caused them to flee.

"Yes, sir," said the servant. "He is one of your soldiers, a member of your royal guard. You gave him that house for his valor in battle. He is now with Joab and the army in the fields near Rabbah."

Trying to appear nonchalant, David took a slice of pomegranate and asked, "And his new wife, what is her name?"

"Her name? Isn't she Bathsheba, sir?"[178] The servant looked surprised at the king's curiosity about the Hittite's wife...especially because the king's mind recently had been filled only with thoughts of the war.

David thought of little else but Bathsheba all day. He went about his usual business, but his mind played and replayed the scenes of the night before. How was it possible that this Hittite, this foreigner, this *mercenary*, was married to the most beautiful woman in David's kingdom? Why had he not known of Eliam's daughter? Why hadn't his counselor, Ahithophel the Gilonite,[179] asked for David's blessing before giving his granddaughter to Uriah? Had this, too, been the work of Joab? Had Joab arranged with Ahithophel for Uriah to marry his granddaughter, Bathsheba? These thoughts kept nagging him throughout the day.

He waited impatiently for the day to end and for darkness to come. As soon as dusk began to descend, he sent his messenger to bring Bathsheba to the palace.[180]

When she caught sight of the messenger, Bathsheba feared bad news about Uriah. That fear was replaced by cold, hard dread when she learned that it was David who had sent for her. Bathsheba knew such a summons at nightfall would mean only one thing. She looked around her frantically. Should she resist? But how could she resist the king? Answering the summons would bring ruin, but defying the king might mean death—not just for her, but for her family as well.

Everyone had heard about how King Saul ordered the murder of all of the priests and their families in the city of Nob because Ahimelech had innocently given David bread and a sword, not knowing he was fleeing from Saul for his life. If a priest who displeased Saul was not safe from a king's wrath, what possible chance would she have if she refused to come when David summoned her?[181]

As Bathsheba saw it, she had no choice but to go to him. Tears welled in her eyes as she turned to get her things. She stopped. Why bother? The king's servant girls would bathe and clothe her appropriately for the encounter.

Bathsheba's steps faltered as she followed behind the messenger. She was a great beauty, but she was also a realistic and pragmatic woman. She knew that neither her husband nor her father could protect her now. Worse still, once she entered the king's palace, she would be completely beyond the reach of anyone. She had only moments to consider her situation, but that was all it took to realize that she was facing inevitable disaster. With each step toward the palace, she placed another layer on the barrier she was erecting around her heart.

The path before her was forbidding. She could escape the king's anger by answering his summons, but, under the law, she might still face death if it became known that David had taken her and she had not cried out in protest. Would the king protect her? No, the question was *could* he? Indeed, could he protect himself? Sorrowfully, she looked back at the home she had so lovingly created with Uriah.

Uriah! She had not yet allowed herself to think about how this despicable summons would affect him. But the thought could not be suppressed. Uriah would be enraged. He would be heartbroken. Worse, he would be *helpless*. This wasn't just a crime against her. It was also a crime against her husband. She stumbled momentarily and paused. What could she do? What could she *do*? There was no choice.

Then, shedding her innocence, she resolutely made her way toward her destiny.

When she came through the front gate, the grandeur of the king's palace added to Bathsheba's anxiety. She entered in a daze. She felt as though she had stepped outside herself to watch numbly as the servants began the preparations for her to come before the king. The gown, she noticed, was of a sheer, luxurious fabric in a style and color that was perfect for her. The maidservant who did her makeup and hair was highly skilled. Bathsheba hardly recognized herself. She ruefully admitted that she now looked fit for the role of a king's paramour.

Too soon she was led to David's bedroom. She hesitated as the servants disappeared. Then steeling herself, Bathsheba drew herself up to her full height and entered.

She stood there a moment, briefly studying the look in the king's eyes. Bathsheba had been told she was beautiful since childhood. It was something she had come to take for granted. But while she was accustomed to being admired and was aware of her physical beauty, she had never fully realized the power it could give her over a man. Her parents adored her, as did Uriah. He told her often that she was beautiful. But her previous sheltered experiences had not prepared her for this moment or for the intensity she saw in David's gaze.

As she stood there, she took a deep breath and began trying to grasp the situation that had burst upon her like a sudden summer storm. She couldn't escape this encounter. She couldn't turn time back. Nothing could make things the way they had been only a few hours earlier.

Indeed, her life would never be the same again. Her relationship with Uriah would forever be marred. Because there was no way to go back, she realized she had to move forward. It was imperative that she please the king. She knew that her future—and even her beloved Uriah's life—depended on it.

She forced a smile. She knew she appeared shaky and tentative, but David smiled warmly in return…and beckoned her. When she stepped forward, she seemed to float as gracefully as a bird soaring on the wind. Before him now, she was even more beautiful than he had been able to imagine. Her features and skin were as flawless as her form.

David admired Bathsheba as she slept in the dim half-light that signaled the approaching dawn. Even in repose, though, her face was troubled. He realized the circumstances of their encounter had been difficult for her. Regardless of that, something in her manner—beyond her beauty—captivated him.

There was the physical, of course, but it was more than that. What was that something, that inner quality? He couldn't quite identify what it was, but he was intrigued. Could he possibly come to love this woman?

David awakened Bathsheba in the predawn stillness to send her back home. Though it was not difficult to know she had pleased him greatly, Bathsheba discovered that neither beauty nor passion was enough. Even the mighty King David did not want them to be found out. What did he fear? She couldn't read his thoughts, but he had ruined her life…and now he was sending her away. The king called a servant to escort her home and sent her out, quietly and unobtrusively, through the back gate.[182] For her, though, there could be no going back.

David strode across the rooftop, stopping in the spot where he had first caught sight of Bathsheba. His stare crossed the city, taking in her house, and then shifted out toward the horizon. Out there, Joab and his men were encamped, loyally following his orders. *Uriah!*

David stared once again at the message in his hand—a simple yet devastating message: "I am pregnant." He read it again and began pacing anew. *What a fool I have been!* How obvious it would be to everyone that this could not possibly be Uriah's child.

What should he do now? He could simply leave Bathsheba to her fate. But certainly the palace servants would know he was the father. However, if he denied it, who would accuse him? He was the king. Who was there to hold him accountable?

Uriah…a warrior, a warrior who even now was distinguishing himself in battle alongside Joab while David stayed behind. Uriah would believe his wife. And Joab would believe Uriah.

His wife. Yes, indeed, Bathsheba was Uriah's—not his. He closed his eyes, and a vision of her as she had been that night appeared before him. *She is so incredibly lovely!* No, he did not wish to leave her to her fate.

And why should he? If he acted quickly, there was time. He would go through the pretense of bringing Uriah back to Jerusalem for a briefing on the progress of the siege. Would this rouse Joab's suspicions? And what if it did! He was the king!

He strode back across the rooftop. He would send a message to Joab to have Uriah brought home from battle.[183] He congratulated himself on the shrewdness of his plan.

The next week when Uriah arrived, David asked him about how the war was progressing, about Joab's spirits, and about the morale of all the other soldiers.[184] After a perfunctory conversation, he sent Uriah away with instructions that he was to go home, wash his feet, and get some rest.[185] Though David was not very subtle in suggesting that Uriah spend the night in Bathsheba's bed, it never occurred to him that strong encouragement on his part would be necessary. David even sent a gift of food and wine so Uriah could enjoy the evening with his wife.[186]

As he watched Uriah leave, David took satisfaction in the skill with which he had solved his problem. He felt a great sense of relief now that things were back under control. He could not, however, escape his irritation at the thought that the Hittite was about to be reunited with Bathsheba. He spent a restless, fretful night tossing and turning.

The next morning, David hurried to find a messenger to carry his orders for Uriah's return to his duties. The messenger returned immediately.

"Sir, Uriah did not go to his home."

"Oh?" David feigned disinterest. "Where did he go?"

"He spent the night outside the palace gates with the servants."

David's head snapped up. "He did *what?*"

"Yes, sir. He slept outside by the gate. He did not go home."[187]

"Send him here immediately."

David paced restlessly while waiting for Uriah. He spoke as soon as the soldier appeared in his presence. "I'm told you didn't go home last night. You traveled such a distance to Jerusalem. Why didn't you go home and get some rest as I instructed?"

Uriah explained that he could not go back home.[188] "My lord's men and my master Joab are camped in open fields. The ark and Israel and Judah are staying in tents. How can I go to the comfort of my house? How can I eat your good food and drink your fine wine? How can I lie with my wife when my fellow soldiers are there in devotion to their duty? As surely as you live, I will not do such a thing."[189]

The king stared at the man. What did this mean? Did Uriah's manner indicate that he thought the king's sudden interest in him was strange, or was it just David's nerves? Was Uriah accusing him of dallying in Jerusalem while his men risked their lives on his behalf? Just what was the implication of Uriah's remarks? Did they reflect what Joab and his soldiers were saying about him staying in Jerusalem? David wondered if perhaps he wasn't letting his imagination get carried away and tried to reason that it was only his own guilt that prompted the thought. But the more he thought of what Uriah had just said, the greater his anger grew. It was anger born of guilt over having attended to his own wishes and needs while his men put their lives on the line for the safety of their land, their homes, their wives, and the children God had given them.

And why did this foreigner mention the ark? The ark symbolized the Hebrew soldiers' reliance on God to give them courage and strength in the midst of battle. The ark in their midst showed that they were depending on God's guidance and protection.[190] Its presence on the battlefield showed that their ultimate confidence was in God, not the king. The ark identified them as the children of Israel, Abraham's seed, God's chosen people—a people whose kingdom belonged not to the king, but to God. At this particular moment, David was not at all happy to be reminded of the fact that it was the anointing by God's prophet Samuel that had made him king.[191]

With that realization, an awful, horrifying question flashed in his mind: *What if Samuel were here today?* He angrily cut short such thoughts and spoke curtly, "Stay here another day before starting your journey. I will send you back tomorrow."[192]

That night David insisted that Uriah dine with him. David kept the wine flowing until he succeeded in getting Uriah drunk. David hoped that with his mind clouded by drink, Uriah's resistance would weaken and he would go home to Bathsheba. But in the evening when he left the king's table, Uriah only staggered out as far as the gate and collapsed on his mat among the king's servants. He did not go home![193]

David was furious. *Enough!*

When Uriah left the next morning, David sent a sealed letter along with him for Joab. In it he wrote: "Put Uriah on the front lines of the fiercest battle. Then leave him there alone where he will be struck down and killed."[194] In his anger, it had been easy enough to write the letter, but now he had to live with a troubling question. What would Joab's reaction be when he received the message?

It had been 12 days since Uriah departed. For the last three days no one had been able to do anything that pleased the king. By David's reckoning, Uriah should have reached Joab in, at most, three to four days. If he pushed hard, and if Joab acted with dispatch, he could easily have mounted the attack David ordered in another two days. If Joab sent news immediately by a fast messenger, word should have reached him in no more than nine or ten days—unless, of course, the weather had turned bad. For the last two days, David had demanded to know if Joab had sent news from the battlefields. When there was none, he ordered a messenger to travel half a day's journey to determine whether a courier from Joab was anywhere to be seen. Late that afternoon, word finally came that Joab's messenger was nearing Jerusalem and would be there within the hour. At this news, David issued orders that sent each of his senior advisors to attend to some task away from the palace. He wanted to be alone when word arrived from Joab.

When the messenger came before him, he told David everything Joab had told him to say. "The men overpowered us and came out against us in the open, but we drove them back to the entrance of the city gate. Archers shot arrows at your servants from the wall, and some of the king's men died, sir. Moreover, your servant, Uriah the Hittite, is dead."

David feigned surprise, "Uriah, dead?"

The messenger nodded.

David turned his back and strode away. He thought to himself, *So Joab's not going to be a problem after all. I've been worried all this time for nothing.* Then he whirled and returned quickly. Addressing the messenger, he said, "Say this to Joab: 'Don't let this upset you; the sword devours one as well as another. Press the attack against the city and destroy it.'"[195] *Joab and Abishai,* David thought, *would as soon fight as eat.*

"Destroy it, sir?"

"Yes. Say this to encourage Joab."

Bathsheba received the messenger with a heavy heart. She knew from his garments that he had come from the battlefield, and from his expression, she knew he brought bad news. "Madam, your husband, Uriah, died in battle. He led the attack and fought heroically. But in the battle, he was struck down."[196]

Bathsheba wept...and wondered. Was there a connection between his recent trip to see King David and his death? Why had he not come home to see her while he was in Jerusalem? Had he died suspecting what had happened? Had he chosen a suicide mission because he no longer wanted to live? Had he died hating her?

Bathsheba thanked the messenger for his kindness and began to mourn her husband, the death of their dreams, and the life they had planned to share together.

When the seven days of formal mourning were over,[197] Bathsheba saw David's messenger approaching her home again.[198] She watched as he came down the pathway, knowing immediately why he came.

"Ma'am, the king has commanded me to bring you to his palace."[199]

"Please let me gather my things. Then I will come with you."

Bathsheba looked around the house she had so enjoyed making into a home. She would never live here again. She tucked a few cherished items into a shawl. She couldn't bear to think of all she was leaving behind. How was she supposed to carry the burden of her memories of this life as she journeyed to the palace of the king? Somehow she had to find the strength to go forward. There was no other choice. It was becoming an all-too-familiar feeling.

Time was of the essence, too, she knew. She longed for a little more time…time to adjust her thinking to what lay ahead and to wander through the memories of what lay behind. Because she was carrying the king's child, people might not count the months as closely as they otherwise would—at least not openly—but haste was, nevertheless, prudent.

Bathsheba was sitting with David when the servant announced a visitor. She greeted their guest and noted that his gaze lingered for an extra, uncomfortable moment. She knew the man named Nathan was a prophet sent from God.[200]

He seemed a kindly man with an impressive, authoritative bearing. She was unsettled by his presence, but Bathsheba was uncertain as to why. He did not seem condemning or judgmental when she greeted him. Rather, his grave, piercing eyes seemed to see more than she wanted anyone to know. He seemed to be looking deep into her soul. He seemed to know her deepest thoughts. It seemed, in that awkward moment, that to this prophet of God everything was an open book. *Just how much has God revealed to him?* she wondered. She discretely departed so that David and Nathan could talk alone.

Bathsheba hoped the great man could reach through the barriers David had erected. David enjoyed her beauty; he made that obvious. He lusted after her, and that was obvious, too. But it was equally obvious that he didn't love her. She wasn't sure he was capable of love—true love.

Yet there *was* one person he loved unquestionably—their son. He adored the child. Everyone marveled at how he doted on the boy. But she wasn't sure he was glad to be married to her. He seemed to be a different man from the one she first saw on that fateful night when she walked through the door into his bedroom. She hoped this prophet would help.

She stopped the rambling of her thoughts when she realized that the prophet was beginning to tell David a story. She stepped close enough to hear through the open door. Nathan was saying,[201]

> There were two men in a certain town, one rich and the other poor. The rich man had a very large number of sheep and cattle, but the poor man had nothing except one little ewe lamb he had bought. He raised it, and it grew up with him and his children. It shared his food, drank from his cup and even slept in his arms. It was like a daughter to him. Now a traveler came to the rich man, but the rich man refrained from taking one of his own sheep or cattle to prepare a meal for the traveler who had come to him. Instead, he took the ewe lamb that belonged to the poor man and prepared it for the one who had come to him.[202]

Bathsheba heard David burst out in anger, "Who is that man? He deserves to die. He must pay for that lamb four times over. What kind of man would do such a thing? He has no pity! As surely as the Lord lives, that man must die."[203]

Bathsheba held her breath. The meaning of the prophet's story was clear to her. She feared what was coming next, and she braced herself for another burst of fury from her husband. All was quiet for a brief moment. Then she heard Nathan's voice, grim as death, announce slowly, "You are the man!"

Hearing no reply from David, Bathsheba shifted her position slightly, for she was desperate to see his face. Fearful that she might have been seen, she flinched when she heard Nathan continue. Only now he was speaking much more rapidly—as though to rid himself of some unwanted hateful thing:

> This is what the Lord, the God of Israel, says, "I anointed you king over Israel, and I delivered you from the hand of Saul. I gave your master's house to you, and your master's wives into your arms. I gave you the

house of Israel and Judah. And if all this had been too little, I would have given you even more. Why did you despise the word of the LORD by doing what is evil in his eyes? You struck down Uriah the Hittite with the sword and took his wife to be your own. You killed him with the sword of the Ammonites. Now, therefore, the sword will never depart from your house,[204] because you despised me and took the wife of Uriah the Hittite to be your own" (2 Samuel 12:7-10 NIV).

Bathsheba gasped and put her hands to her mouth. She had, of course, wondered if David had been instrumental in Uriah's death, but to hear the truth so bluntly from the prophet…all the grief she had not had opportunity to express swept over her like a raging flood. She thought that it was more than she could endure, but Nathan was not finished:

This is what the LORD says: "Out of your own household I am going to bring calamity upon you. Before your very eyes I will take your wives and give them to one who is close to you, and he will lie with your wives in broad daylight.[205] You did it in secret, but I will do this thing in broad daylight before all Israel" (2 Samuel 12:11 NIV).

Bathsheba heard a sound—somewhere between a groan and an agonized cry. It was unlike anything she had ever heard before. Then she heard David wheeze in utter horror, "I have sinned against the Lord." David's bitter anguish seared her soul.

She watched through her tears as Nathan moved to the side of David, who had fallen to his knees. The king's body convulsed with great sobs of guilt and shame. Then Nathan spoke again, his voice full of both pain and compassion, "The Lord has taken away your sin. You are not going to die."[206]

Bathsheba let out the breath she had been holding in a long sigh of relief. Her emotions were a tumult. She needed to grieve Uriah and the terrible injustice of his death. At the same time, to her surprise, she wanted to rush to David. She hesitated only a moment. But as she reached for the doorpost to steady her step, she heard Nathan continue,

"But because by doing this you have made enemies of the Lord show utter contempt, the son born to you will die."

The words hit Bathsheba like a blow to the stomach. She couldn't breath. Her head reeled, and she gasped for air. Her frantic thoughts ran wild. She could no longer control her emotions. She wanted to rush to Nathan and plead for mercy, but her feet were swiftly carrying her away and up the stairs to where her son lay sleeping. Quickly, she gathered the little boy in her arms, held him tightly against her breast, and sobbed as she rocked back and forth. After several minutes, she regained her composure, for the child continued to sleep peacefully in her arms. Bathsheba was reassured as she gazed lovingly at the sleeping child.

Faintly, she heard footsteps outside. She tiptoed softly to the window and watched the prophet depart. Nathan's head hung low as he walked away. Bathsheba clutched her baby tightly and watched until he was out of sight.

The same night, when Bathsheba checked on her son before retiring for the evening, she felt his fever rise.

David therefore pleaded with God for the child, and David fasted
And went in and lay all night on the ground.
Then on the seventh day it came to pass that the child died.
Then David comforted Bathsheba his wife, and went in to her and lay with her.
So she bore a son, and he called his name Solomon.
And the Lord loved him.
And He sent word by the hand of Nathan the prophet;
so he called his name Jedidiah,[207]
because of the Lord.
2 Samuel 12:24,25 NIV

Epilogue

Meanwhile Joab fought against Rabbah...Joab then
sent messengers to David, saying, "I have fought against Rabbah
and taken its water supply. Now muster the rest of the troops
and besiege the city and capture it. Otherwise I will take the city, and it
will be named after me." So David mustered the entire army and went to
Rabbah, and attacked and captured it.

2 SAMUEL 12:26-29 NIV

The Power of Beauty

Her children arise and call her blessed;
her husband also, and he praises her:
"Many women do noble things, but you surpass them all."
Charm is deceptive, and beauty is fleeting;
but a woman who fears the LORD is to be praised.
Give her the reward she has earned,
and let her works bring her praise at the city gate.
PROVERBS 31:28-31 NIV

In October 1999 renowned wood engraver Barry Moser released a new illustrated Bible. The wood engravings feature the "unbeautified human face" of biblical characters. Within two weeks the first printing of 50,000 Bibles sold out. Moser's work was heralded because, said one critic, faces like those portrayed in Moser's art help us to learn to value individuals and, thus, to value ourselves.[208]

Moser's work is but a recent example of our human struggle to come to grips with the contradictions between physical beauty— those inherited qualities that we can help along with good hygiene, nutrition, and cosmetics—and inner beauty—an accomplishment that is the sum of decisions grounded in moral principles and love. In those whose life is one of discipline and devotion, inner beauty increases with age while external physical beauty fades, a victim of the passage of time.

One of the oft-repeated sayings from Murphy's Law is that "beauty is only skin-deep, but ugly goes clear to the bone."[209] Jean Kerr commented on that law in her own inimical way, "I'm tired of all this non-sense about beauty being only skin-deep. That's deep enough. What do you want—an adorable pancreas?"[210]

Kerr got one thing right: However deep it goes, beauty is deep enough. Of all the powers available to women, beauty may be the strongest. A woman's beauty can have dramatic impact on people's lives—even on strangers. And feminine beauty can change history, as Bathsheba's story shows us.

Nevertheless, beauty has always been a mixed blessing for women. Throughout the ages few philosophers have had anything positive to say about feminine beauty. In fact, neither have most of the artists or theologians. Beauty has always been intrinsically connected to sexual temptation and often has been depicted as the source of men's downfall.[211] In spite of the fact that we, as human beings, are drawn to beautiful people, great Christian thinkers have often viewed beauty as a pitfall.

Running concurrent to this view is a parallel historical debate that has raged about whether beauty is inevitably good. In fact, our human tendency is to describe the behavior of the beautiful as good, and to attribute bad actions to those whom we consider physically unattractive. Six hundred years before Christ, the philosopher Sappho wrote, "What is beautiful is also good, and who is good will soon be beautiful." Ralph Waldo Emerson later added, "Beauty is the virtue of the body, as virtue is the beauty of the soul."

Even today Christians have ambivalent reactions to beautiful women—alternately fawning over them or criticizing them, either drawn to them or afraid of them. Some Christians deny the impact of beauty. Others consider it irrelevant, even trivial, thus making themselves vulnerable and easy prey to the powers of temptation. Beauty, like money, power, sex, and alcohol, can be seductive. Many a life has crashed on these dangerous shoals.

Shakespeare wrote, "She's beautiful; therefore to be woo'd, She is a woman; therefore to be won."[212] Such was David's desire for . Bathsheba. Her ravishing beauty captivated his imagination. As king, of course, David's pursuit did not require tender or considerate wooing. As absolute monarch, all he had to do was summon any of his subjects, and they had to obey. He was answerable only to God.

Since Eve women have been blamed for enticing, tempting, and seducing men. At many periods of history, godliness was equated with celibacy. The rejection of beauty as an evil temptation to draw men away from God is a recurring theme from ancient times.

Yet we must not denigrate physical beauty. It is part of God's creation and a part of His divine plan. Wherever we turn we see His handiwork exhibiting great beauty—wondrous beauty.

A Season of Beauty

One of the highlights of spring in Washington, D.C. is the short period during which the cherry blossoms are in full bloom. With literally hundreds of trees in flower around the monuments—especially around the Tidal Basin—the sight is breathtaking. But the spectacle is also very brief—particularly if a hard spring rain comes along at the height of the season. Under the best of conditions, the blossoms are at their peak for only a few days. Like the physical beauty of youth, the cherry blossoms are temporary and fragile.

After the blossoms' brief and sensational parade comes the hard work. If the cherry trees are to survive, the roots—out of sight and unheralded—must push down into the soil, penetrating into the dirt, stones, and muck to extract the moisture and nutrients the tree needs to live. The branches and twigs must reach upward, lifting the budding leaves to the light in good weather and bad. All during the long hot days of summer and into the fall until the frost comes, the roots, branches, and leaves must do the grubby, ordinary, day-to-day work to sustain the life of the tree and prepare it for bringing forth the next spring's blossoms. Though less dramatic, these life-sustaining processes are no less miraculous and certainly no less essential than the fertilization phase that was initiated by the blossoms with their outrageous, glorious, but transient, display of beauty.

The transient nature of the blossoms' beauty is not to be faulted for its brevity. It is that way by God's design. Neither is it to be exalted to the neglect of the maintenance and pruning of the tree. Likewise, the physical attractiveness of youth is genuinely beautiful. There is no skin so wondrous as that of an infant. President Teddy Roosevelt said that the most beautiful thing he had ever seen was a baby's hand. There are no eyes as bright as a child's—save perhaps those of a young woman in love. There is nothing more glorious than a young man's strength. This list goes on and on, but each item has one thing in common: They all last only briefly.

The physical attractiveness of youth, like the beauty of the blossoms, is part of God's design. All of the attributes of beauty related to youth have their function, and they flourish for their season. We err, however, when we elevate beauty's significance out of all proportion or fail to accept that it is transient. Though physical attraction is usually the basis for romance, more mundane and less-glamorous processes are required for romance to become long-lasting love.

In the initial stages of romance, selflessness and putting the beloved first can seem effortless. But in time resisting the temptation to elevate one's own needs, wishes, and desires to priority over those of the beloved requires a conscientious and determined effort of the will. Habits of self-denial and a humble attitude of service are necessary for a relationship to grow and flourish.

Like the roots of the tree, the unheralded habit of sacrificial love is the channel by which a relationship is nourished. Sacrificial love is the indispensable means by which the love that was first fueled by physical attraction and passion can be sustained. However, our own selfish desires are like low branches that needlessly consume the resources needed by higher branches that lift the leaves to the life-sustaining light. We must submit to the Master's pruning of our lives if we are to thrive.

The Importance of Pruning

God's pruning of our lives—though for our own benefit and essential for a healthy relationship—is always painful. We often resist it strenuously. And we do so in two ways: through anger and denial. First, we become angry with God when He takes away something we hold dear—something He knows is sapping our energy and limiting our personal growth or keeping us from giving to others. Additionally, we chafe and stew like spoiled children when God asks us to wait instead of providing something we want immediately.

Remember that Ruth's amazing vow to follow Naomi's God came *before* He gave her children, and even more astonishing, *after* her husband's death had left her a childless widow. What a contrast! Peaceful acceptance and gracious submission to God's plan instead of raw resistance enables an entirely different dynamic in our lives. When we are angry with God, we are in much the same situation as children who are angry and resist their parents' discipline. When a family is full of love and affection, disagreements and anger are usually temporary. Though hostile emotions are dangerous and potentially damaging, if they are brought into the open and hashed out fairly and honestly, they can lead to deeper and richer relationships. Childish temper tantrums spoil the natural radiance of a two-year-old's joy! Are we any different from God's perspective? Constructive discipline promotes growth and weeds out our tendency toward childish rebellion.

The second means of resisting pruning poses an even greater threat. This form of resistance surfaces in a denial to face reality. *What we refuse to face, even God Himself cannot repair.* At times we can be quite adept at avoiding the things God wants us to deal with in our lives. We can suppress or paper over things through self-deception. Rationalization is deeply ingrained in us from childhood: *"But he started it...!"* We can become so skilled at this process that we sometimes hide from the truth as long as possible—just as David did after he sinned by taking another man's wife.

But God is faithful. He pursues us. He is merciful. He will often give us multiple opportunities to submit to His skillful hand and see our sin through His eyes. Through Tamar, God brought Judah face-to-face with his faithlessness. Through Samuel and Nathan, God confronted both Saul and David with their disobedience. When the moment of truth arrived, one king continued to rationalize while the other faced the truth and made a full confession of his sin.

The Seductiveness of Beauty

We can be assured—from observing the rest of God's creation—that Adam and Eve were the most beautiful physical specimens of humanity ever created. Generations later, even after the fall, there is something about every human being that is beautiful.

While appreciating and acknowledging God's work in creating human beauty, we cannot, at the same time, worship physical beauty, as our contemporary culture does. Americans have made the Barbie doll image our ideal. "The quest for a fit, fat-free body," writes one observer, "has become an American obsession."[213] Young women feel this pressure most acutely. One of today's teen pop-idols, Christina Aguilera, is a size 2 and regularly has to have her stage costumes taken in. Thus the average woman—at size 12—diets or starves herself in a hopeless quest to look like popular actresses, models, and performers.

Physical beauty is a gift to be appreciated and valued, but it is not an asset to be craved at the expense of virtue. Using beauty to manipulate

and exploit others, and promote oneself, may provide a fleeting triumph, but is ultimately a pitfall that ends in anger and alienation—and
even humiliation. Think of the countless women, propelled by their
beauty, who have followed the modern trajectory of celebrity, grabbed
their 15 minutes worth of fame, and landed finally in the pages of
Playboy. Their beauty becomes an object of exploitation.

Viewed as a vehicle for fame and a tool for seduction, the glory of
beauty is in this way corrupted. Beauty, of course, is one of the prime
ingredients in physical attraction and is usually a significant factor in
courtship. But it isn't an enduring foundation for a faithful love. In our
own day and time, the breakup of the marriages of the "beautiful
people"—sports figures, musicians, television and movie stars—are
"Exhibit A" for the case that beauty, privilege, fame, and material
wealth are inadequate by themselves to sustain relationships in the
face of the corrosive effects of selfishness and pride.

When conflict arises, as it inevitably will, separation and divorce—
rather than apologies, forgiveness, and reconciliation—are too frequently seen as the solution. The same is true of all human
relationships. Estrangement and alienation among family and friends
are tragically common. Nothing is more certain than the necessity for
forgiveness if marriages and other vital relationships are to survive.
Without the reality of grace in our lives, at a minimum, we will err in
judgment. We will misunderstand. And, worse still, we will act selfishly. Our pride will hold us back from the apologies that are essential
ingredients in putting damaged relationships back together again.

Adam and Eve were the two most perfect human specimens who
ever walked on this planet—how stunning they both must have been!
Yet their sin meant that the rest of us live as marred beings. We were
created for perfection in form and in relationships. Because God created Adam and Eve for each other, we can be sure that before they
sinned, they experienced the greatest passion ever known. But after
they sinned, they began blaming each other, and the unity of their
relationship was fractured. Before they sinned they had been confident without even knowing it. Afterward they felt vulnerable and
exposed. The harmony and joy of their relationship changed to fear
and alienation.

Though their bodies retained much of the original capacity for
pleasure, their spirits could no longer freely relate with the same lack

of inhibition they had enjoyed because uncertainty and mistrust became barriers that had to be overcome. When sin enters the picture, relationships are weakened regardless of whether there is strong physical attraction or not.

At the outset David was certainly attracted to Bathsheba's beauty, but there is not even the slightest possibility that there was any trust or respect between them. How could there have been? Their relationship sprang from David's lust and his selfish determination to have the object of his desire, even though she was another man's wife. Indeed, the deceptive seduction of beauty's power may have contributed to Bathsheba's downfall, as we shall see in the next chapter on the power of endurance.

It is noteworthy that after the birth of Solomon Scripture makes no further mention of David and Bathsheba's relationship until David lies dying. At that point, another woman—a very young woman, specifically chosen for her beauty—is attending to his needs. Bathsheba's once-unparalleled beauty is not powerful enough to sustain her position by David's side.

A Beauty That Lasts

As Christian women we want to rediscover the power of true beauty—the beauty of inner loveliness. True inner beauty comes from righteousness, wisdom, devotion, obedience, and godliness—inner qualities that have eternal rewards. Keeping our focus on God and on the future He has for us is the key to letting Him develop this true beauty within us. It is also the key to keeping our perspective on the meaning and value of true beauty.

There are only a handful of women in the Bible who are described as physically beautiful. Abigail and Queen Esther are two of them. Both women's stories were given to us as an illustration of women who used their beauty—coupled with discernment—to achieve God's purposes.

Esther, of course, was the gorgeous young Israelite woman who married a Persian king, Xerxes, and, through her astute and careful interaction with him, saved the Jews from annihilation. Her looks and position never turned her head. Her humility was exhibited by the fact that, even after she was made queen, she still followed the wise instructions of her Uncle Mordecai, who had raised her after her parents died.

At the risk of her life, she went unbidden into the presence of the king to request an audience with him and ultimately to ask that he lift the death sentence all the Jews had been placed under. Not only was she bold enough to face death, she was also wise and strategic in her method of approaching the king. The result was the salvation of her people. As we shall see shortly, this stands in sharp contrast to how Bathsheba's life ended. In Bathsheba's life, we see the danger inherent in beauty when good judgment is lacking.

Abigail, too, is introduced as a woman of beauty and "good understanding." When her husband offended King David, endangering the entire household with his stupidity and evil wickedness, the servants ran immediately to Abigail! They knew she was a wise woman.

Abigail went to David, and, with winsome words and gifts of food, she soothed his fury. "Blessed be the Lord God of Israel who sent you to meet me!" cried King David. "And blessed is your advice and blessed are you, because you have kept me this day from coming to bloodshed and from avenging myself with my own hand." God Himself punished Abigail's wicked husband with death. Following his death, David married Abigail, and she became the mother of his second son.[214]

These women were beautiful. But more importantly, they were wise and devoted to God. They were women willing to be obedient to His call on their lives and willing to risk their safety to pursue righteousness boldly. It was their qualities of sacrifice and obedience that enabled them to become powerful women—women with a different kind of strength. And these qualities can bring true inner beauty to our lives as well. As women of God, we can resist the temptation to follow the secular pattern of making the pursuit of outward beauty the priority of our lives and a consuming pursuit of our everyday endeavors.

The ancient, golden-voiced orator, John Chrysostom, had words of wisdom for women who desire true beauty, "Let all your zeal be directed toward making your souls comely, that they may shine forth with a brighter beauty." And 1 Timothy 2:10 advises women to adorn themselves with good deeds and a whole collection of virtues. In this verse, the apostle Paul emphasized the splendor crafted in women through spiritual discipline. What a powerful insight, reminding us that beauty comes from character!

The Path to Beauty

Even the most beautiful among us know beauty is ephemeral. Proverbs reminds us: "Charm is deceptive, and beauty is fleeting."[215] Beauty can be wiped out in moments by an accident or disease. And, inevitably, with age beauty fades.

Or does it? There is an old saying that after 40 we all have the face we've earned! Think for a moment of the most beautiful woman you've ever known. For some of us, the image that appears in our mind's eye is not a youthful one. The face has a forehead that has been creased by trouble and kissed by fortune. The face of incomparable beauty is hard-won and has laugh lines around the eyes—eyes that have endured pain and sorrow, that have witnessed many more triumphs; eyes that give us *not* the fresh promise of the beginning, but eyes that reflect the quiet content of the end. They are eyes that turn our gaze toward the eternal.

On the other hand, we all know women who were beautiful in their youth, but who, in their old age, have let bitterness and anger become frozen into the lines of their faces. Sharp words and a sour disposition often determine the characteristics of their interaction with others.

Ruth Baird Shaw wrote a poem, "The Old Woman in My Future," that beautifully captures the choice that confronts us all:

Someday, somehow, somewhere in time
She's waiting, I will see
An old woman, time is making
Time is making, out of me!

Will she be a sad complainer,
A fretful tenant of the earth?
Or a kind, productive person
Filled with happiness and mirth?

Please be patient, God is making
Molding slowly, out of me
A shining portrait, He has promised.
Just you wait and see.

He is smoothing out the roughness
Polishing the dreary places
Filling life with joy and gladness
Pouring out His gifts and graces.

God remake me, in Your image.
I want to like her, when I see
That old woman, time is making.
Time is making, out of me!
—RUTH BAIRD SHAW, 1984

How, then, do we get a proper perspective of beauty? That is a difficult task in a culture that is as beauty obsessed as ours. Can we appreciate beauty as a gift of God while avoiding the snares we shall see entangled Bathsheba?

Our study of the biblical stories of these five women of Christ's genealogy has increased enormously our appreciation for the subtle meanings that are often conveyed in terse words and in the sequencing of events in the biblical accounts. Most writers romanticize the encounter between David and Bathsheba. They picture Bathsheba as an eager participant in the liaison, at the very least—if not as a seductress who deliberately enticed David.

In our imaginary account, however, we portray the relationship between David and Bathsheba as the powerful taking advantage of the powerless. This interpretation can be supported with the details that are part of the biblical account.[216] Scripture gives no indication of Bathsheba's feelings, but it does show that she suffered, along with David, from God's judgment. And because God blessed them with another son, we believe that Bathsheba repented—just as David did when confronted with the sin.

Bathsheba's dreams died. Her dream for love, and marriage, and children ended in the death of her husband, Uriah, and then again in the death of her firstborn child with David. Yet, she had the blessing of a second chance.

Somewhere in the quiet of an intimate moment, David, her king and lover, promised that someday their son would sit upon the throne of Israel. This was an unparalleled honor. David had many wives and a full complement of ambitious sons from whom to choose his successor. But there was something about Bathsheba. In the enjoyment of her physical beauty, David had found something deeper—a companionship that compelled him to make her his queen and her son his heir. God, too, could have chosen another woman to fulfill His plans, but, with her repentance, God restored Bathsheba and placed Uriah's wife in the genealogy.

God offers us a second chance as well. When our dreams die, and we face an uncertain future that appears empty—as Tamar did, or as Rahab, or as Ruth, or as Bathsheba did on that moonlit night when David set his plan in motion—we can harden our hearts in anger and bitterness and resist God's pruning, or we can turn our hearts toward the Lover of our soul.

In Leo Tolstoy's great novel *War and Peace*, there is a haunting scene where a group of Russian soldiers in the Napoleonic wars of 1808 gather at a campfire. Tolstoy describes the bloody horror of the battles raging around the soldiers. Yet there they sit, enjoying a brief respite. It is a time of reminiscing and of telling tales of "moral beauty." How fascinating. They are surrounded by the ugliness of war, yet they sit in their haven celebrating the beauty that God can develop within those whose hearts are turned to Him.

We live today in the midst of a culture that spends, literally, billions of dollars to achieve physical beauty. Yet our inner spirit remains uncultivated and distracted by trivial desires and withers from neglect. Tolstoy's tale of good and evil is a vivid and poignant reminder that, unlike physical beauty, inner beauty is nourished by those deep, moral streams that can feed the soul and sustain us in the midst of the world's ugliness.

Our prayer is that you will accept the grace God offers us through Jesus—grace to transform our hearts and thus our countenances so that, regardless of our external features, others will see Christ shining through us. For only He can create in us a beauty that is truly radiant and lasting. Only He can create in us beauty that is a different kind of strength.

The Power of Endurance

And we pray this in order that you may live a life
worthy of the Lord and may please him in every way:
bearing fruit in every good work,
growing in the knowledge of God,
being strengthened with all power
according to his glorious might
so that you may have great endurance and patience.
COLOSSIANS 1:10,11 NIV

The story of David and Bathsheba has many facets: beauty…temptation…lust…sin…confrontation…confession…repentance…forgiveness…judgment…mercy…restoration.

With all of these elements, Bathsheba's story should have ended in triumph and joy. After all, she and David experienced the miracle of God's forgiveness and restoration. And they had the incredible joy of being blessed with a second son after losing the first, who died so tragically after Nathan confronted David about his sin. But the final chapter in the life of Bathsheba, though vital for our instruction, is not a happy story. Further, its themes are not consistent with godly feminine strength and power.

Instead, the end of Bathsheba's story is sad and a little pathetic in its banality. A woman who captivated a king and secured a kingdom for her son ends in ignominy. Bathsheba did not endure. The glory of her beauty and the wonder of God's forgiveness in giving her another son, Solomon, are overshadowed by her foolishness at the height of her power—her life illustrates a tragic cycle: threat…victory…pride…oblivion. Her dreams had been revived, only to end in ashes.

First, Bathsheba got the oft-desired second chance in life, but she squandered the opportunity. Her example reminds us that though we obtain forgiveness, it is yet possible to self-destruct.

Second, Bathsheba was the only one of the five women included in Matthew's genealogy to attain a position of power. *And* she was also the only one to end up disgraced. With all of the preeminence given in our culture to attaining positions of influence, these two seemingly contradictory facts are worth pondering. Indeed, we need to analyze and try to understand what went wrong in Bathsheba's life that caused her life to end so pathetically.

It is worthwhile to look at the closing chapters of Bathsheba's life because life is a race, and the final laps are important ones. There is no triumph in starting strong and being favored to win. The victory is in reaching the finish line in triumph. If we are to claim God's victorious power in our lives, we must be faithful, endure, and persevere to the end.

> Let us run with perseverance the race marked out for us. Let us fix our eyes on Jesus, the author and perfecter of our faith, who for the joy set before him endured the cross, scorning its shame, and sat down at the right hand of the throne of God. Consider him who endured such opposition from sinful men, so that you will not grow weary and lose heart (HEBREWS 12:1-3 NIV).

There are numerous instances in the apostle Paul's writings where he utilizes the imagery of running a race to instruct us regarding Christian endurance. In the race of life, however, we are not in competition with others for the crown. The crown is available to us all. Our struggle is with ourselves and against our common enemy, the deceiver. Therefore, our battle is with the external and internal forces that would confound and neutralize or defeat us.

To the human eye, paradoxes abound. The law is the law. The God of Scripture is a holy God who pronounces judgment on sin. Yet God is also plenteous in mercy and slow to anger. Even so, it is made abundantly clear that we must not presume upon His grace. Further, we must face the fact that though the merciful Father does not reject us when we cry out to Him in repentance, He does not exempt us any more than He did David from the consequence of our disobedience. God's justice requires accountability; His judgments are unsearchable.[217] He is the one God who describes Himself as faithful and true. "I am He," God says, "who searches the minds and hearts" (Revelation 2:23 NASB). Godliness is about faithfulness and truth "in the innermost parts" (see Proverbs 20:27,28). "I know your works," God says.

The last recorded events—the "works"—of Bathsheba's life are particularly sad. She manages to snatch defeat from the jaws of victory. Bathsheba's final scenes have two interrelated preludes, and each stems from the aging King David's failing condition in his last days.

The Glory of a Woman's Influence

In the first prelude, we learn that when David was old he could not keep warm even with extra covers over him. So his servants said to the king, "Let us look for a young virgin to attend the king and take care of him. She can lie beside him so that our lord the king may keep warm."[218] They searched throughout Israel for a beautiful girl and found Abishag, a Shunammite, and brought her to the king. Abishag was very beautiful. She took care of the king and waited on him. But he never knew her intimately.

In the second prelude, the prophet Nathan came to visit Bathsheba during a time of tumult. David's son Adonijah had declared himself king. The prophet counseled Bathsheba to go to David and tell him what was happening in order to save her life and the life of her son, Solomon. Following Nathan's instructions, Bathsheba went to David and said, "My lord the king, did you not swear to me your servant: 'Surely Solomon your son shall be king after me, and he will sit on my throne?' Why then has Adonijah become king?"[219]

Next, Nathan came in to see David and confirmed what Bathsheba had said. David responded by ordering the priest to anoint Solomon as king and place him on the throne. When Adonijah heard this news, he rushed to the temple for sanctuary. He caught hold of the horns of the altar and begged, "Let King Solomon swear to me today that he will not put his servant to death with the sword."[220] Solomon replied, "If he shows himself to be a worthy man, not a hair of his head will fall to the ground; but if evil is found in him, he will die."[221]

Then Solomon sent men who brought Adonijah down from the altar. Adonijah came and bowed down to King Solomon. Whereupon Solomon said, "Go to your home."[222]

What a glorious example of a wife's positive influence on her husband! In this instance, Bathsheba used her position to encourage King David to do the right thing, and David's humble heart responded in obedience. He honored the pledge that he had made to her before God.

Bathsheba Loses Perspective

Now the curtain rises on the dramatic conclusion of the story of Bathsheba's life. After these sad events there is no further record of her. This one who began so well was not able to finish the race set before her. Adonijah comes on the scene once more—and trips her up as she heads into the final lap.

Rather than remain at home out of sight and out of trouble, Adonijah hatched another scheme. He knew of Bathsheba's role in convincing David to have Solomon installed as king. Hoping to improve his standing in the court, Adonijah went to Bathsheba, assured her that he came in peace, and played the role of supplicant. He persuaded her that he desired and needed her help. Pleased by his deference to her, she agreed to hear him out.

"As you know," he told her, "the kingdom was mine. All Israel looked to me as their king. But things changed, and the kingdom went to my brother, for it has come to him from the LORD. Now I have one request to make of you. Do not refuse me" (1 Kings 2:14-16 NIV).

"You may make it," she answered...apparently relishing her newly elevated position as the Queen Mother.

So Adonijah continued, "Please ask King Solomon—he will not refuse you—to give me Abishag the Shunammite as my wife."[223]

"Very well," Bathsheba replied. Obviously flattered by his acknowledgment that she had access to and influence with the king, she accepted Adonijah's overture immediately. She did not seek wise counsel. She did not ponder the merits of the request. She did not consider the ramifications, nor did she wonder about Adonijah's motivation. She quickly replied, "I will speak to the king for you."[224]

How incredible! Her foolish, irresponsible, impulsive response meant that Bathsheba chose sides *against* her own son!

When Bathsheba went to Solomon to speak for Adonijah, the king stood up to meet her, bowed down to her, and sat down on his throne. Then, he had a throne brought in for his mother. Thus, Bathsheba sat in a prestigious position. She was at King Solomon's right hand.

It must have been a heady experience! She was at the height of power, and all the court could see her exalted position. She was no longer just one among David's many wives. She was now seated on a throne beside her very own son, Solomon...*King* Solomon!

Then, inexplicably, she proceeds down an incredibly foolish path.

"I have one small request to make of you," she said to Solomon. "Please do not refuse me."

The king replied, "Make your request, my mother; I will not refuse you."

So she said, "Let Abishag the Shunammite be given in marriage to your brother, Adonijah."

Stunned by her request, King Solomon answered his mother, "Why do you request Abishag for Adonijah? You might as well request the kingdom for him—after all, he is my older brother."

Then Solomon swore by the Lord: "May God deal with me, be it ever so severely, if Adonijah does not pay with his life for this request! And now, as surely as the LORD lives—he shall be put to death today!"[225]

Why indeed would Bathsheba make such a foolish request? She surely knew court intrigue and understood matters of succession because she had been married to King David and because her son was now king. How could she not see that a marriage between Adonijah and Abishag would give the appearance that Adonijah was the successor to his father, King David? Did she not understand that such an action would strengthen his claim to the throne? He was, after all, older than Solomon and had many supporters. Solomon immediately understood the implications of his mother's request.

We cannot know Bathsheba's motivation. There is no logical explanation. However, her foolishness would appear to be one of two things. First, it could have been ego. She could have been so enthralled by her newly elevated position that she heedlessly seized upon the first opportunity to be seen by all in the court as a person of importance and influence.

Alternatively, it could have been jealousy. She could have been so terribly jealous of the beautiful young woman who had been brought in to care for David that she was determined to get her rival out of the palace…whatever the cost.

Either, or both, of these motivations could have clouded her judgment.

Bathsheba had but one moment on the throne beside her son, and she turned it from glory to ignominy by foolishly flaunting and squandering her power.

This account is the last mention of Bathsheba by name in Scripture. Though she is mentioned in Christ's genealogy, the account in Matthew refers to her, not by name, but as "the one who had been Uriah's wife." Interesting. No mention of her as David's wife. No mention of her as Solomon's mother. She "had been Uriah's wife." What a world of implication and tragedy is in that statement!

Running the Race

Bathsheba's humiliating end leaves us with some very pertinent messages for today's women—lessons that will help us as we strive to endure to the end of the race…and win the prize.

We are told in Scripture that we should "forget what is behind and strain toward what is ahead" in order to win the prize for which God has called us. Further, we are given even more specific instructions for running the race successfully. We are to live up to the level we have already attained and join with others who are following Christ's example. Why? Because there are times when our motivation and faithfulness will wane or falter—times when we will need to be buoyed up by fellow believers.

We are to pattern our lives after Christ. Our aim is not this world. Rather, we are to live for Him and for the crown that He will give us when we enter His presence and see Him face-to-face. "Blessed is the man who endures temptation," wrote James, "for when he has been approved, he will receive the crown of life which the Lord has promised to those who love Him."[226] We are to rejoice and let our faith and commitment be evident to all who come in contact with us. We are told to bring our prayers and petitions to God in times of need. We are to guard our hearts and minds at all times by thinking on good things—the noble, right, pure, lovely, and admirable. We are, above all, to put excellence and praiseworthiness into practice.

Aim for eternity. This is a high goal, indeed, but one sure to hold us steady—even in the worst turbulence and buffeting of the winds of trouble, tragedy, or pain.[227] Paul wrote to Timothy to remind us, as one who knew firsthand, that "all who desire to live godly in Christ Jesus will suffer persecution." Paul was writing from a prison cell. Yet after cataloguing his suffering, he concluded that, "out of them all the Lord delivered me."

That is real faith! That is real endurance! Even while yet in prison, Paul was rejoicing in the Lord's provision. In Hebrews 5:13,14 we are told that "living on milk" is for infants and that as adults, we should be on "solid food." Further, we are cautioned that those who are mature will maintain a diet of solid food in order to be "trained themselves to distinguish good from evil."

Later, we are instructed that the only way to keep from "falling away" in the race is to "show this same diligence to the very end, in order to make your hope sure." We are warned against becoming lazy and advised to "imitate those who through faith and patience inherit what has been promised." This hope is, we are promised, "an anchor for the soul, firm and secure."[228]

So our training must rise above the level of "elementary teachings about Christ." Instead, we are to go on to maturity. All of us have wondered at how easy it is to know the will of God early in our Christian lives. Usually, there is an open or a closed door, and the choice is relatively simple: We either go through an open door to seize an available opportunity or stop because a door has been closed, eliminating that option.

But, as we mature, decision making often becomes more complicated. It becomes increasingly more difficult to choose. Making wise decisions requires prayer and discernment to determine God's leading because our choices are often no longer simple. Because the enemy will most certainly supply tempting trifles to trip us up, we must diligently develop our abilities to know and understand God's leading. Endurance, persevering to the prize of God's calling, requires that we train by saturating our minds with scriptural truth and by developing our heart's sensitivity to God's still quiet voice so that we may carefully follow His leading in our lives.

And what is the "gain" when we apply these principles? These disciplines are the way we prepare ourselves to react in a godly way to what Shakespeare called the "slings and arrows of outrageous fortune."

None of us can know what the future will require of us. We all know friends or loved ones who live with tragedy or pain. While their load is extraordinarily heavy, each of us will face some challenge to our faith. Each of us will reach a crisis point at some time in our Christian walk. As C. S. Lewis put it: "God whispers to us in our pleasure, speaks in our conscience, but shouts in our pains; it is His megaphone to rouse a deaf world."[229]

Only those determined to live Christ's way and who have trained their hearts and minds will be able to persevere through the "pains" with endurance to win the prize. If we miss the prize, we will have missed it all.

Crossing the Finish Line

Isn't that what endurance boils down to? Holding steady and experiencing God's grace and power during adversity and challenges are at the heart of endurance. Coaches often challenge athletes to "keep on pressing on" by telling the story of Florence Chadwick, a swimmer whose goal was to break a record by swimming the 26-mile stretch from Catalina Island to California in 1952. Florence endured the cold, the fog, and shark attacks for 25½ miles. Just a half mile from the shore, she quit. When she discovered that she had almost reached her goal, she was devastated. Florence learned a lesson about endurance from that experience, however. She later went on to become the first woman ever to swim the English Channel in both directions.

We need to persevere, like the Thessalonians of the early church, and become an inspiration and standard-setter. We need to aspire to be worthy of Paul's words, "We always thank God for all of you, mentioning you in our prayers. We continually remember before our God and Father your work produced by faith, your labor prompted by love, and your endurance inspired by hope in our Lord Jesus Christ....You became imitators of us and of the Lord; in spite of severe suffering, you welcomed the message with the joy given by the Holy Spirit. And so you became a model to all the believers in Macedonia and Achaia [and everywhere!]."[230]

Do you not know that in a race all the runners run,
but only one gets the prize?
Run in such a way as to get the prize.
Everyone who competes in the game goes into strict training.
They do it to get a crown that will not last;
but we do it to get a crown that will last forever.
Therefore I do not run like a man running aimlessly;
I do not fight like a man beating the air.
No, I beat my body and make it my slave
so that after I have preached to others,
I myself will not be disqualified for the prize.
1 CORINTHIANS 9:24-27 NIV

When Life Seems Overwhelming

The Power of Purity
The Power of Humility

Mary

When Life Seems Overwhelming

*M*ary was happier than she had ever been. She could not wait to get home to tell her mother about the progress Joseph was making on the furniture he was building for the little house they would live in after they were married. It had been a perfect day. As she walked she noticed the sun sinking through a bank of clouds, creating one of the most beautiful sunsets she had ever seen.

As soon as she entered her home, Mary rushed into the kitchen, filling the air with details of the chest for her things, a table for her to work on, and the bed. Her mother's faint smile at the mention of the bed made Mary blush furiously as the memory of her mother's recent instructions about the duties of a wife flashed into her mind. Hannah quickly busied herself with her work on the evening meal and pretended not to notice Mary's crimson cheeks.

Mary's happiness moved Hannah so that she felt tears welling up in her eyes. Hannah had all but given up the hope of having a child when she had finally conceived. Mary had been a gift from God. She had filled their lives with so much joy that Hannah ached to think of the gaping void the approaching wedding day would bring to their home.

Joseph was a wonderful young man, and Hannah was confident he would be a devoted husband. Even so, it was hard to let go of this heaven-sent child who had filled the house with songs and laughter. Hannah cherished her memories of Mary as a little girl, and now the thought of her daughter being ready to take on the responsibilities and burdens of womanhood was not easy for a mother to accept. Mary caught a glimpse of her mother's burning heart and pretended not to see her tears.

The night was uncommonly still. Mary lay awake for a long time thinking and planning. It was so quiet she could hear the deep, steady breathing of her father in the next room.

Then, without warning, the stillness was contested. One instant all was dark and calm, and then something luminous very quietly began to intrude. At first it was faint—like when her mother would move through the house in the night with her small oil lamp, walking very softly so as not to awaken her father. Then, very quickly, the room was suffused with light as the dim glow turned as brilliant as silver reflecting the sun. Mary blinked rapidly, trying to adjust to the full force of the dazzling change. When the form of someone standing in her room came into focus, she was too terrified to make a sound. At that moment she heard a voice—a voice more beautiful than any music she had ever heard—saying, "Hail, thou that art highly favored, the Lord is with thee: blessed art thou among women" (Luke 1:28 KJV).

Hearing these curious, exalted words of greeting, her fear melded into confusion. Mary could not begin to guess who her visitor might be or to understand the purpose of the visit. Like the sound of the voice, the beauty of the form was too incredible for words. As she tried to fathom the meaning of the greeting, she noted that the being's countenance appeared as gracious as his words. He had not moved any closer than when she had first seen him.

Curiously, her terror was dissipating, and her confusion was turning into wonder. One thing seemed certain: Her visitor was not a human being! He seemed to sense when she had absorbed the greeting and was prepared for him to speak further. Realizing this, she felt a rising sense of eager anticipation. The jubilation of Gabriel's tone lifted her spirit as she heard him continue, "Fear not, Mary: for thou hast found favor with God. And, behold, thou shalt conceive in thy womb, and bring forth a son, and thou shalt call his name Jesus. He shall be great, and shall be called the Son of the Highest: and the Lord God shall give unto him the throne of his father David: and he shall reign over the house of Jacob forever; and of his kingdom there shall be no end" (Luke 1:30-33 KJV). Though she couldn't remember moving, Mary realized when the visitor paused that she was now sitting up.

The room seemed full to bursting from the light radiating from the figure. This magnificent presence could only be a heavenly being, an angel. Gradually she became aware that her fear had turned to wonder as an overwhelming feeling of peace enveloped her.

Mary stared at her visitor for several moments. She was relieved that he did not seem the least bit impatient with her as she struggled to take in all he had said. His message left her puzzled at the very thought that she had found favor with God. Her mind seemed curiously detached as she replayed his words and tried to fathom the mystery of their meaning.

She knew her parents had waited a very long time before they had been able to have a child. Was the angel telling her that when she married Joseph she would not have a problem conceiving? "A son," he had said, "and you shall call his name Jesus," he added firmly. *It is a beautiful name,* she thought. *But, of course, it is not a family name. Will Joseph like it,* she wondered?

Her mind raced on to Joseph. Joseph would be so happy to have a son. And Mary was certain he was going to be a wonderful father. In her mind's eye, she could see Joseph's strong hands steadying the tools in their little boy's hands as he taught the child how to shape the wood and join it carefully together.

Then it struck her. The angel had not said, "You and Joseph are going to have a son." He had said only, "You will conceive in your womb...the Son of the Most High."

Puzzled, and with a growing sense of consternation, Mary's thoughts floundered. How could what the angel was saying be true? She could not conceive. She was not yet married. She was still a virgin. She started at the visitor's movements. He seemed to be nodding in agreement with her. Yet, as far as she could tell, her lips had not moved. Neither had her voice made a sound. Had she spoken to the angel? Was she awake?

Then God's messenger spoke again. This time, however, his tone was compelling, and he spoke very deliberately, accenting each word with great clarity and force, "The Holy Ghost shall come upon thee, and the power of the Highest shall overshadow thee: therefore also that holy thing which shall be born of thee shall be called the Son of God" (verse 35 KJV). The angel had been so intense that Mary was relieved when he paused for a moment to let his words sink in and to be certain, from her expression, that she had understood him exactly. When he continued at last, his tone was once again warm and gentle, "Behold thy cousin Elizabeth, she hath also conceived a son in her old age: and this is the sixth month with her, who was called barren. For with God nothing shall be impossible" (verses 36,37).

Bewildered and astonished, Mary stared at the angel. He seemed to be waiting patiently for her to respond. The Son of God? The Messiah? Surely she was dreaming. How could this be?

Many devout Hebrews dreamed of the coming of the Messiah...but mostly in the distant future. Like other Hebrew girls, she had tried to imagine being chosen to be the mother of the Messiah. But, of course, those had only been idle musings. Yet now there was no question as to Gabriel's message, "Thou shalt conceive in thy womb...the Son of the Highest...and the holy thing which shall be born of thee shall be called the Son of God."

Quietly her visitor waited.

Where her answer came from, Mary wasn't quite sure. Her mind was too stunned by all that she had just been told to frame a reply. But her heart, the "heart for God" that had been nurtured in her since her birth, lifted its song of obedience, "Behold, the handmaid of the Lord," Mary whispered. "Be it unto me accordingly to thy word."

Then the angel vanished.

Listening intently for any sound, Mary's eyes swept the room. She searched for evidence that what she had experienced had been real. Then, in the silence and darkness that followed the angel's departure, Mary felt the presence of God surrounding her and filling the room.

God's presence was as warm as the noonday sun, yet He could not be seen. His presence was as perceptible as an earsplitting clap of thunder, yet it made no sound. Her mind was mute with awe, but her spirit felt an exhilarating freedom such as she had never experienced before.

In an instant the glory of the Lord dispelled the darkness, illuminating everything. Every nook and cranny was ablaze. Her spirit overflowed with joy and peace and began to rise and sing. Her mind tried to understand the words of her spirit's song, but the meaning was beyond her grasp. Strong as an earthquake yet soft as a gentle breeze, Mary felt the Holy Spirit come upon her. At that moment she heard the simple melody of her heart change to harmony, and her spirit soared.

Sensing the power of the Highest overshadow her, her mind reeled. Her senses were awash with feelings unlike anything that she had ever known. Mary was totally overwhelmed. Shaken, she gasped for breath, and her song turned into tears of joy.

In that divinely appointed moment, the Prince of Glory left heaven. Time was cleft by eternity. The Word who was in the beginning with God, the One by whom all things were made, the Life and Light of the world, the Only Begotten of the Father, the Lamb of God was clothed in human flesh and conceived in Mary's womb.

Her strength spent, Mary lay quietly. She again became aware of the passage of time measured by the rhythmical beating of her heart. Her soul, mind, and body seemed once again to be intertwined in a complete whole. She lay there a long time in wonder and awe before she began to perceive God's Presence slowly receding from the room. Though she longed to, she could not hold on to her acute sense of God's Presence, still the glory lingered...for she now carried in her body the very Son of God.

Mary was completely awash in her memories of the night's mysteries. From this moment on, there was no room for doubt that the angel's message had been fulfilled. As incredible as it seemed, she knew that these events were no mere dream. In the morning she might question whether she had really been awake, if the vision had been real, but at this moment she felt more awake, more alive than she had ever been in her entire life.

Mary lay there replaying all that had happened and pondered it in her heart. She wanted desperately to capture in memory every single, precious detail. She looked around the room to see if there were any changes. She could see very little in the darkness that now wrapped itself around her, but what she could see indicated that nothing had been disturbed.

Yet something *had* changed! She held on fiercely to the words of Gabriel, "Thou shalt conceive in thy womb, and bring forth a son, and shalt call his name Jesus. He shall be great, and shall be called the Son of the Highest: and the Lord God shall give unto him the throne of his father David: and he shall reign over the house of Jacob forever; and of his kingdom there shall be no end." How could it be that her life would never again be the same—and yet nothing had been disturbed?

Everything else might appear to be the same...for now. But *she* was different, and everything else was profoundly changed as well even though the effects weren't yet visible. Now she bore in her womb an infant king, conceived by the Holy Spirit.

Mary's breathing was no longer ragged. She felt an overpowering thirst. She eased off of her bed and moved as quietly as she could through the darkened house, trying not to disturb her mother, who had never failed to hear her cries in the night. She managed to find a cup in the darkness, but her hands trembled as she tried to fill it with water. Then she saw the faint light of an oil lamp. As always, her mother was coming to care for her. Relieved, she welcomed her mother's arms around her.

"Mary, you are ill?" Hannah asked fretfully. "Your skin is clammy, and you're trembling. You shouldn't be out of bed. You should have called me."

"Mother, I love you so much. Thank you for coming to me," Mary said softly, trying not to awaken her father, "but I'm really not sick. That's not the problem."

At that moment, she saw her father enter the room. He looked distressed at the sight of her—pale and talking about having a problem. She took a drink from the cup her mother had filled for her, then she hesitated, knowing that what she was about to say would not strike nearly so responsive a chord with her mother as with her father.

"I had a vision." She paused and looked at the floor. "An angel appeared to me." Mary suddenly realized that she had launched into this accounting without time to think it through. Now she wondered if she was supposed to tell anyone what the angel had said to her.

Sensing her hesitation, Jonadab took her hand and asked quietly, "Did you understand what the angel said to you?"

"Well, yes," she replied. "But he said some things that are hard to explain. There was one thing in particular, Mother, that you will be very happy to hear."

Her mother, who was not nearly as sympathetic as her father to the idea of visions and angels, asked a little stiffly, "And what is that, dear?"

Mary drank the rest of the water in the cup, handed it back to her mother, and asked for more. Jonadab was relieved to see the color coming back into her face. Gathering her thoughts, Mary plunged ahead saying, "Mother, the angel told me that in spite of her age, Elizabeth has conceived and is going to have a baby boy. She is already in her sixth month. Can you believe that?"

Her mother dropped the cup to the floor. Mary was so surprised to see that it did not break that she missed what Jonadab saw—his wife's bewildered look and her face turned ashen. As Hannah stumbled to a chair, he caught her by the shoulders and helped her sit down.

"Mother, what is the matter? I thought you would be happy," Mary moaned.

"Hush, child. I'm okay. I am happy. Now you two stop your fussing over me. I could use some of that water, though. Did the cup break when I dropped it? That was so foolish of me. I don't know what happened to me." Mary picked up the cup as her mother kept talking aimlessly, saying nothing. Washing it off and refilling it from the jug nearby, she handed the cup of water to her mother.

Jonadab looked at Hannah thoughtfully. Then very firmly he said to her, "Hannah, you do know why you dropped the cup. I've never known you to not know what was bothering you. Tell us what has upset you so."

Hannah offered no resistance and answered immediately, "Jonadab, I would have told you earlier over supper, but Mary came in so excited about all of the wonderful things Joseph was making that it just didn't seem like the right time. Just this afternoon while Mary was visiting Joseph, a message arrived from Judea. It was from Elizabeth… she is pregnant…and in her sixth month."

They were all silent as the significance of the information sunk in.

Finally, Hannah continued, "I suppose Elizabeth hasn't heard of the wedding yet, because she sent word to ask if Mary could come and take care of her during the last three months of her pregnancy."

Taken aback by all of these midnight revelations, Jonadab struggled to put together a sensible response—not only to Mary's account, but also to the miraculous news from Elizabeth. "I don't know what we should do about Elizabeth's request. Joseph has waited so long to marry Mary. I don't think it's fair to ask him to wait any longer. I would be embarrassed to ask him to postpone the wedding now," he finally responded.

Hannah broke into Jonadab's rambling. "Besides, what would everyone in the village think? Still, I don't see how we can say no to Elizabeth either. If I were able, I would go myself."

"No, no, Mother," Mary cut in, "that wouldn't do. I'm the one who needs to go."

Jonadab was eager to pursue a conversation with Mary about her encounter, but realized he had to first think about the practicalities of the moment. "Do you want me to speak to Joseph in the morning, or do you want to discuss this with him yourself?" he asked Mary gently.

The thought of talking to Joseph stirred Mary's emotions into a turmoil. Jonadab saw the frantic look on her face and wondered if something had happened between her and Joseph.

"I think it would probably be best if I talked to him. Would you like that?" he volunteered.

Mary nodded a yes as her eyes welled up with tears.

Jonadab stood up and put his arms around his daughter, knowing that words were useless at a time like this. Mary laid her head on his shoulder, and he could feel her weeping softly. He looked at Hannah for guidance, but she only raised her hands emptily and shook her head.

After a few moments, Hannah rose and took Mary in her arms. Though she experienced her own share of heartache and disappointment, she thought there could be no greater pain than seeing your child's heart hurting. She led Mary back to her room where she sat with her as she had done so many times when she was a child. Hannah patted her brow until she felt Mary go limp at last with sleep.

Hannah kissed her child as she gently laid her head to rest. In her heart, she softly prayed that the morning light would bring with it the peace of knowing that she was being true to her duty in going to care for Elizabeth and that this knowledge would erase some of this night's pain and confusion.

The first day of the journey passed uneventfully. Mary talked about everything she could think of…except what was really on her mind. They had risen before daybreak in order to travel as far as possible before stopping to rest from the midday heat. Jonadab took the route that went south and east to follow the Jordan Valley. It was not as direct as the route leading straight through Samaria, but this way eliminated the steep hills until the end of the journey, when they would have to climb into the Judean hills from down in the Jordan Valley. Either route, the ascent in these hills was a climb of 1,500 feet!

The second day's journey was much like the first. They were making good time. Jonadab was pleased to see that Mary had recovered from her vision, if that's what it was. From his perspective, she seemed to show no ill effects.

It was the final day of their trip, and Mary was tired of riding the donkey. Early on, she had walked more than she had ridden, and now she was sore and stiff and the idea of walking again seemed a welcomed change. So when their brief rest stop was finished, she decided to walk beside her father.

As they traveled, Mary had replayed the memories of the angel's visit again and again, searching for the right words to describe to her father the parts of her vision she hadn't yet shared with him. It wasn't that she didn't want to tell him. They had always been complete confidants, and not telling her father the details of something as important as this felt like a breach of trust that made her so miserable she could not stand it. If it all just weren't so fantastic and unbelievable, it wouldn't be such a problem. *Is there any way,* she wondered, *that I can make him understand?* At last when she couldn't contain it all any longer, Mary simply blurted out, "Father, I just have to tell you something!"

Hearing the distress in her voice, Jonadab stopped so abruptly that the donkey's head bumped into his shoulder. "Whatever is the matter, Mary?" he asked as he turned to search her face with his loving eyes. He had been worried all along that this trip to Elizabeth's might be too much for her. "Are you feeling ill?" he asked gently.

"No."

"Did you drink enough water when we stopped?"

"Yes. I'm not sick, Father, but I do feel terrible. There is something I haven't told you that you need to know."

Jonadab nodded, not wanting to interrupt her. He knew his daughter, and he had been sure that her impersonal chatter for the last three days had meant that she was distracted by something. He had never known it to take this long before the dam had burst. But now that the floodgates were open, he knew if things ran true to course that she would tell him everything without much prompting.

"The other night when I saw the angel, and he told me that Elizabeth was six months pregnant, I didn't tell you everything he said to me. Things were happening so fast, and Mother was in such a state that I decided to wait until morning to tell you the rest. But then the next morning, you were up and gone to see Joseph before Mother and I were up."

Mary paused in her rapid-fire explanation and took a few deep breaths. Jonadab could tell that she was trying to get everything out at once. "When you came back and told us that Joseph had agreed to postpone the wedding, I started crying. You didn't know what to say because you knew Elizabeth needed me but..."

Mary's voice weakened, and Jonadab could see tears rolling down her cheeks. "Father, the reason I started crying then...was not what you thought. I was thinking that when Joseph found out what the angel told me that he might not want to marry me at all."

Jonadab looked at his daughter in disbelief. He knew the deep and tender love that Joseph had for her, and he recalled how patiently

Joseph had waited for her to come of age to marry. Joseph was a good man, a just man. Jonadab could not imagine his affections waning.

His thoughts were interrupted as Mary blurted out, "Father, the angel told me I was going to have a baby."

"But that's wonderful, Mary! Your mother and I will be so proud and happy when you...when you are able to have a child." Jonadab's words came awkwardly as he remembered the long, anxious years of waiting before Hannah had finally been able to conceive.

They had both been overjoyed when Mary was born. He had worried for years that she would be spoiled from their doting on her. If it hadn't been for her mother's common sense, he guessed he would have ruined her. But Mary had inherited her mother's good judgment and had never been selfish or proud. It had been a source of unending joy to him, however, that she also inherited his love for the wisdom and poetry of the Scriptures. She never seemed to tire of learning more, and she had a prodigious memory. She seemed to remember every line of Scripture he ever taught her, and she could quote more of the promises about the coming of the Messiah than most priests or rabbis.

Mary's plaintive tone cut into his thoughts, "Oh, Father, you don't understand. When the angel told me I was going to have a baby, I asked him how this could be since I'm not married and still a virgin. He answered and said to me, 'The Holy Ghost shall come upon thee, and the power of the Highest will overshadow thee.'" She paused briefly, looking for words. Then she blurted out, "Father...I'm pregnant!"

She took a deep breath and seemed ready to say something more. But, at this moment, Jonadab took her hand in his and said very gently, "Mary, take it easy. Slow down. You're pregnant?"

Jonadab was mystified and perplexed by what he was hearing. He would have liked to sit in the shade and rest his weary feet, but he knew that he shouldn't stop the momentum of the conversation. But in an effort to, at least, slow the pace of the conversation, he said, "Mary, start over again and tell me everything you can remember. Don't leave anything out—not even the tiniest detail."

Mary could tell from her father's tone that he didn't know what to make of all of this any more than she had when the angel appeared unto her. She wanted to tell him everything that she had bottled up inside for the last few days, but she realized that she needed to pace herself. She knew, too, that she needed to be as calm as possible, so she tried to talk slowly. She was confident that if anyone could tell her what to do, it would be her father. He was a kind, gentle man, and everyone in Nazareth knew him for his godliness, faith, and wisdom. During her childhood, she had watched the men of the village come to talk with him when they had problems, to ask his advice and counsel.

Mary struggled for a moment to remember exactly how the angel's greeting began. When she remembered, her modesty made her reluctant to repeat his words. She faltered. Her father, who was watching her intently now, squeezed her hand gently as he said to her, "It's okay. Take your time."

He saw her face grow pink as she stammered, "This angel…greeted me by…saying, 'Hail, thou that art highly favored, the Lord is with thee: blessed art thou among women.'"

Mary drew a deep breath and looked at her father. She hadn't known what he would think of her account of being called "blessed among women," but he did not seem upset. Despite her determination to stay calm, she hurried on, wanting to let him see that she hadn't meant to sound proud by repeating this about herself. His gaze never wavered, so she continued, "When he said that, I couldn't figure out what he could possibly mean. Then he went on and said, 'Do not be afraid, Mary; for you have found favor with God. And behold, you will conceive in your womb and bear a son, and you will name Him Jesus. He will be great and will be called the Son of the Most High; and the Lord God will give Him the throne of His father David; and He will reign over the house of Jacob forever; and His kingdom will have no end." Mary paused and looked intently at her father to assess his reaction. She still saw no hint of disapproval, only his familiar, loving smile.

"Is that all?" he asked in a knowing tone that said, "Tell me the rest."

"Well, Father," she said smiling weakly, feeling tremendously relieved to see that he didn't think she was being prideful to relate that the angel had called her "highly favored" or that he had said that God would give her son the throne of King David, "I asked the angel how this could be possible since I am still a virgin."

Jonadab suddenly took a deep breath as it finally dawned on him that the angel's words were the words of the prophet Isaiah. But before he could sort out his thoughts, his mind raced to catch up with Mary as she continued.

"Father?" she asked.

"Yes, dear," he said, "I'm sorry. I was just thinking about something you said. Go on. I'm listening."

After a moment's hesitation, she continued in a voice so soft he had to strain to hear over the clip-clop of the donkey's feet walking behind them. She continued, "The angel's answer was that the Holy Spirit would come upon me and that the power of the Most High would overshadow me. And...and," Mary paused, then said, "the angel said that the holy child I would bear would be called the...the Son of God." As she spoke, her perplexity was obvious. "I guess he could see how confused I was by this. That's when he told me about Elizabeth. And then he said 'nothing is impossible with God.' After that he stopped speaking and looked at me as if he were waiting for me to answer."

She paused. Jonadab, not wanting to interrupt this time, listened intently.

Mary began again, "The angel stood there waiting and waiting. I was trying to think what else I needed to ask so that I would know what I was supposed to do. But even though I tried as hard as I could, I couldn't think. Now I wish I had thought to ask him what I am supposed to tell Joseph."

After another moment of silence, Mary, who was now emotionally spent, continued, "Finally, I just said the only thing I knew to say. 'Behold the handmaid of the Lord; be it unto me according to thy word.' Then the angel just vanished. Father," she pleaded anxiously, "did I say the right thing?"

Jonadab felt her squeezing his hand with all of her strength. Immediately, without thinking, he heard himself answer hoarsely, "Yes, Mary, you said just the right thing."

They walked a little way in silence. Then she asked in a flat tone that indicated that she wasn't really expecting a reply, "How will I ever explain this to Joseph?" Her voice was full of despair as she answered her own question by saying, "He is never going to believe this."

She was finished for now. She was drained from the ordeal of her confession.

They walked on in silence with Mary's words ringing in his ears. "He is never going to believe this." Jonadab had held his breath fearing what her next words might be. Mercifully, those words had not come. He struggled to frame an answer to the question she had not asked. What could he have honestly said if she had asked him the question, "Father, you believe me, don't you?"

Without a doubt he believed that she was telling him exactly what she *thought* had happened. Of that much he was certain. And he had to admit that somehow she had gotten it exactly right regarding Elizabeth. But the rest of her story was so astonishing that it was hard to believe. His Mary? The mother of the Messiah? Could it possibly be?

What if she were just imagining this angel visitation? He himself had taught her the prophecies of Isaiah. If her vision were just in her imagination, then by the time she returned to Nazareth there wouldn't be any need to explain any of this to Joseph.

But even if Mary didn't have to tell Joseph that she was with child, Jonadab still had a problem. Why was his sweet Mary imagining things? He was going to have to tell Hannah about her vision—even if it weren't true.

He wished he could just wait this all out to see if Mary really was pregnant. He knew that he was going to have to come up with a way to tell Hannah everything Mary had told him. They had a long-standing disagreement over Mary because Hannah had not approved of the way he had educated their daughter. She had feared that no good would come from him filling Mary's head with the Scriptures. "Why must you persist in filling her mind with these things?" she questioned him constantly. "It's not as though she's a boy in training to be a rabbi."

Hannah would listen proudly to Mary reciting the psalms to Jonadab. But then afterwards, privately, she would complain to him that he was trying to make Mary into the son they had not been able to have. He would try to soothe his wife by pointing out that Mary could sew and cook as well as any woman in the village—except her mother, he always hastened to add.

He challenged Hannah to name one girl in Nazareth, or any other village in the world for that matter, who was more graceful and feminine than their Mary. This would temporarily silence her, but then she would always come back with the complaint that Mary had a Scripture for everything, for everything! "She sounds just like you, Jonadab," Hannah would always scold.

As they walked along, each lost in thought, Jonadab could hear Mary's voice in his mind reciting prophecy after prophecy that he had taught her about the Messiah. He knew when he told Hannah the rest of the story about Mary's angel visitation that Hannah would say, "You've crammed so much prophecy into her head that it has made her delusional."

Had Hannah been right all this time? Maybe such a tenderhearted young girl should not have been burdened with such weighty matters. Maybe it had all been too much. Maybe it had affected her mind. What had he done? How could he undo the problem he had created?

Jonadab walked along in torment at the thought that Mary's delusions were of his making. Still, he could not seem to purge from his mind the memory of a little girl's singsong voice reciting the words of Isaiah from his mind, "Therefore the Lord Himself will give you a sign; Behold, a virgin shall conceive, and bear a son, and shall call his name Immanuel. Butter and honey shall he eat, that he may know to refuse the evil and choose the good."

A sign. The prophet had said that the virgin conceiving would be a sign of the coming of the Messiah. Could it be? Could his Mary be that virgin? Could this actually be possible?

Mary broke into his thoughts by saying that she wanted to ride for a while and save her strength for the work she would need to do in the days ahead. *So practical,* he thought, *just like her mother.*

When they stopped for Mary to mount, Jonadab studied the terrain. They had been climbing now for quite some time and were well into the Judean hills. He knew from the position of the sun that very little daylight was left. But as he considered the length of the light remaining before dusk and the distance left to travel, he thought they could make it to Zacharias' house before sunset if they kept up a good pace.

The thought of Elizabeth's miracle baby raised his spirits a little. He wanted to talk with her about Mary. He knew Elizabeth to be a devout and wise woman. Perhaps she would give them both some insight. Certainly, a solution was beyond his understanding. *Besides,* he thought, *Mary needs a woman's counsel.*

A short distance from Zacharias' house, Mary asked her father to stop again so she could get down. She was tired of sitting again and wanted to walk the last little bit.

When Mary and Jonadab approached the house, no one came out to greet them. Jonadab guessed that Zacharias must be in Jerusalem at the temple and that Elizabeth would be inside resting. The donkey began braying at the smell of water, so Jonadab let it loose to drink at the animals' watering trough beside the well and to forage around the area. The animal was too tired from the journey to wander away.

As they entered the house, Mary began calling, "Elizabeth, Elizabeth. Are you here, Elizabeth?" Jonadab watched as Elizabeth walked stiffly from the back room where she had been resting. Her face was aglow with joy at the sight of Mary.

Mary and Elizabeth had a special, affectionate relationship. Mary had visited here many times before when he and Hannah had made the long trek to Jerusalem to celebrate Passover or Pentecost.

Still, as familiar as this home was, Jonadab suddenly felt strange. This time, something stopped him as he moved into the room. Mary, too, stopped abruptly. They both were startled when Elizabeth began speaking in a clear, loud voice. Her words made chills run down Jonadab's spine, "Blessed art thou among women, and blessed is the fruit of thy womb. And whence is this to me, that the mother of my Lord should come to me? For, lo, as soon as the voice of thy salutation sounded in mine ears, the babe leaped in my womb for joy. And blessed is she that believed for there shall be a performance of those things which were told her from the Lord."

Jonadab felt rooted to the spot where he stood. He watched in amazed reverence as he saw the glow of joy that he had first seen on Elizabeth's face begin to suffuse Mary's face. She stood quietly for a few moments as tears welled up in her eyes. Jonadab saw her take a deep breath and compose herself. Once again, he felt a spine-tingling chill as he heard Mary's musical voice start softly and then begin to soar:

> My soul doth magnify the Lord,
> And my spirit hath rejoiced in God my Savior.
> For he hath regarded the low estate of his handmaiden:
> For, behold, from henceforth all generations shall call me blessed.
> For he that is mighty hath done to me great things;
> And holy is his name.
> And his mercy is on them that fear him from generation to generation.
> He hath shewed strength with his arm;
> he hath scattered the proud in the imagination of their hearts.
> He hath put down the mighty from their seats,
> And exalted them of low degree.
> He hath filled the hungry with good things;
> And the rich he hath sent empty away.
> He hath helped his servant Israel,
> In remembrance of his mercy:
> As he spake to our fathers,
> To Abraham, and to his seed forever.
> (See Luke 1:46-55 KJV.)

When Mary finished, the three of them stood quietly, not wanting to let go of this rare and priceless moment. God's Holy Spirit had spoken. None of their lives would ever be the same. Both Elizabeth and Jonadab had listened many times to Mary quoting the psalms, but they had never heard anything like this from her before.

When the transcendent moment had at last ebbed away, Jonadab felt Elizabeth's eyes on him. Looking at her now, he saw a different person than he had seen moments earlier. Her countenance was again that of the gentle, modest woman he had always known. She was warm and motherly as well, despite the fact that she had never had children of her own...at least not until now. He had known Elizabeth nearly his whole life, and he remained astonished by the transformation he had seen in her a few moments earlier.

And Mary. He couldn't begin to comprehend the change he had seen in his own daughter. She was his daughter still, but now she was more than that. God had opened his eyes through Elizabeth's words, "The mother of my Lord." He was working to absorb the full meaning of her words when Elizabeth caught his gaze again and then swung her eyes to Mary.

This time he caught the meaning of her unspoken question. She wanted to know if he could place the source of Mary's song in Scripture. He replayed the words in his mind. They were all so familiar, and yet he had never heard them put together in quite that fashion.

He shook his head no and Elizabeth beamed with pleasure. Her suspicion was confirmed. The Holy Spirit had given Mary the song, a song as beautiful as any ever written by King David himself.

Later, when he was alone caring for the donkey, Jonadab remembered his journey that day with Mary. What a fool he had been. What a blind, unbelieving fool. Once again, the words of Isaiah stirred his heart, the same words that had been echoing in his mind earlier that afternoon: "Therefore the Lord Himself will give you a sign; Behold a virgin shall conceive, and bear a son, and shall call his name Immanuel."

He had always believed that God would one day fulfill this promise. He had even prayed that he might live to see the day when it was fulfilled. But never in his wildest imagination had he ever thought that his Mary might be the one chosen by God, the virgin prophesied by Isaiah. Even when she told him of the angel's words, he had not believed.

He felt ashamed. Looking back, it distressed Jonadab that he had lacked the faith to believe Mary when she told him about what the angel had said to her. If it had not been for the revelation that came through Elizabeth's words, would he have ever believed? What would he have said when it finally became obvious that Mary was pregnant? Would he have believed her story then?

Jonadab had said his goodbyes to Elizabeth, and now it was time to say goodbye to Mary. He had thought that they would have time to talk before now, but that time hadn't come. Mary had been busy taking care of Elizabeth and cleaning the house. Like her mother, she was a diligent worker and would not stop until she had things in good order.

Jonadab sought a moment to talk as preparations were made for his departure. He needed to know whether or not she wanted him to talk to Joseph. Also, he had to know what she thought he should tell Hannah when he got back.

Mary had said she didn't see any benefit from burdening her mother with all that the angel had said because there was nothing that could be done at the moment. She felt that it would be just as well to wait until she returned to talk about the upcoming birth of her baby. She thought her mother likely would just fret over whether or not Mary was actually pregnant until her condition was obvious. Considering everything, she thought it best to wait until they could all talk face-to-face. This view certainly made good sense to Jonadab. He was relieved.

And Joseph? It came as no surprise to him to hear Mary say she had been thinking about that constantly. She turned to him and looked intently into his eyes, "Father, if you couldn't believe me when I told you what the angel said, how can I expect Joseph to believe?"

"Mary, I am so..."

Mary stopped him before he could finish his apology, saying, "I don't blame you, Father. Who could believe such a fantastic story? I knew you were trying as hard as you could to believe me."

"Mary, you know me too well. I can't hide anything from you," he said, winning a heartwarming smile from her.

"Father," she continued, her face once again earnest and deadly serious, "I can't tell you what a tremendous relief it was to me when I heard the words of Elizabeth's greeting. I was holding on to the angel's words so tightly. God knew I needed her confirmation and support. He knows the struggle I am having over how I'll ever be able to face Joseph. I believe that is why He revealed to Elizabeth that the child I am carrying is the Son of God, just as the angel had said to me."

Her voice sounded strong and assured, but when he looked down, he saw that her fists were tightly clenched.

"It seems to me," she continued, "if Joseph is ever going to believe that this child is of the Holy Spirit, it will have to be because God reveals it to him. If God doesn't see fit to do that, then I don't think you or I, or anyone else, would ever be able to convince him. It was part of God's plan for Elizabeth to conceive in her old age and for me to bear a child even though I am still a virgin. So if it is part of His plan for Joseph to understand, then God can and will make that happen as well."

Jonadab wrapped his arms around her and kissed her on each cheek. "Don't get so busy taking care of Elizabeth that you neglect yourself. Send word when it is time for me to come and get you," he said.

Mary hugged her father fiercely. Releasing him, she smiled and said, "God be with you, Father." Mary warmed his heart as always. But leaving her today was a bittersweet experience. Mary was no longer a transparent child—his little girl. She would never again be *just* his daughter, for God had elevated her to an exalted status. God had chosen her for the awesome responsibility of being the mother of the long-awaited Messiah. It was such a weighty burden she had taken up so innocently...and yet so soberly.

Jonadab headed off toward the pathway with his donkey plodding behind. His head was full of the events of the last days, and his heart was full of wonder.

Mary stood there smiling and waving as he turned down the trail. Her smile was not the lighthearted smile he was used to seeing when he left her for a joyful visit with her beloved Elizabeth. Nor was it a hollow smile, for the three of them had rejoiced together from the moment they arrived, exulting at the miracle of both Elizabeth's and Mary's pregnancies.

Instead, her smile reflected her concern over the simple practicalities related to this wondrous unfathomable miracle. Pregnant and not knowing what would become of her wedding plans with Joseph, she was burdened about her uncertain future. Jonadab could see this clearly now as he thought of her smile. The somberness of this goodbye traveled with him many hours. The solitude of the journey home was made all the more sobering by contrast to the memories of Mary's presence with him on the journey to Elizabeth's. What a fool he had been not to believe her when she had at last opened her heart to him!

These thoughts made for miserable traveling companions. "Thank God," he sighed at last, "for the revelation that came through Elizabeth!" As he breathed these words of thanksgiving, the memory of Mary's beaming face lit up his mind, and he could hear her song again:

> *My soul doth magnify the Lord,*
> *And my spirit hath rejoiced in God my Savior.*
> *For he hath regarded the low estate of his handmaiden:*
> *For, behold, from henceforth all generations shall call me blessed.*
> *For he that is mighty hath done to me great things;*
> *And holy is his name.*

The memory of the heavenly glow on Mary's face in that moment made Jonadab's heavy heart cease its aching for what was past. Hard on the heels of this memory, he heard again a little girl's earnest voice reciting the words of Isaiah: "Behold a virgin shall conceive and bear a son, and shall call his name Immanuel."

His Mary...his very own Mary was the virgin who would bear the long-desired Messiah! Still, for all of this, in his heart, Mary would never stop being his little girl. What did the future hold for her? What did it hold for them all?

And, the *Messiah?!*

Immanuel...God with us!

What would this child be like, the long-awaited Messiah?

His grandson! What would He be like? IMMANUEL!

Now the birth of Jesus Christ took place in this way.
When his mother **Mary** had been betrothed to Joseph,
before they came together
she was found to be with child of the Holy Spirit;
and her husband Joseph,
being a just man and unwilling to put her to shame,
resolved to divorce her quietly.
But as he considered this, behold, an angel of the Lord
appeared to him in a dream, saying,
"Joseph, son of David, do not fear to take **Mary** your wife,
for that which is conceived in her is of the Holy Spirit;
she will bear a son, and you shall call his name Jesus,
for he will save his people from their sins."
All this took place to fulfill what the Lord had spoken
by the prophet:
"Behold, a virgin shall conceive and bear a son,
and his name shall be called Emmanuel"
(which means, God with us).
When Joseph woke from sleep,
he did as the angel of the Lord commanded him;
he took his wife,
but knew her not until she had borne a son;
and he called his name Jesus.
Matthew 1:18-25 rsv

The Power of Purity

Whatsoever things are true, whatsoever things are honest,
whatsoever things are just, whatsoever things are pure,
whatsoever things are lovely, whatsoever things are of good report;
if there be any virtue, and if there be any praise,
think on these things.
PHILIPPIANS 4:8 KJV

In ancient times St. Augustine of Hippo offered the intriguing idea that Mary first conceived Christ in her heart by faith before conceiving Him in her womb. The heart, of course, is the source of who we are. Only God knows our hearts—our inward thoughts and feelings. Scripture reminds us that, "Man looks on the outward appearance, but the LORD looks on the heart."[231] Doubtless, as God looked for the virgin who could give birth to the Son of God and nurture Him as the Son of Man, He looked for someone with a pure heart.

In common parlance, the word "pure" means to be free of dirt and foreign matter. It can also mean to be clean and free of filth and iniquity. Either meaning carries the implication that nothing is in the mix that shouldn't be there. In the beatitudes, God says that those who are pure in heart—pure, not just on the surface, but all the way through to the depths of their hearts—are blessed. He found that kind of single-minded devotion in Mary, the mother of Jesus. While Scripture does not deify Mary, she was unusually worthy of honor and respect. The fact that she was chosen for this awesome responsibility means that her devotion to God and the purity of her attitudes and behaviors are an example that we should study and emulate.

At first glance, God's choice of Mary seems an odd one. She was young. She had not had much time to mature—to gain experience and develop wisdom. She was from humble circumstances. Mary lived a very ordinary life in common surroundings. A closer look, though, reveals that Mary had the qualities of heart and spirit that made her ideal for the high honor and calling to be the mother of Jesus. The pure in heart, we are told, desire God's presence in their lives. They have heard and understood the words of the psalmist: "Who shall ascend the hill of the LORD? And who shall stand in his holy place? He who has clean hands and a pure heart, who does not lift up his soul to what is false...." Their response with David is, "Create in me a clean heart, O God; and renew a right spirit within me."[232]

Let's begin by looking at Mary's reaction to that momentous night when Gabriel visited and announced that she was to be the mother of the Messiah, the Son of God.

A Servant's Heart

Some depictions of Mary's encounter with the angel place emphasis solely on the elements of spiritual ecstasy. Yet Mary's reaction throughout was also characterized by clear reason and solid logic. We can compare Mary's encounter with the angel to that of others in Scripture who interacted with angels, such as Moses, Jonah, and Jacob. We see that none of them was so overpowered that they were incapable of reasoning, even arguing—or as in the case of Jacob, wrestling—over the instructions that were given to them. Neither was Mary.

Mary was lucid enough in the presence of the heavenly being to understand what she was being told and to ask legitimate and reasonable questions. For instance, she asked the most basic question: How she, as a virgin, could have a baby. When we read her conversation with the angel, it sounds as coherent as that between any two humans. The type of questions she asked revealed her simple trust in and reliance upon God. It was obvious that, to her, God's goodness was so complete that she just expected Him to provide all that would be needed. So she didn't have to ask further questions or try to negotiate any conditions before accepting His plan.

Hers was a simple trust that flowed from a pure heart and from a knowledge of God. She stated plainly and without any apparent reservations, "I am the Lord's servant....May it be to me as you have said" (NIV). Her response provides us with a perfect example of what it means to be purely and completely devoted to God.

This is not to say that Mary understood all that was involved in God's plan, that she didn't have questions about how things were going to work out, or that she never had to struggle or face the temptation to doubt. After all, uncertainty and temptation are part of the human condition. Even her divine Son, Jesus, was tempted in the wilderness and had to contend with the half-truths of the enemy who tried to ensnare Him and derail Him from the mission given to Him by the Father.[233]

But when Mary needed assurance, God provided the witness of Elizabeth to strengthen her for the task that lay ahead. Her expectation that God would supply everything she needed was fulfilled completely. Unlike Moses, whose reply to God—when he encountered Him at the burning bush[234]—was, "Not me, Lord," Mary's answer to the angel was, "I am the Lord's servant." The response tells all. She had a right conception of God. She understood—as well as a human being can—who God is. By knowing who God is, it was plain to her who *she* was created to be: the servant of the most high God.

From her understanding of who she was in light of who God is, the second half of her answer logically follows: "May it be to me as you have said." What it took years for Moses to achieve—the role of "servant of God"—Mary purposed to be from her youth. Like Samuel, who became one of the mightiest prophets in the Old Testament, Mary had learned in her youth to say, "Speak, LORD; for thy servant heareth."[235] Mary was so totally devoted to God that she did not hesitate as Moses did. Her highest goal was to always do the things that pleased God.[236]

Peace Comes Through Perspective

If we put ourselves in Mary's place, what would our reaction have been? Joy? Uncertainty? Fear? Indecision? There are several issues that come to mind when we consider Mary's encounter with the angel. What questions would we have asked? What objections might we have raised? What conditions might we have stipulated before agreeing to God's plan?

God had the angel tell Mary *what* He was going to do. In addition, He explained *how* He was going to accomplish it. But to the amazement of the natural human mind, Mary did not ask *why*. Nor did she say, "Okay, Lord, I'm completely supportive of what You're planning to do here, but there are one or two minor adjustments in the plan I'd like for You to consider before we finalize this arrangement. Like, first, how about if we just wait a few days until the ink is dry on the marriage license. Don't You think it would really make things a lot simpler for everybody?"

Here we see how Mary's right conception of God—and in turn her relationship to the Most High—comes to bear. Most of us would have had the temerity to demand that the all-wise God justify His plans to us, to demand that the Author of all that is good defend to our satisfaction the worth and validity of His intentions. Not Mary. She had a right understanding that God was the Good Creator and she was His creature. God had made her with the freedom to choose, and she chose to be the Lord's servant.

Had we been there, and able to think as clearly as Mary in the terrifying, awesome presence of the angel, we would have wanted to know how to explain this to Joseph! We would have wanted to know how we were supposed to cope with the embarrassment of people believing that we had been impure. We would have asked how to deal with the scorn of the hometown folks who would be counting on their fingers when it became known that we were pregnant. We would have wanted to know what to do about our parents' embarrassment.

With the benefit of hindsight, we know that God provided for the problem with Joseph by sending an angel. It is beautiful to think that the angel's message to Joseph included the same instructions regarding the infant's name as the angel's instructions to Mary, so that when the two of them got around to discussing this matter, they would receive yet another confirmation that they were a part of God's unfolding plan.[237]

In hindsight, we also know that the scorn of the local town folk was not going to turn out to be the problem Mary might have expected. Through the means of Caesar Augustus' decree that dictated that there be a census taken,[238] God was going to get Mary and Joseph out of Nazareth and on to Bethlehem in time for the birth. After that, He was going to send them to Egypt to get them away from Herod's

murderous rampage.[239] Everything would be done to completely ful-
fill all of the prophecies about Christ. By the time they returned to
Nazareth, the length of time between their marriage and the date of
Christ's birth was no longer a relevant issue.

But we know all these things, of course, by looking back. They are
not things Mary could have known when she was talking with the
angel. From our perspective today, it seems remarkable to think that
Mary, with her limited years of experience and without the advantage
of hindsight, believed so completely in God that she knew without
any doubt that He is totally reliable and that He could be trusted to
work out all the details of His good plan—indeed His perfect and
astonishing plan.

Pure but Not Passive

Most of us would have asked God to explain why He hadn't considered using Plan B! All through the Old Testament, we see one
example after another of God speaking to one of the prophets who
then tells the king or announces to the people "this is the word of the
Lord." Most of us in Mary's situation would have said to God, "Don't
You think people would connect with this whole Messiah idea better
if You gave a message to a prophet or a priest and have them announce
in front of everybody that You are going to give me—still a virgin—
this miracle baby, one who is not going to have a human father? That
way, God, I won't be embarrassed, my parents won't be embarrassed,
and everyone will understand this whole deal a lot better. Don't You
see, God, that we are accustomed to having You speak through
prophets? After all, that's the way You've always done it!"

Some might want to argue that Mary's limited response to the angel
does not indicate a high degree of trust in God as much as it shows
that she was simply a very passive person. There is just one problem
with this view of Mary's personality. We have evidence that it is not
true.

Consider the situation about 30 years later when Mary, along with
Jesus and His disciples, are invited to a wedding. When the host ran
out of wine, Mary approached her Son with the problem. Now notice
that when Mary learned of this problem, she did not passively accept
the looming embarrassment of the host who likely was a close friend,
or perhaps even a relative. Then consider what followed next. Jesus'

first response to His mother's suggestion that He provide a solution to the problem was to say, "Why do you involve me? My time has not yet come."

Do we see Mary passively accepting her Son's attempt to deflect her request for Him to get involved? Hardly. While she does not urge Him to reconsider, that doesn't necessarily mean she didn't give Him the "look"—the one that says: Hello, this is important to me...this is Your mother here, the one who changed Your diapers, remember. Whatever the case may have been, despite having received no words of encouragement from Jesus that might cause her to proceed further (we can't even guess what she might have seen in His face), she turned to the servants and instructed them, "Do whatever He tells you to do." With the servants eyeing Him for instructions, Jesus set in motion the steps by which He turned upwards of 180 gallons of water into wine![240] (All of this was done so unobtrusively that the servants were the only ones who knew how the supply of wine was replenished.) Score an A+ for Mary's persistence.

As this incident clearly shows, Mary was definitely not a passive person. We are not told how she knew, but it is quite evident she understood something of her Son's capabilities. (Though we have to wonder if she was expecting Him to go to such lengths in remedying the problem.) Moreover, she was prepared to push Him when, in her judgment, the situation warranted His attention. The picture we see of Mary in this story is certainly not that of someone with a passive personality. That being the case, the only viable explanation we have so far for Mary's response to the angel is that she was devoted to God and trusted in His goodness.

Preparation for Purity

But what of God's actual plan as compared to our hypothetical this-is-the-way-we've-always-done-it Plan B? Why did God change course and speak directly to Mary rather than through some prophet as He had done so often in Old Testament times? At first glance it does seem as though it would have made things easier on Mary. Easier, but not better. That is the problem. There is something in our nature that finds the easier solution more appealing. Usually, easier just seems better to us. But since when has our experience shown us that anything of great value can be obtained without great effort?

No athlete builds strength by doing easy things. True, athletes engage in some easy stretching at the outset of a workout to maintain flexibility, but then they move on to exercises that involve sweat and strain. These are the indispensable ingredients for building strength. Though "easier" is more attractive to us, it is not better for us because it does not produce growth, increase strength, or prepare us for the trials yet to come.[241]

Had Plan B been the way God operated at the outset of this drama, then Mary and Joseph would not have been prepared to receive and act upon further messages from God. Some time after the birth of Christ, an angel appeared to Joseph in a dream and instructed him to get up immediately and flee to Egypt to keep Herod from murdering the baby Jesus. Another time, an angel appeared to Joseph to tell him that it was time to return to Israel. A third time, Joseph was warned to go to Nazareth in Galilee rather than return again to Judea where Archelaus, Herod's son, was now ruling.[242]

Another aspect of Mary's purity was her willingness to confirm God's message to her through those who were more mature. She went to Elizabeth, someone of deep and abiding faith who knew her, understood her, and had her best interests at heart. Mary's action was not that of a person who doubted God. Her heart understood what her eyes couldn't see and her mind couldn't grasp. Her desire for confirmation was the action of someone who trusted God with deep reverence, but was wise enough to know that human interpretations are vulnerable to the influence of our own wishes and desires and hence should be handled with care to ensure that we are not simply hearing what we want to hear.

Mary understood accountability and recognized that God promised to give wisdom generously. "If any of you lacks wisdom, he should ask God, who gives generously to all without finding fault, and it will be given to him."[243] Mary knew Scripture and the prophecies. Her mind and heart were filled with God's words. She worshiped God with her whole heart.

In the first chapter of Luke, we find Mary's song that describes her adoration of her God who is mighty and strong, holy and merciful, who cares for the needy and empowers the lowly, who is the Savior and Lord. The description of Mary in every specific indicates that she was a young woman who was willing to be used by God in any way

He deemed best. She was pure in heart and bowed in reverence and obedience to God.

The Path to Purity

In the beatitudes, Jesus says that the pure in heart are blessed because they shall see God. If seeing God is the height of blessedness, then keeping a pure heart should be a high calling for every Christian. Some of the ancient philosophers thought that the pure in heart were able to see the spiritual world more clearly than those less pure, whose view was limited to the physical world. Perhaps the pure in heart see God more clearly because that is where they focus their attention. And, in the light of God's holiness, our own unworthiness is made plain. As C. S. Lewis once wrote: "To know God is to know that our obedience is due Him."[244] Meekness and the fear of the Lord are, then, natural results of seeking the Lord with all our heart and mind.

Mary's purity reminds us that when we clothe ourselves in God's righteousness rather than relying on our own strength and wisdom, we become conformed to the image of His Son. The apostle Peter called us, as the children of God, to "participate in the divine nature" of God so that we can "escape the corruption in the world caused by evil desire." Mary serves to remind modern women that it is possible to put on the spirit of Christ, that God promises we can participate in His divine nature. The apostle Peter admonishes us that we need to make every effort to add to our "faith goodness; and to goodness, knowledge; and to knowledge, self-control; and to self-control, perseverance; and to perseverance, godliness; and to godliness, brotherly kindness; and to brotherly kindness, love." Peter added, "For if you possess these qualities in increasing measure, they will keep you from being ineffective and unproductive in your knowledge of our Lord Jesus Christ."[245]

We inevitably end up focusing our lives on some set of ideas or principles. The ultimate irony is that even those who think they are creating their own way, their own truth, their own life, experience the greatest bondage: addiction and enslavement to their own urges and the chaos that are the wages of sin and disobedience. Paul admonished the Romans: "Don't you know that when you offer yourselves to someone to obey him as slaves, you are slave to the one whom you obey—whether you are slaves to sin, which leads to death, or to obedience, which leads to righteousness?"[246] Mary's life shows us how much better that it is to serve our heavenly Father, who knows our frame and holds our best interest in His hands.

Faithfulness to Christ brings wonderful freedom in our lives—the freedom that comes from a pure heart. And, in the end, we can say with Paul, "I have fought a good fight, I have finished my course, I have kept the faith."[247]

The Power of Humility

The Magnificat
My soul magnifies the Lord,
And my spirit has rejoiced in God my Savior.
For He has regarded the lowly state of His maidservant;
For behold, henceforth all generations will call me blessed.
For He who is mighty has done great things for me,
And holy is His name.
And His mercy is on those who fear Him
From generation to generation.
He has shown strength with His arm;
He has scattered the proud in the imagination of their hearts.
He has put down the mighty from their thrones,
And exalted the lowly.
He has filled the hungry with good things,
And the rich He has sent away empty.
He has helped His servant Israel,
In remembrance of His mercy,
As He spoke to our fathers,
To Abraham and to his seed forever.
LUKE 1:46-55 NKJV

Mary was fully aware of the honor bestowed on her by God. Her selection to be the woman to give birth to the Son of God—the Messiah—was an unparalleled event in human history. God would not have chosen her had she not been pleasing to Him—pleasing in her attitudes and her actions, in her beliefs about Him and her worship of Him, in her disposition, and, most especially, in her character. Everything about the angel's visit to Mary confirmed her purity, humility, and devotion. She responded exactly the way a faithful servant should: In spite of any uncertainties she might have felt, she embraced the Lord's will for her life.[248] Given that Mary was so pleasing to God, we should all want to know and understand as much about her as we possibly can.

Though we have only fragmentary knowledge of her life, there are, nevertheless, some things about her that appear evident from the few events that are recorded. There is no indication that either she or Joseph came from anything more than modest means. Joseph, we know, was of the tribe of Judah (a direct descendent of David), and both he and Mary lived in Nazareth in Galilee where Joseph was a carpenter by trade.[249] While Jerusalem was the center of Israel's religious life, Nazareth was a place of such corruption and low repute that, when he learned that Jesus came from there, Nathaniel asked, "Can any good thing come out of Nazareth?"

In his Gospel Luke tells us that Mary had a relative named Elizabeth who was married to a priest named Zacharias, both of whom were descendents of Aaron.[250] Luke also takes the time to say that "Both of them were upright in the sight of God, observing all of the Lord's commandments and regulations blamelessly."

It seems strange that Luke would take the pains to describe the character of the parents of John the Baptist in greater detail than that of the mother of Jesus, but Scripture is full of surprises! Given the affectionate relationship that apparently existed between Elizabeth and Mary, it seems obvious that Mary followed the example of her relative Elizabeth and that she lived according to the same precepts. Otherwise would Mary have gone to see Elizabeth immediately upon having been visited by the angel?[251]

These few details exhaust the little we know about Mary's background. Everything else we must deduce from her words and her actions.

Holy Is His Name

In addition to her conversation with the angel, Luke also recorded for us Mary's song, the Magnificat. Here we find a gold mine from which we can learn much about her. The first thing that is obvious is the artful, poetic beauty of the language and its multiple references back to the Old Testament writings—including echoes of Hannah's prayers from the book of Samuel[252] and recitations of the promises of God. That information tells us that Mary was not—as some have described her—an ignorant peasant girl. Her language is elevated and refined, and her mind was obviously saturated with the teachings of the law and the prophets.

Consider, for example, her opening lines: "My soul magnifies the Lord, and my spirit has rejoiced in God my Savior." Compare them with David's words in Psalm 70:4 (KJV) where we read: "Let all those that seek thee rejoice and be glad in thee: and let such as love thy salvation say continually, Let God be magnified." The similarities are clear, yet upon hearing Mary's words there is no sense whatsoever that she is imitating or mimicking a better poet than herself. Her themes of "magnifying the Lord" and "God as Savior" are common ones from Scripture, but they are never stated in more lyrical terms.[253] For example, we read in Isaiah 45:21 (KJV): "There is no God else beside me; a just God and a Saviour; there is none beside me." Similarly in Hosea 13:4 (KJV) we find: "Thou shalt know no god but me: for there is no saviour beside me." We would be remiss in looking at the poetic quality of her words if we lost sight of the fact that here Mary is expressing her deep devotion and great joy in her worship of her God and her Savior.

Mary's statement regarding the fact that all generations would call her blessed shows that—far from being a naïve, ignorant young girl who wasn't quite sure what she was caught up in—she clearly understood the nature of the child she was bearing and that she further understood at least something of the meaning of the coming of the Messiah. It is important to see the context of this statement.

First we need to recognize that despite her age and spiritual maturity, Elizabeth has just deferred to Mary's newly elevated status—as one might to royalty—by asking, "But why am I so favored that the mother of my Lord should come to me?" Then we need to see that Mary's opinion of herself has not changed one whit from the moment when she replied to the angel, "I am the Lord's servant....May it be to me as you have said." Though she clearly understood what Elizabeth had just said about her new role, she still saw herself as a humble servant and prefaces her remark about being called blessed by calling attention to that fact. Humility is one of Mary's dominant characteristics. It flows as a natural consequence from her concept of who God is combined with her commitment and devotion to Him.

How did Mary see God? As Savior. God *could be* her Savior because He was mighty. She knew God *was* her Savior because He had "done great things for me." She didn't see God as Someone who was interested only in Israel as a corporate body, only as a nation. Mary saw God in very personal terms: *my* Savior who has done great things for *me!* But she immediately balances this familiar, personal viewpoint with one of great reverence, respect, and awe: "And holy is His name."

Mary sees the implication of the fact that God is holy: except for His great and tender mercy, we would be lost, totally alienated from Him by our sin and without hope. In fact, the mercifulness of God is so important to Mary that she speaks of it in two separate places in her song. When we come to see our sinful pride and willful disobedience in the light of God's holiness, we know—like Adam and Eve—that we are not fit to stand before Him. There is—and should be—fear when we have our eyes opened. But the fear of the Lord—He who is both mighty and holy—is the beginning of wisdom (Proverbs 9:10). And the wise see that God has revealed Himself to be the merciful Father who has compassion on His wayward children.

There Are No Words

At one point David said, "My sin is ever before me." That, however, was not the end of David's story, for we also hear him say in words that Mary echoes in her song, "But the steadfast love of the LORD is from everlasting to everlasting upon those who fear him, and his righteousness to children's children, to those who keep his covenant and remember to do his commandments."[254] Note that David links his confidence in the mercy of God to the keeping of the covenant and remembering to do God's commandments. David had gained this wisdom through a very bitter experience. Mary also recalls the covenant in her second mention of mercy when she makes the point that God in His mercy helped Israel just as He promised when He spoke unto Abraham.

If we put aside the poetic beauty of the opening line of Mary's song and instead focus strictly on the logic of the statement, we find a problem. In what literal sense can we as mere human beings magnify or glorify the Almighty? We can, and we should, proclaim His glory and praise His terrible majesty, but our praise adds no more to God's infinite glory than putting a thimbleful of water in the ocean would increase its vastness. Still, those who have experienced God's grace and mercy cry out as best we can to try and give expression to our appreciation for the goodness of God.

Our language, which seems so rich to us when we read the poets and philosophers, is bankrupted when it comes to conveying the nature of God. When God told Moses at the burning bush that He was sending him to Pharaoh to bring the children of Israel up out of Egypt, Moses tried to evade the moment of decision by asking God what he should tell the Israelites when they asked him to give the identity of the God of their fathers. God replied to Moses, "I AM WHO I AM." Philosophers and theologians find endless meaning in this opaque statement. To those who are good at ferreting out the meaning of poetic utterances, this statement is a source of endless delight and speculation. But to those who interpret things literally, it is difficult to understand the meaning of this name for God.

This instance of the limitation of human communication in interacting with God is not unique. When we pray, we speak to the all-knowing God as though we need to inform Him about the nature of our problems. In fact, we tell Him—and it is proper that we do so—not because He needs to be told, but because we need to do the telling, even though He already knows.

Consecrated by Humility

Our limited ability to convey meaning with words is not confined to our attempts to interact with God. There are times of grave significance on a purely human level when we exhaust the limits of language. Such was the case when President Abraham Lincoln journeyed to Gettysburg, Pennsylvania, to attend the ceremony to mark the dedication of the cemetery there.

After three days of hot, deadly battle in early July 1863, the fields of Gettysburg were soaked with the blood of thousands of men. As the Union forces celebrated a victory that proved to be a turning point in the Civil War, it was the president of the beleaguered United States, Abraham Lincoln, who observed that the day, July 4, was the anniversary of the Declaration of Independence. Lincoln believed that the Union soldiers had died defending "the principle that all men are created equal." And as the end of the war began to seem imminent, Lincoln became focused on how to communicate that vision to an embattled country and rebuild a nation. When he was invited later that year to give remarks at the dedication of the cemetery at Gettysburg, Lincoln seized the occasion as an opportunity to frame the ultimate purpose of the national conflict that had cost so much.[255]

Still, on the way to Gettysburg, Lincoln was troubled about his role in dedicating this battlefield-turned-cemetery. Nothing anyone could say, he believed, would add any real meaning above and beyond what had already been forged there in the heat of the deadly battle that had raged in those bloody days in July. He began drafting the speech, writing in longhand on White House stationery, in Washington. But he had trouble concluding the speech, and he boarded the train for Gettysburg with his address still unfinished. When he did complete the address, it was only 272 words long. It took him only two minutes to deliver. Former senator Edward Everett, who preceded Lincoln on the podium, spoke for two hours. It is Lincoln's brief words, however, that are now remembered and recognized as a masterpiece of the English language.

His words were few, but carefully chosen. Lincoln rose to speak deliberately and, observers commented, somberly. His voice, which was "penetrating," rang out:

> ...In a larger sense we cannot dedicate—we cannot consecrate—we cannot hallow this ground. The brave men, living and dead, who struggled here, have consecrated it far above our poor power to add or detract.

Here we see the essence of humility—an accurate sense of proportion, a proper assessment of the weight of our finite contribution to the fulfillment of God's eternal purposes. This, too, was Mary's great strength. If anything, however, she underestimated her own significance. She was, after all, the one woman in all of human history chosen by God Himself to bear His son.

A Covenant of Intimacy

We do the best we can with our puny human language and limited logic, but they are totally inadequate as we approach the

Almighty. We cannot encompass Him with our words or capture Him in the net of our categories. We are finite, and He is infinite. If we are to know God, He must come down to us. We cannot rise up to Him. We catch a bare glimpse of His glory in the awesome scope and beauty of His creation. We sometimes sense the beauty of His presence in a song. These experiences are fleeting and quickly slip from our grasp. The possibility for us to be in a relationship with the awesome Creator of the universe exists because He chose to reveal Himself to us in ways that we could understand. He is great, and apart from Him we are insignificant.

In moments of reflection we understand our insignificance. Yet at other times we hold up our views as the measuring rod by which God is to be measured—to which He must be accountable. Instead of bowing in humility before God as Mary did, we demand that He be answerable to us, that He conform to our wishes and expectations. All this despite the fact that we are so small that we cannot give glory to God any more than the moon can give light to the sun. All glory is already His, and our efforts do nothing to add to or take from that glory. We can, at most, praise Him, and we can, at most, in thanksgiving enumerate all that He has done for us—as Mary did in her song.

Mary ends the Magnificat with reference to Abraham's seed. The most marvelous thing we could ever comprehend is that Almighty God has offered us a covenant relationship with Himself, a covenant whereby He is our God and we are His people. In His covenant God promised Abraham, Isaac, and Jacob a land to be their possession. In this land they could be free. There they could work, live, and raise their children. We are foolish to take so lightly God's offer to be our God. We should daily give thanks to Him for the privilege He offers us to be joint-heirs with Christ.

The apostle Paul wrote: "The Spirit Himself bears witness with our spirit that we are children of God, and if children, then heirs—heirs of God and joint heirs with Christ; if indeed we suffer with Him, that we may also be glorified together. For I consider that the sufferings of this present time are not worthy to be compared with the glory which shall be revealed in us" (Romans 8:16-18 NKJV).

And what is the source—no, *Who* is the source—of the glory that shall be revealed in us? We receive glory by virtue of our connection to the all-glorious Father, Son, and Holy Spirit. Where will this occur? In a new land. In a new city. In a new home.

Understanding True Humility

Mary was faithful, but at the same time she was strong. These two qualities enabled her to fulfill her high calling to be the mother of Jesus. Her true strength, however, was born of humility before God and devotion to Him.

Mary's song is remarkable not only for its poetic beauty and the praise to God that comes straight from her soul, but it is also remarkable for what it tells us about her. She is not pretentious. She sees herself as lowly, as a servant. Most of us, from time to time, utter words by which we portray ourselves as being humble, even though in our hearts we really think otherwise.

It is a mistake to think that being humble is the same thing as having low self-esteem—or to use a more old-fashioned term, the same as having an inferiority complex. Some even equate humility with self-loathing. But it isn't necessary to think poorly of yourself or to dislike who you are in order to be humble. True humility is an inner attitude. It is recognizing our unworthiness before Christ. Humility is acknowledging that it is not our loveliness that gives us value, but God's love of us. He loves us not because of who we are (what our nature is), but He loves us because of who He is (what His nature is). We are "God's workmanship."[256] We need to bring before God all the glory, honor, and praise for who He is and for His willingness to call us His children.

John Ruskin, a nineteenth-century British writer, once gave an excellent explanation of humility when he said, "I believe the first test of a truly great man is his humility. I do not mean by humility doubt of his own power or hesitation in speaking his opinion. But really great men have a feeling that the greatness is not in them, but through them; that they could not do or be anything else than God made them." In a similar vein, Andrew Murray said, "The humble man feels no jealousy or envy. He can praise God when others are preferred and blessed before him. He can bear to hear others praised while he is forgotten because...he has received the spirit of Jesus, who pleased not Himself, and who sought not His own honor. Therefore, in putting on the Lord Jesus Christ he has put on the heart of compassion, kindness, meekness, longsuffering, and humility."

Mary's song is dominated by her humility. Mary rejoiced that God "has been mindful of the humble state of his servant."[257] As we look at her reaction to the angel's visit and to the news that she is to be the mother of Jesus, we see the importance of humility as a Christian trait. God, once again, turns human values upside down. He shows through Mary's responses that His kingdom consists of those who have a different kind of strength. Those who were insignificant became powerful. Those who were poor became great. Those from the wrong place in Israel, those who recognized their dependence upon God, and those who hungered after His righteousness were lifted up.

The Path to Humility

Mary's response to the angel is a model for us of true humility: God has the right to arrange my life however He chooses, whenever He wants to intervene. Because Mary's attitude was one of willingness to serve, God could use her to do the miraculous. What could He do with us if we were willing to come before Him in humility to say, "Be it according to me as You wish, Lord?"

Lloyd Ogilvie, former pastor of the Hollywood Presbyterian Church in California, likes to tell the story of an unforgettable introduction he received before speaking at a large convention. The person introducing him gushed that their guest was someone who could sense a person's needs and meet them immediately. He could heal hurts, and he was an extremely compassionate, wise, and sensitive communicator. Dr. Ogilvie describes how flattered he was by her comments, but also how nervous he was becoming as the woman completed her introduction. *How in the world,* he wondered, *can I ever live up to her extravagant remarks?* The woman concluded, "In our midst tonight is the supreme lover of people, Jesus Christ. And here is the Reverend Lloyd Ogilvie who will tell us about Him!"

This wise woman's introduction provides us with the key to an attitude of humility—approaching every situation with the sole purpose of reflecting Jesus Christ. In the great hymn, "The Church's One Foundation," there is a line describing a different kind of strength. "Lord, give us grace that we, like them the meek and lowly, on high may dwell with Thee." Mary recognized that only the meek and lowly would see God. She was willing to accept that role and to glory in serving Him—whatever the role and whatever the capacity. That is the same mind and spirit of humility that we need when we approach the Almighty. Mary recognized that He alone is all-wise and all-knowing. Who are we, with our mere human perspective, to think that we know what is best? Once we internalize that heavenly view, God can use us powerfully, too, for His purposes.

At the manger in Bethlehem, the wise men fell down and worshiped Mary's baby boy. These learned men acknowledged the power and majesty of God embodied in the Christ child. Suddenly, everything was new and different. The old categories and status symbols were reversed. The insignificant had become significant. The powerless had become powerful. The weak had become strong. Behold, all things had become new. That is the different kind of strength that Christ brings to our lives when we are willing to bow before Him in humility and adoration.

A Different Kind of Strength

Pursue righteousness, godliness, faith, love,
endurance and gentleness. Fight the good fight of the faith.
1 TIMOTHY 6:11 NIV

They that wait upon the LORD shall renew their strength....
ISAIAH 40:31 KJV

*A*s we pondered the lives of the five women mentioned in Matthew's genealogy of Christ, we discovered that a different kind of strength is available because we serve a different kind of Lord. Christ is the one of whom Isaiah said: "He was wounded for our transgressions, He was bruised for our iniquities."[258] Christ is the One who called Himself the "good shepherd: the good shepherd giveth his life for the sheep."[259] John the Baptist called Jesus the "Lamb of God, which taketh away the sin of the world."[260] In Hebrews, we are told that "we do not have a High Priest who cannot sympathize with our weaknesses...."[261] Jesus Christ took on human form and became like us so that He might show us the Father and demonstrate how incomparable is His love for us. It is God Himself, through the sufferings of His Son, who saves us. Our Lord loved us enough to take on our pain—and triumphed over it.

He is risen! He is risen, indeed! "Let us therefore come boldly to the throne of grace," says the author of Hebrews, "that we may obtain mercy and find grace to help in time of need."[262] Mercy, we think we understand. But what of grace? Theologians define God's grace using words, but God chose to show us the meaning of grace through His actions. And there is no more beautiful example of God's mercy and grace than His rescue of Rahab the harlot from the doomed city of Jericho...by faith.[263]

We serve a God who is both great and good! When we look back at the stories we have shared with you, we marvel and delight to see how God worked. It is breathtaking to see how He used what looked like shattering blows to produce something of extraordinary strength and beauty in the lives of Tamar, Rahab, Ruth, and Bathsheba. Mary, too, along with the other four women, faced situations that required her to struggle, to grow, and to become stronger. From their pain and difficulties, though, God brought lasting joy and deep meaning.

Yes, God is great...and He is so good! It is critical that He be both great and good. If God were only great and not good, we would have every reason to fear Him as the pagans fear their gods, but there would be no reason to love Him. If God were only good and not great, we might have reason to love Him, but we could not trust in and rely upon Him as Mary so evidently did.

Even in the midst of our difficulties, we must accept that God is the author of everything of true value, and we must not try to hold Him hostage to our ideas of what is good. God's commands and His dealings—the ultimate realities of our faith—will not always seem reasonable in terms of our human logic. Our logic—as useful and powerful as it is—is not adequate to deal with the transcendent, the divine, the miraculous, the God who names Himself the "I AM."

We see in the stories we have studied together how God was always at work in all of the details—small as well as large to create something good out of what seemed only difficult and painful. From the story of Rahab and the destruction of Jericho, as well as those of Tamar and

Ruth, we see perfect illustrations of how God can redeem the bad things that happen to us and how His plans are better and grander than we could ever imagine. Tamar and Ruth's stories show us how God uses struggle and waiting to build patience and fortitude. Mary's story shows us the perfection of God's plans. Because God is good, His plans for us are good. Because He is great, we can be confident that His purposes will prevail.

The Beauty of Victory

If there is one lasting impression that these women leave as a group, it is one of profound beauty...attractiveness that goes far deeper than surface appearance. They challenge us with the loveliness and radiance of their lives. These were women who had whole hearts, who joined with the psalmist in his cry: "Give unto the LORD the glory due His name...worship the LORD in the beauty of holiness" (1 Chronicles 16:29 KJV).

It is a challenge and blessing to see God's faithfulness in these very human lives. God plucked Ruth out of a pagan culture and—through suffering and strain—molded her into one of the most exemplary women of history—an Old Testament forerunner of Mary. Just as God miraculously used Tamar, Rahab, and Bathsheba against all odds, He can use you and me. We see from their examples that when we fear the Lord and set our hearts toward obedience, the guiding hand of the heavenly Father moves above the circumstances and directs our way despite our weakness and frailty.

As these five women lived out their faith in God in the everyday situations in which He placed them, they overcame and achieved, they persevered and triumphed, they held firm in the face of the challenges that confronted them, they endured. God delights in us when we see that our own human effort is inadequate to face life. He takes so much pleasure in providing strength and power when it is sought that Christ instructs us to ask, to seek, to persist! We marvel at the ingenious ways God strengthens and uses humble, ordinary women who fear Him and are committed to obeying Him. We praise God for their faithfulness and for the godliness of their examples. God took their devotion and, through His power, made it righteousness.

If we look for unblemished virtue and perfect achievement in any Christian example offered as a source of hope and inspiration, we will inevitably come away disappointed and perplexed. More often than not, what we find are imperfect, flawed human beings very much like ourselves. Again, we reiterate the truth that the real inspiration of the stories about these ancestors of Christ, however, rests not primarily in the character or achievements of the human personalities occupying the foreground, but it rests fundamentally in the boundless grace, mercy, and forgiveness of the heavenly Father who is working in the background. The blessing of these stories is that they show us God's faithfulness in these women's lives—especially through their struggles and in the uncertainties of their circumstances.

The stories that we have considered are ultimately accounts of the aspects of the women's lives that provided a challenge or hindrance to their role in Christ's lineage. These stories are chiefly victorious ones—told to inspire us and strengthen our faith. These were women who overcame and achieved; they persevered, they endured.

The Challenge of Fear and Despair

Still, it is one thing to look back on God's provision and rejoice to see how perfect and wonderful it has been. But it is quite another to turn and face our own uncertain future and not feel fearful, over-whelmed, and sometimes even angry. If we can see in these biblical role models that God's way proved to be the best way, then why do we still struggle? Why do we feel so weak, so frustrated? Why are we so depressed, so anxious? And why are we so angry?

How is it that we can come to a correct understanding about who God is and what He is like—believe all the right things about God—and still lack faith? In our human frailty, we lose hope when we try to use our own strength to contend with life's circumstances. There are two ways we can fall short: by facing the unknown with fear and by confronting the known with despair.

When things are already going badly, the unknown future can be frightening. We can think of all sorts of other things that could go wrong as we look ahead. Some of these are merely imaginary, but many are real. We need look no further than the morning news to see the reality all around us—sickness, crippling disease, accidents, marriages falling apart, bankruptcies, and foreclosures. When these images cloud our minds, our hearts cry out in *fear,* "No, God!"

The flip side of fear is despair. Sometimes everyone is healthy, and we're managing to pay the bills, but...it doesn't seem enough. We lose hope when our reality doesn't match our dreams and expectations. Faith can be replaced by frustration and depression at what our lives are turning out to be in comparison to what we hoped and wanted, what we were determined they would be. We think we know what would make us happy! And we become disappointed and disillusioned when the things we desire are either beyond our reach or are taken away.

Fear and despair are very human emotions. Even the great man of faith, the apostle Paul himself, wrote to the Corinthians: "For we do not want you to be ignorant, brethren, of our trouble which came to us in Asia: that we were burdened beyond measure, above strength, so that we despaired even of life" (2 Corinthians 2:8 NKJV). Even Paul struggled against despair when he found himself beyond his own *strength* to endure! That's the human reaction to adversity. For this reason, just as it is important to know who God is, we must know who we are.

The Power of Choice

If we were creatures of reason only, it would be relatively simple to say, "Because God is infinite and I am finite, I will always choose His way for my life." That is the logical response. But it pleased God to make us in His image with a capacity not only for thought and choice, but with the capacity for love and many other emotions as well. God did not choose to create mere sentient thinking machines—computers with bodies.

God chose to make us with some very dangerous capacities. One of those is the capacity to want what seems desirable to us, what appeals to our eyes, our imaginations, and our hearts. We are most definitely creatures of emotion as well as reason. Our emotions are part of God's design and not, therefore, inherently bad. They were put in us for a purpose. And nowhere can we see this reality more clearly than in the way a woman's emotions give her the capacity to make the sacrifices that it takes to be a mother.

So our emotions, particularly fear and despair, are natural, but they are also powerful. And when they overwhelm us, they can be dangerous. In their presence, reason can become unreliable. They can contaminate the logic of our thought processes and strip us of objectivity. When we see the extent to which we are capable of behaving self-destructively, it is enough to make us wonder why God took the risk of creating us with strong creative powers and then gave us the freedom to use them either for good or for evil.

On the other hand, His gift of freedom is not so surprising when we stop to think about how we treat our own children. We let them ride bikes, skate, and climb trees knowing they will occasionally get scraped and bruised. We try to teach them to be careful and keep the risk manageable, but we delight too much in their joy to raise them in an overly protective hothouse environment. We watch them stretch and grow with a mix of anxious fear and joy. When they fall, we watch intently to see if they can make it back up on their own. If they need help, we fly to them.

And what of God? Does He watch us intently? The psalmist describes Him in these terms: "As a father pities his children, so the LORD pities those who fear Him. For He knows our frame; He remembers that we are dust."[264]

We are God's children, and He allows us to sometimes be bruised, but never broken. "We are hard pressed on every side," Paul said to the Corinthians, "yet not crushed; we are perplexed, but not in despair; persecuted, but not forsaken; struck down, but not destroyed...." And then Paul gives us the key—"...always carrying about in the body the dying of the Lord Jesus, that the life of Jesus also may be manifested in our body!"[265]

We have a High Priest who knows our sufferings! "Therefore...we do not lose heart," Paul proclaimed. "Turn your eyes upon Jesus," reminds the beloved hymn, "look full in His wonderful face. And the things of earth will grow strangely dim, in the light of His glory and grace...."

Accessing God's strength—even once we know it is available and once we acknowledge that we need His supply—requires that we focus on Him, that we seek to know Him by understanding more of His character, His ways, His Word. This understanding will give us the capacity to hear His voice, to recognize His path, and to cooperate with His plan.

Turn Your Eyes Upon Jesus

A different kind of strength begins with a different focus: When we set our gaze on Jesus, He will direct our attention toward others in need and away from our own concerns. When a woman concentrates simply on her own many wants and needs, she will never have the focus of a woman who has a sharply defined goal and purpose. When we spread our attention around over all the things that we desire, our energy is diffused and dissipates. But when we concentrate on a purpose outside ourselves, God can strengthen us and make us a great power for good.

Think for a moment of the light provided by a candle. It is unfocused light that gently illuminates in all directions, but it never attains the power of a halogen flashlight with its parabolic mirror that reflects its beam outward. Moreover, neither the candle nor the flashlight comes anywhere near the focused power or reach of the laser beam.

The laser provides us with a wonderful object lesson about how to increase strength. First introduced in 1958 by Charles Townes and Arthur Schawlow in scientific journals, the laser is a device that creates and amplifies a narrow, intense beam of "coherent light." The two brothers-in-law, Townes and Schawlow, began research on the laser beam in 1948 at Bell Laboratories. Both men won Nobel Prizes in physics for their work that kept a light beam "within a line width" and eliminated bouncing so that there was "not even slight off-angle motion."[266]

The formal description of a laser is instructive: "Normally, [atoms] radiate their light in random directions at random times. The result is incoherent light—a technical term for…a jumble of photons going in all directions. The trick in generating coherent light…is to create an environment in which they can all cooperate—to give up their light at the right time and all in the same direction."[267]

The marvelous invention of the laser has enabled scientists to focus light narrowly enough to reach the moon and reflect back to the earth. They have created lasers with such force that the beam can cut through steel and with such precision that delicate surgery can be accomplished with minimum physical invasion. Such is the potential of coherent light.

Like the laser, our key to force, strength, effectiveness, and power lies in focusing. All of us as "atomic" Christians need to be flowing in the same direction—in proper alignment with Christ, the "light of the world." Jesus explained that the basis of His power lay in His relationship—and alignment—to the Father. He said, "I do always those

264 A Different Kind of Strength

things that please Him."[268] Here we see that the ultimate focus for our lives should be to *please the Father*. The more we commit together in this common purpose, the more we achieve alignment and the power of the body of believers grows stronger and stronger.

When we are tempted by fear, frustration, despair, and anger, we are feeling the pull of darkness. But we must resist with all of the strength God provides. "For you were once darkness," Paul wrote to the Ephesians, "but now you are light in the Lord. Walk as children of light" (Ephesians 5:8 NKJV).

Walk as Children of the Light

God is good, and God is great...and we are His children—children of the light. This knowledge, this assurance, is the source of a different kind of strength. This is a strength that is challenged by life's hardships but is unbowed by fear and despair. "For you did not receive a spirit that makes you a slave again to fear, but you received the Spirit of sonship. And by him we cry, 'Abba, Father,'" proclaims Paul to the Romans. "Now if we are children, then we are heirs—heirs of God and co-heirs with Christ, if indeed we share in his sufferings in order that we may also share in his glory" (Romans 8:15,17 NIV).

From the examples of the women of faith we have studied, it is clear that at some point obedience will require sacrifice. But achieving such a lofty goal as being joint-heirs with Christ deserves stripping away everything that is false or frivolous in your life. It also often requires letting go of the "good" in order to reach the "best." Far more often than not, achievement—like character—hinges not on the occasional big decision but on a multitude of small choices.

The Importance of Ending Well

In the story of Tamar and Judah, the two major figures barely escape a tragic ending. If Judah had not faced up to the truth regarding his role in Tamar's condition and taken responsibility, he would never have become the leader God intended for him to be. Instead, he would have killed his own unborn twin sons by whom his line was to continue through to David—sons who replaced the two sons, Er and Onan, whom God took because of their wickedness.

Neither Bathsheba nor her eminent son, Solomon,[269] ended well. Solomon's father, David—like King Saul before him—abused the office God gave him. Unlike Saul, however, David repented and was forgiven—though not without incurring judgment. The child conceived in sin died, but God gave Bathsheba and David another son, Solomon—a son particularly loved and blessed by God from birth.[270] God restored David and Bathsheba, but in the end Bathsheba's role in Solomon's court was cut short by her foolishness.

Bathsheba's life provides two very pertinent messages for women. First, Bathsheba received the oft-desired second chance in life, and she squandered the opportunity. Her example reminds us that though we obtain forgiveness, we may still self-destruct.

Second, Bathsheba was the only one of the five women included in Matthew's genealogy to attain an influential position. With all of the emphasis in our culture today on women gaining power, we do well to ponder the fact that only Bathsheba—among the women mentioned by Matthew—ended up disgraced.

Perhaps one reason Scripture uses the race metaphor is to draw attention to the finish line: It is important to end well. Paul tells us we are to "hold fast the confidence and the rejoicing of the hope…firm to the end!" Though we serve a mighty God who has no shadow of turning, who has ever been and ever shall be…the story of man has a Genesis and a Revelation. But we are not left to write the story alone…God gave us His word…and He gave us *the* Word.

Jesus tells us, "I am the Alpha and the Omega."

He is the Beginning and the End.

"Surely I am coming quickly," He promises.

Yet we must persist until then.

"Amen. Even so, come, Lord Jesus!"

The Path to True Strength

In Revelation, John assures us that the culmination of the Great Story in which we all play our parts will be the establishment of the New Jerusalem. At the end there will be a new beginning! And who will enter the holy city? Not the perfect, but "he who overcomes." We would not be called to be overcomers if there were not a challenge to be faced, if there were not a battle to be waged, if there were not a race to be run. "He who has an ear, let him hear what the Spirit says to the churches." When the First and the Last speaks to the churches through John, the theme is clear: We are to persevere; we are to overcome. We must endure.

"Behold, I am coming quickly! Hold fast what you have, that no one may take your crown" (Revelation 3:11 NKJV).

Sometimes the challenges we face in life seem too daunting. Sometimes life falls apart...sometimes life seems empty...sometimes it seems as though there is no way out...and sometimes our dreams die. "Do not be afraid," God says, "I am the First and the Last." God has a story that He wants to write with our lives. It is only through pursuing His will and His purposes that we gain the power to achieve lasting joy, meaning, and fulfillment.

In all that we face, in all that we are, God is there. He is the God of the second chance. He is the faithful one. He is the eternal I AM. And we call Him "Abba, Father."

If we are to be powerful women—powerful forces for good, for the building of Christ's kingdom—it will only be in, and through, the God who is great, who is always there and always good.

Notes

Finding Strength When Life Falls Apart
1. Isaiah 30:15,16 NKJV.
2. *Newsweek*, January 8, 2001, cover.
3. Ibid., p. 40.
4. Richard Zoglin, "Lady with a Calling: Oprah Winfrey," August 8, 1988, p. 4, www.time.com/time/time100/pro-file/winfrey_related4.
5. *Newsweek*, p. 48.
6. Ray B. Browne, ed., *Contemporary Heroes and Heroines* (New York: Gale Research, Inc., 1990), p. 398.
7. As quoted in Courtney Macavinta and Rebecca Vesely's article "Gloria Steinem's True Self," www.societypoli-tics,chickclick.com, p. 2.
8. Matthew 28:18; Luke 9:1.
9. Judith Hennessee, *Betty Friedan: Her Life* (New York: Random House, 1999) p.xv.
10. Galatians 3:28 NKJV.
11. 2 Corinthians 9:8 NIV.

When Life Falls Apart
12. Genesis 49:8-12.
13. 1 Samuel 17:34-37.
14. Revelation 5:5.
15. Genesis 38:1.
16. Genesis 35:16-20.
17. Genesis 37:31-35.
18. Genesis 19:1-29.
19. Genesis 37:12-36.
20. Genesis 34:1-29.
21. Genesis 12:11-20; 20.
22. Genesis 14:8-24.
23. Genesis 38:1.
24. Genesis 34:1,2.
25. Genesis 38:7.
26. Genesis 38:8.
27. Genesis 38:9.
28. Genesis 38:10.
29. Genesis 38:11.
30. Genesis 38:12.
31. Genesis 38:12.
32. Genesis 38:14.

The Power of Courage
33. Genesis 44:18-33.
34. First, Judah had turned aside to her; second, he had arrived there with no available means of payment, third, she had had the inspiration to ask for his signet and staff as a pledge, fourth, he had not become angry and taken offense at her demand, fifth, he had not recognized her, and finally, she had conceived a child from the single encounter. Any one of these by itself might be taken as mere happenstance but all of them together showed clearly that God's work to fulfill His covenant lacked for nothing. There had been no thunder or light-ning, no dreams or visions but her desperate high-risk plan had, against all odds, succeeded, and not just barely! God had not only allowed her to become pregnant; He had also provided her with hard evidence to prove that she had been the woman that Judah had "come in unto" on the way to Timnah to shear his sheep.
35. See Genesis 38:25.
36. 1 Kings 18:18-38.
37. 1 Kings 19:3-18 RSV.
38. C. S. Lewis, *The Screwtape Letters* (Great Britain: Fontana Books, 1942), p. 148.
39. 2 Corinthians 12:9 NLT.

The Power of Fortitude
40. Daring is a form of courage that can be displayed in an instant, and it can disappear just as quickly. When Jesus told Peter he would deny Him before morning, Peter averred that he was ready to die with Christ and we know he meant it because in the Garden of Gethsemane, Peter drew his sword and set about to defend Christ; but in the flickering firelight in the court of the High Priest, Peter's daring evaporated in the chill light of dawn (see Matthew 26:34-74 and John 18:10-27). Fortitude, on the other hand, is forged in our characters only through an extended period of struggle.

Beyond daring, there is recklessness (that is, taking risk without proper consideration of the potential consequences). Tamar possessed both fortitude and daring, but she was not reckless. Tamar's action did not spring, therefore, from recklessness born of a mindless, hysterical feeling of desperation. Tamar brilliantly showed her mettle when called upon to improvise in the matter of obtaining a pledge from Judah that was supposedly to guarantee the payment he promised. If she had been driven by mere heightened emotions rather than the determined resolve to see things through despite the very real risk of being discovered, in all likelihood she would have panicked and lost the will to carry on.

It is far easier to see Tamar's boldness and daring than her fortitude. Her daring we see in her actions, but her fortitude we have to see by implication. How do we know she possessed fortitude? Had she given herself over to despair during the long period of waiting she would not have been alert to the possibility for action. Had she given up hope, she couldn't have seen that there was a possibility for action when the news came that Judah was on his way to Timnah to shear his sheep.

41. 1 Samuel 17:26-51.
42. William Jennings Bryan (1860–1925), Speech at the National Democratic Convention, Chicago, 1896.
43. At the end of their confrontation, Saul said to David, "And now, behold, I know that you shall surely be king, and that the kingdom of Israel shall be established in your hand. Swear to me therefore by the LORD that you will not cut off my descendants after me, and that you will not destroy my name out of my father's house" (1 Samuel 24:20,21 RSV).
44. See 1 Samuel 24:1-17.
45. In the instance where David confronted Saul after the incident in the cave where unbeknownst to Saul David cut off part of his robe, David respectfully addressed Saul with the term "my father" and referred to himself as no more important than "a dead dog" or "a flea" (1 Samuel 24:11,14). In the instance where David confronted Saul after the incident where David slipped into Saul's camp and took his spear and cruse of water, David respectfully addressed Saul with the term "my lord the king" and referred to himself as being of no more importance than "a flea" or "a partridge" (1 Samuel 26:19,20).
46. In Genesis 17:17 we read that Abraham laughed upon hearing God's promise that he at age 100 would sire a son by Sarah who was then 90. But then in Genesis 18:13-15 we read that Sarah also laughed when she overheard this promise that she would bear a son at her advanced age, and it is recorded that the heavenly messenger confronted her for her unbelief and disrespect.
47. On two occasions Abraham represented Sarah as being not his wife but his sister: Genesis 12:11-20 and 20:2-18.
48. Sarah laughed at the idea that she would have a child in her old age and then when confronted about her cynicism, denied that she had laughed: Genesis 18:10-15.
49. Isaac represented Rebekah as being not his wife but his sister: Genesis 26:7-11.
50. Rebekah conspired with her son Jacob to deceive Isaac and steal Esau's blessing: Genesis 27:1-41.
51. Jacob disguised himself and told his father Isaac that he was Esau in order to steal his brother's blessing: Genesis 27:1-41.
52. Rachel stole her father Laban's household images (gods) and then concealed them when he came searching for them: Genesis 31:19-35.
53. Judah and his brothers sold Joseph into slavery and then tricked their father into believing that Joseph was killed by a wild animal: Genesis 37:13-33.
54. Deuteronomy 25:5-6. Note also that in the story of Ruth, the custom was extended to the nearest of kin.
55. A particularly poignant case was that of Rachel who, though she was Jacob's favorite wife, remained barren all the time her sister Leah was bearing Jacob four sons, the fourth of which was Judah. Rachel became jealous of her sister and pleaded with Jacob, "Give me children, or I shall die!" Jacob became angry with her and said, "Am I in the place of God, who has withheld from you the fruit of the womb?" (Genesis 30:1,2 RSV). Also we read that when Boaz married Ruth, "the LORD gave her conception, and she bore a son" (Ruth 4:13 RSV). Note also an opposite case. David's wife Michal—the daughter of Saul—saw him leaping and dancing before the Lord as the Ark of the Covenant was brought into Jerusalem and "despised him in her heart." The scriptural account seems to imply that it was a consequence of her sinful pride that she "had no child to the day of her death" (2 Samuel 6:16,23 RSV).
56. Job 13:15 KJV.
57. Job 19:25 KJV.
58. Job 42:10 KJV.
59. Job 42:7,8.
60. Ruth 4:12 NKJV.
61. Genesis 34:25-31.
62. Genesis 35:22.
63. Genesis 37:27,28.
64. Exodus 3:11 KJV.
65. Exodus 4:14.
66. Romans 8:29 KJV.
67. Philippians 4:13 NKJV.

When There's No Way Out
68. Numbers 21:21-32; Deuteronomy 2:26-37.
69. Numbers 21:33-35; Deuteronomy 3:1-11.
70. Exodus 14:10-30.
71. Deuteronomy 2:36–3:7.

72. Joshua 2:1.
73. Deuteronomy 2:34.
74. Examination of the lunar history of the last 300 years indicates that the full moon in the month of March rises in the East with a variation of plus or minus 12 degrees, i.e., its azimuth is in a range of 78 to 102 degrees where 90 degrees equals due East.
75. Numbers 22:1-6.
76. Joshua 4:13.
77. Four thousand ranks (of 5 men per rank) spaced three and a half feet apart would create a column 28,000 feet long or a little over 5 miles, which is about the distance from ancient Jericho to the Jordan River.
78. An examination of the moon's orbit for the last 300 years indicates that the full moon in the month of March stands at 50 to 60 degrees altitude in the south southeast in the middle of the night.
79. Archaeological excavations have revealed that a portion of Jericho's north wall did not collapse.

The Power of Wisdom
80. Proverbs 4:5.
81. Proverbs 8:11.
82. Job 32:9.
83. Francis Bacon, Essay #12, "Of Boldness."
84. Joshua 5:13-15; 6:1-20.
85. James 2:25.
86. Hebrews 11:31.
87. Joshua 2:11.
88. Matthew 8:8-10; Luke 7:2-10.
89. John 14:6.
90. John 8:32 KJV.
91. Romans 5:12; 7:18-21.
92. Luke 10:27 KJV.
93. 1 John 4:20 KJV.
94. Proverbs 9:10 KJV.

The Power of Boldness
95. The production of linen thread from flax requires not only drying but numerous other steps as well. After being dried, the flax must be drawn through a rake to remove the seed. Then the flax straw must be wetted and rotted seven to ten days to expose the inner fibers. After this the outer hull of the stalk must be beaten and crushed without damaging the inner fibers. The broken stalks must then be removed and the fibers scraped clean of debris. In a final step before the fibers are ready to be spun into thread, they must be combed (hackled) to remove any remaining bits of flax straw and short fibers. All together, making linen thread from flax is a lengthy, painstaking process that must then be followed by weaving the thread into cloth.
96. An incident in the experience of Deborah reminds us that laying a trap is not beyond the capability of a woman in this culture. Jael, the wife of Heber the Kenite, in fulfillment of Deborah's prophecy, assassinated Sisera who was fleeing from Barak after she had provided Sisera a place to hide in her tent.
97. Joshua 5:2.
98. Joshua 5:13-15.
99. Judges 3:15-30.
100. Judges 4:8 NIV.
101. See Job 28:28; Psalm 111:10; Proverbs 9:10.
102. There is a long-standing argument about whether in the absence of direct revelation, God's creation is an adequate basis for understanding the nature of God and the difference between good and evil. Also philosophers and theologians debate whether there is anything that is innately known or if everything is learned. What most parents know for certain is that they didn't have to teach their children about property rights; "sharing" may have to be taught, but saying "mine" comes straight out of the genes. Even the youngest children feel that their rights have been violated when someone takes away one of their toys or a favorite blanket, something they identify as "theirs"; the protests this provokes are usually immediate, loud, and angry; and as most parents are dismayed to learn, it is not unusual for their beautiful "innocent" child to become violent when something valued is taken away from them. Human beings know about their rights. The converse of this is that they understand that violating another child's rights is a "wrong." While we are fallen creatures, there remains within us a part of the Divine image that recognizes right and wrong, that there is an innate moral order, and that we do evil when we violate that order.
103. Deuteronomy 30:19 KJV.
104. 1 Samuel 16:7 KJV.
105. Joshua 6:25 KJV.
106. Ruth 4:21,22 KJV.
107. Matthew 1:5.
108. Samuel M. Shoemaker, *By the Power of God* (New York: Harper & Brothers, 1954), p. 155.

When Life Seems Empty
109. Ruth 1:2.
110. Numbers 21:10-26; 22; 23; 24; Judges 11:15-26.
111. Numbers 21:29; Jeremiah 48.
112. Ruth 4:10.

113. Ruth 1:4.
114. Ruth 1:13.
115. Ruth 1:5.
116. Ruth 1:6,7.
117. Ruth 1:7.
118. Evans, *Women of Character*, p. 165.
119. Ruth 1:8,9.
120. Ruth 1:9.
121. Ruth 1:11-13.
122. Ruth 1:14,15.
123. Evans, *Women of Character*, p. 166.
124. Ruth 1:16-18 NIV.
125. Ruth 1:19.
126. Numbers 20:2-13.
127. Ruth 1:20-22.
128. Ann Spangler and Jean E. Syswerda, *Women of the Bible* (Grand Rapids: Zondervan Publishing House, 1999), p. 139. Moses' welfare system is described in Leviticus 19:9; 23:22; Deuteronomy 24:19-22.
129. Ruth 2:1-4.
130. Ruth 2:4.
131. See Ruth 2:5-12.
132. See Ruth 2:13-21.
133. Ruth 2:22,23.
134. See Ruth 3:1-5.
135. See Ruth 3: 6-8.
136. See Ruth 3:9-15.
137. See Ruth 3:16-18.
138. Judges 1:11-13.
139. Judges 3:9-11.
140. Ruth 4:1-4.
141. Ruth 4:5.
142. Ruth 4:6-10.
143. Ruth 4:11,12.

The Power of Devotion

144. Ruth 1:16,17 NIV.
145. Ruth 4:16,17. These words were prefaced by the women saying, "Blessed be the LORD, which hath not left thee this day without a kinsman, that his name may be famous in Israel. And he shall be unto thee a restorer of thy life, and a nourisher of thine old age: for thy daughter in law, which loveth thee, which is better to thee than seven sons, hath born him" (Ruth 4:14,15 KJV).
146. James 1:8 NASB.
147. Isaiah 50:7; Luke 9:51.
148. As quoted in a review by Susan R. Garrett, *Christian Century*, Dec. 16, 1998 of Leo G. Perdue, Joseph Blenkinsopp, John J. Collins and Carol Meyers, *Families in Ancient Israel*. (England: Westminster/John Knox), p. 285.
149. Barker, *The NIV Study Bible*, p. 364.
150. Spangler and Syswerda, *Women of the Bible*, p. 140.
151. Micah 6:8 RSV.
152. Job 3:25 KJV.
153. Job 1:8 KJV.

The Power of Obedience

154. John 12:24 NIV.
155. Mark 8:34 KJV.
156. Numbers 12:3.
157. Numbers 12:8; Deuteronomy 34:10.
158. Exodus 17:4 NIV: "Then Moses cried out to the LORD, 'What am I to do with these people? They are almost ready to stone me.' "
159. Exodus 17:6 NIV.
160. Numbers 20:8.
161. Numbers 20:11.
162. Numbers 20:12; Deuteronomy 3:23-26; 32:48-52.
163. Deuteronomy 3:27; 34:1-4.
164. 1 Samuel 13:8-12. Saul fails to wait for Samuel to arrive. Instead, he offers the sacrifice himself.
165. It is noteworthy that both here (1 Samuel 15:15) as well as in verses 21 and 30 that Saul in talking to Samuel refers not to the Lord *our* God but to the Lord *your* God.
166. 1 Samuel 15:22 NLT.
167. Saul had another problem: he had brought back King Agag alive as a trophy (1 Samuel 15:20). Samuel remedied this act of disobedience by personally executing Agag (1 Samuel 15:33).
168. Thomas Nagel, *The Last Word* (England: Oxford University Press, 1999).

169. Gilbert Meilaender, "Books in Review," *First Things 94*, June/July, 1999, pp. 45-50.
170. Romans 6:12,13.

When Your Dreams Have Died
171. 2 Samuel 11:4.
172. 2 Samuel 11:1.
173. 2 Samuel 11:2.
174. 2 Samuel 3:26-30.
175. 2 Samuel 3:31-38.
176. 2 Samuel 3:12-21.
177. 2 Samuel 10:7-14.
178. 2 Samuel 11:3.
179. 2 Samuel 23:34.
180. 2 Samuel 11:4.
181. 1 Samuel 21 and 22. It is noteworthy that the Israelite soldiers would not obey Saul's order to slay the priests and that Saul had to turn to Doeg, an Edomite, to kill all 85 of the priests and their families.
182. 2 Samuel 11:4.
183. 2 Samuel 11:6.
184. 2 Samuel 11:7.
185. 2 Samuel 11:8.
186. Ibid.
187. 2 Samuel 11:9.
188. 2 Samuel 11:11.
189. Ibid.
190. Barker, *The NIV Study Bible*, 2 Samuel 11:11.
191. 1 Samuel 16:13.
192. 2 Samuel 11:12.
193. 2 Samuel 11:13.
194. 2 Samuel 11:14,15.
195. 2 Samuel 11:23-25 NIV.
196. See 2 Samuel 11:26.
197. Barker, *NIV Study Bible*, 2 Samuel 11:27.
198. See 2 Samuel 11:27.
199. Ibid.
200. 2 Samuel 12:1.
201. Barker, *NIV Study Bible*, 2 Samuel 12:1. Barker identifies Nathan's parable as "one of the most striking in the Old Testament."
202. 2 Samuel 12:2-4. Note that in Nathan's parable Bathsheba is portrayed as an innocent lamb.
203. Barker, *NIV Study Bible*, notes that payment of "four times over" conforms to the requirements of Exodus 22:1.
204. In fulfillment of this prophecy, three of David's sons died violent deaths—Amnon (2 Samuel 13:28,29), Absalom (2 Samuel 18:14), and Adonijah (1 Kings 2:25).
205. This prophecy is fulfilled at the time of Absalom's rebellion (2 Samuel 16:22).
206. David responds to Nathan with repentance, in contrast to Saul's response to Samuel, which was to try to justify his behavior. Because David repented and humbled himself before God, Nathan said that God would extend mercy and release him from the death penalty that was mandated by law for murder and adultery.
207. The name Jedidiah reveals Solomon's special favor with God and, with its connection to David's name, is reassurance to David that he is forgiven and that his line will continue to the Messiah (Barker, *NIV Study Bible*, notes, p. 440).

The Power of Beauty
208. Catherine Madsen, "A Terrible Beauty: Moser's Bible," *CrossCurrents*, Spring/Summer 2000, vol. 50, issue 1-2, pp. 1-5. Reporting on "Engraving from the Holy Bible: King James Version" (Barry Moser, Illustrator).
209. As recorded by Arthur Block, 1977, *Murphy's Law*.
210. Jean Kerr, "Mirror, Mirror, on the Wall, I Don't Want to Hear One Word Out of You," *The Snake Has All the Lines*, 1960.
211. These ideas are explored in detail in Karen Lee Thorp's article, "Is Feminine Beauty Dangerous: A Brief Look at Our Theological Legacy," *Mars Hill Review*, issue 9, Fall 1997, pp. 39-48.
212. *Henry V*, iii, 78 and *Titus Andronicus*, II, I, 82, where he phrases it, "She is a woman, therefore may be woo'd, She is a woman, therefore may be won."
213. Roberta Pollack Seid, *Never Too Thin: Why Women Are at War with Their Bodies* (New York: Prentice Hall, 1989), p. 15.
214. 1 Samuel 25:3-42.
215. Proverbs 31:30.
216. In Nathan's parable, Bathsheba is portrayed as an innocent lamb. Also, our depiction of Bathsheba as fearful for her life and for her husband's life proved all too accurate. David did, indeed, order Uriah to be killed. And while we do not know enough to divide the blame between David and Bathsheba, we know that God allowed Bathsheba to conceive in an era when barrenness was a punishment for sin—not just the first time, but again after that child's death. The second son, Solomon, was especially loved by God and was endowed with wisdom. In contrast, Michal, whose sin was pride, was punished with lifelong barrenness.

The Power of Endurance
217. Romans 11:33.
218. 1 Kings 1:2.
219. 1 Kings 1:13,14.
220. 1 Kings 1:51.
221. 1 Kings 1:52.
222. 1 Kings 1:53.
223. 1 Kings 2:17.
224. 1 Kings 2:18.
225. 1 Kings 2:23,24.
226. James 1:12 NKJV.
227. Philippians 3 and 4.
228. Hebrews 5 and 6.
229. C. S. Lewis, *The Problem of Pain* (London: Geoffrey Bles, 1940), p. 81.
230. 1 Thessalonians 1:2,3,6,7 NIV.

The Power of Purity
231. 1 Samuel 16:7 RSV.
232. From Psalm 24:3,4 RSV; 51:10 KJV.
233. Luke 4:1-13.
234. "And the angel of the LORD appeared unto him in a flame of fire out of the midst of a bush: and he looked, and, behold, the bush burned with fire, and the bush was not consumed" (Exodus 3:2).
235. 1 Samuel 3:9,10.
236. Jesus speaking to the Pharisees said, "And he that sent me is with me: the Father hath not left me alone; for I do always those things that please him" (John 8:29 KJV).
237. Matthew 1:20-25.
238. Luke 2:1 NASB.
239. Matthew 2:1-16.
240. John 2:3-10.
241. God put this issue in slightly different slant when He says (loosely translated) to Jeremiah, "If you have raced with foot soldiers and they have worn you out, how do you expect to be able to compete against horse-drawn chariots? And if you stumble in safe, familiar country, how will you manage in thickets of the Jordan in flood tide?" (See Jeremiah 12:5.)
242. Matthew 2:13-23.
243. James 1:5 NIV.
244. C. S. Lewis, *Surprised by Joy* (London: Harcourt Brace & Co., 1956), p. 34.
245. 2 Peter 1:4-9 NIV.
246. Romans 6:16 NIV.
247. 2 Timothy 4:7 KJV.

The Power of Humility 3
248. Luke 1:38.
249. Luke 1:26; Mark 6:3.
250. Luke 1:5,6.
251. Luke 1:39.
252. 1 Samuel 1:11; 1 Samuel 2:1-10.
253. "My soul shall make her boast in the LORD: the humble shall hear thereof, and be glad. O *magnify* the LORD with me, and let us exalt his name together" (Psalms 34:2,3 KJV, emphasis added). "I will praise the name of God with a song, and will *magnify* him with thanksgiving" (Psalm 69:30 KJV, emphasis added).
254. Psalm 103:17,18 RSV.
255. David Herbert Donald, *Lincoln* (New York: Simon and Schuster, 1995), pp. 459-63.
256. Ephesians 2:10 NIV.
257. Luke 1:48 NIV.

A Different Kind of Strength
258. Isaiah 53:5 KJV, emphasis added.
259. John 10:11 KJV.
260. John 1:29 KJV.
261. Hebrews 4:15 NKJV.
262. Hebrews 4:16 NKJV.
263. Hebrews 11:31.
264. Psalm 103:13,14 NKJV.
265. 2 Corinthians 4:8,9 NKJV.
266. Lucent Technologies, Bell Laboratories, "Invention of the Laser: Schawlow and Townes Invent the Laser," www.bell-labs.com/history/laser.
267. Lucent Technologies, Bell Laboratories, "What Is a Laser," www.bell-labs.com/history/laser.
268. John 8:28 KJV.
269. 1 Kings 11:1-13.
270. 2 Samuel 12:24,25.